Out *of* Line

Out *of* Line

—————————•—————————

A Life of Playing with Fire

BARBARA LYNCH

ATRIA BOOKS

NEW YORK   LONDON   TORONTO   SYDNEY   NEW DELHI

ATRIA
BOOKS

An Imprint of Simon & Schuster, Inc.
1230 Avenue of the Americas
New York, NY 10020

First Atria Books hardcover edition April 2017

ATRIA BOOKS and colophon are trademarks of Simon & Schuster, Inc.

For information about special discounts for bulk purchases, please contact Simon & Schuster Special Sales at 1-866-506-1949 or business@simonandschuster.com.

The Simon & Schuster Speakers Bureau can bring authors to your live event. For more information, or to book an event, contact the Simon & Schuster Speakers Bureau at 1-866-248-3049 or visit our website at www.simonspeakers.com.

Interior design by Kyoko Watanabe

Manufactured in the United States of America

10 9 8 7 6 5 4 3 2 1

Names: Lynch, Barbara, 1964- author.
Title: Out of line : a life of playing with fire / Barbara Lynch.
Description: New York : Atria Books, [2017]
Identifiers: LCCN 2016029684 (print) | LCCN 2016040375 (ebook) | ISBN 9781476795447 (hardcover) | ISBN 9781476795454 (pbk.) | ISBN 9781476795461 (ebook) | ISBN 9781476795461 (eBook)
Subjects: LCSH: Cooks--United States--Biography. | Women cooks--United States--Biography.
Classification: LCC TX649.L96 A3 2017 (print) | LCC TX649.L96 (ebook) | DDC 641.5092 [B] --dc23
LC record available at https://lccn.loc.gov/2016029684

ISBN 978-1-4767-9544-7
ISBN 978-1-4767-9546-1 (ebook)

To my beautiful daughter, Marchesa,
with love and protection

CONTENTS

Out *of* Line

PROLOGUE

"Where did you come from?" my mother shouted, Benson &
Hedges twitching between her fingers. She meant, "Didn't I raise
you better than that?" She wished.

My friends and I were canning—knocking on doors in Old
Harbor, our South Boston housing project, with tin cans labeled
BAND UNIFORMS, to score spare change. Then my pain-in-the-
ass neighbor stuck her nose in: "I didn't know Barbara played an
instrument."

"She doesn't," said my mother. "What the hell? What band?"

Busted. We were scrounging cash to get the fried Tendersweet
clams at Howard Johnson's, which I loved. My mother dumped
out my hard-begged loot and made me give it all back. I burst
into furious tears at the injustice. "It was all my idea!" I raged.
"And now everyone but me is eating clams."

Years later I learned the secrets of those HoJo's clams from the
chef who perfected them: Jacques Pépin.

● ● ●

Old Harbor—and most of Southie—was solid Irish. My one non-Irish friend, Tina, who is Italian, lived in Old Colony, the adjoining project. All of us project rats grew up hard and fast. From ages twelve, thirteen, fourteen, we were drinking, drugging, and stealing. My friend Tina's mother forced her into Alcoholics Anonymous, fearing that, even by Southie standards, she was too wild.

I'd tag along to meetings to check out the better-looking guys, who, unlike my friends, were sober (more or less), seemed old enough to have jobs (cash), and had no missing teeth. To get to know them, we planned a little party. I wanted to make pesto, which I'd never tasted but must have come across in my mother's treasured stash of women's magazines.

Fresh basil—the main ingredient—was exotic in Southie. To buy it I had to go to the Italian neighborhood, the North End, where I also got olive oil, boxed spaghetti, and a hunk of Parmesan cheese. Then I needed pine nuts. Christ, were they expensive. I palmed a few packets and shoved them down my pants.

When I served my spaghetti with pesto, all the guests went, *"Ewww!* What's the green shit? You eat that?"

The brave ones tried it and were shocked. They loved it. That was an *aha!* moment, when I first realized that I could surprise, even excite people with food. But no way could I revel in the victory. No one ever let you get too "jumped up" or full of yourself in Southie. The tone was more, "Lynchie, who the hell do you think you are?" *"Where did you come from?"* someone cracked.

When I got established as a chef, I went back to J. Pace & Son to pay for the stolen pine nuts. I apologized, and we laughed. But that was just one stop. I also had to confess at the shop where I boosted a rolling pin and pie pan—no way could I bake a pie in some tinfoil piece of shit—and few other stores where I sticky-fingered this and that . . .

●　●　●

When I got a James Beard Award nomination for Best Chef: Northeast, I was reminded of where I come from (as if I could forget). Dying to tell someone—maybe celebrate—I went down to the Quiet Man, a classic Southie pub co-owned by my brother Paul. It was right across the street from Triple O's, the bar where Stephen "the Rifleman" Flemmi, a partner, ran crime boss Whitey Bulger's loan-sharking operation, along with deadlier schemes. Once, Triple O's bouncer Kevin Weeks, a Bulger mob enforcer, flung an ax into the back of a brawler with what Weeks called Irish Alzheimer's—the disease that drives out all memories except grudges. The place was packed, but Southie Alzheimer's, the code of silence, kept patrons from calling an ambulance or the law. The guy survived.

The Quiet Man served a less volatile, cop-and-politician clientele, as well the Triple O's riffraff. It was a beloved neighborhood joint with *America/Love It or Leave* stenciled on the windows. Its food was great: incredible steak tips, roast turkey, and twin boiled lobsters stored in a white Igloo cooler on the floor. For serious eaters, there was the John Wayne Platter, with three meats—grilled sausage, chicken, and steak tips—hot pickled cherry peppers, and thick-cut steak fries.

But mainly it was a homey neighborhood pub, where guys hung at the bar reading the *Herald* and drinking "beers"—always with an "s"—from plastic cups. You could get your cup "chilled," meaning that the barman would shove it down in the ice bin and give it a twist. On Fridays, when I took my aunt Mary there for lunch, she'd bring her own vodka so they could make her a martini, and I'd lug a bottle of wine with my own glass.

As we ate, union guys would come by to pay respects: "Hello, Jim Kelly, Sheet Metal, Local Seventeen"; "Mrs. Lynch, Billy O'Donnell, Iron Workers, Local Seven. I know Stephen. Say hi for me." Stephen Lynch, my cousin, was their hero—the youngest-ever president of the Iron Workers Union before he went to law school and then to Washington as our congressman from Southie.

When I got to the Quiet Man the night of the Beard nomination, half the neighborhood was there. It was all kisses and backslaps and "Hey, Barbara, what's going on?"

"Well," I said, "I think I'm up for a James Beard Award."

"Beard—I don't know him. Did he live in Old Harbor?"

"James? Jimmy? What? Some guy you slept with?"

"I think she said Jimmy Fucking Beard . . . right?"

"Who the fuck is this Jimmy Fucking Beard?"

I had to laugh.

● ● ●

The Quiet Man was the place where, a few years later, I staked my claim to Southie. Over lunch, my landlord asked, "Is it true that you're opening a restaurant in New York?"

"God, why would I do that? I have five restaurants now. I don't need any more."

"That's a shame," he told me. "Because I have more than a million square feet of warehouse space in Fort Point Channel." It was a stretch of Southie waterfront that I hadn't explored in years. In spite of myself, I was curious.

Fort Point Channel was once the textile district, though most of that trade had dried up. The most thriving business left was Gillette World Shaving Headquarters, one of Southie's major employers when I was young. Artists had carved lofts out of the beautiful vacant factories. A lot of those buildings were designated landmarks: elegant examples of industrial design from the nineteenth and early twentieth centuries. After dark, the area had an eerie frontier feeling. The streets were desolate.

As we set out on foot, I flashed back on walking that route with my mother: from Old Harbor down Old Colony Avenue to A Street. Then we stopped in front of a building that I knew well. It was the point where my mother and I would turn left for Downtown Crossing and the big department stores: Filene's, Gilchrist's, and Jordan Marsh. On a good day, she'd buy me a Jordan Marsh blueberry muffin. They were legendary. I'd pick at my muffin all the way home, savoring every crumb.

The building my landlord owned had once housed Boston Costume, which moved long ago. When I was a kid, the windows had thrilled me: jeweled masks, mannequins of Big Bird and Dorothy from *The Wizard of Oz*. It was like a fairyland.

"How many square feet?" I asked.

"What do you want? A thousand feet? Fifteen hundred?"

"No, all of it," I said. All fifteen thousand square feet—a whole city block.

It was a vow of commitment to Southie, an act of love.

• • •

Now I'm embedded, more deeply than ever, in the place where I was born. I built out the space into a sporty Italian trattoria, an artisanal cocktail bar, and a French/Italian fine-dining restaurant, where I continue (I hope) to surprise people with food. My full-block nightlife destination helped spearhead the revitalization of an area that, for decades, had been a derelict wasteland, left for dead.

I've never left Southie, and I can't: Southie is in me, in my fuck-you, make-me, prove-it attitude; in my wicked foul mouth, accent busting out if I don't control it. Its rhythms stoke my fierce stamina and drive, my sense of honor, the ironclad allegiance of my lifelong friendships. It throbs in my veins in brash, daredevil impulses that I can't shake—for better or worse—in life and love.

That's Southie: where I come from.

1

THE LOWER END

South Boston or Southie is an island connected to Greater Boston by a double handful of bridges and a few tunnels. Only seven minutes away from anywhere in Boston you'd want to go, it's a separate, self-contained world. It got a bad name during the Boston busing crisis of the 1970s, when the federal court forced students from two equally proud, isolated cultures (white Southie and black Roxbury) to switch schools. Images of screaming white parents mobbing school buses of black children, spitting at the intruders or throwing stones, ruled the TV news, matched by reports of stabbings and black kids dragging a white driver out of his car to beat him, crushing his skull. The mix created a classic case of "contents under pressure," with predictable results—*Boom!*

Today, Southie's congresswoman is homegrown, but Irish-by-marriage and African American. So times have changed, but still, there are scars.

• • •

The Southie of my childhood had been overwhelmingly working-class Irish American for generations. One of the oldest neighborhoods in America, it was settled by immigrants fleeing Ireland's potato famine in the 1800s. So it's not surprising that Southie is spiderwebbed with social connections. The first question anyone asks when you meet is, "Are you related to . . . ?" I got to know Mary, one longtime friend, on the Southie Riviera— Carson Beach—when she hit me with, "Hey, are you related to Kenny Lynch, my brother's friend?" And the second question you always get is, "Where do (or did) you live?" The answer brands you because different stretches of our two-mile-long spit of land—not to mention, nearby Dorchester—were like different villages, each with its own character.

The east or "city" side of Southie—the section fronted by Boston Harbor that faces downtown, full of historic warehouses resettled by Fort Point artists (and now, techie startups)—has gentrified beyond imagination. Even when I was a kid, though, being from City Point on the east side meant money. My home turf was the west side, called the Lower End. It's dominated by housing projects, Columbia Point (mostly black), D Street, and most important to me, Old Colony and Old Harbor (renamed for housing advocate Mary Ellen McCormack, mother of the speaker of the house in the 1960s). The last two each had twenty-two large three-story apartment buildings, and for big families, Old Harbor also offered about 150 two-story row houses.

My family qualified for a row house at 51 Devine Way, near the rotary separating Old Harbor from Old Colony. I was the youngest of six children born to Barbara Kelleher and Philip "Yapper" Lynch. From what I hear, Yapper was a hard-working taxi driver. He'd been class president at South Boston (Southie) High, which is where he met my mother. He loved to play baseball, and he loved to drink. Even on benders, though, he was charming, with the gift of blarney his nickname implied. He died at age thirty-four, shortly before I was born, so I never knew him. Still, whenever I said the Lord's Prayer, "Our Father, who art in Heaven . . .," I imagined that I was talking to him, as well as God, asking for his help and protection.

As a child, I believed that my father had a heart attack. As an adult, I learned the truth: that at some point my mother had to throw him out, and he'd spent a year in a halfway house, fighting to get sober. He'd died of alcoholism, the Irish scourge.

That left my mother with six kids to raise alone. Phyllis, the oldest, was born when my mother was just eighteen. Three boys followed—Paul, who would co-own the Quiet Man; Gerry, nick-named Jazz, who became a bookie then a cop; and Kenny, the cute one, who loved cars, especially BMWs, and is a truck driver. Then came Beth, my troubled sister, and, four years later, me. By the time I was old enough to know my siblings, Phyllis was nine-teen and married, living in her own house in Braintree.

With Phyllis gone, the burden of childcare must have been crushing for my mother. Since she refused to go on welfare, unlike many of our neighbors, she also had to support us. How the hell she managed, I can't even guess. For as long as I can remember, she worked two or three jobs: waitressing by day, col-lating from 7:00 p.m. to midnight for Winthrop Press, a company that made flash cards; and on the side selling Avon or Mary Kay cosmetics. She and her friends often met at our house, scheming ways to boost profits. They all aspired to Grand Achiever status at Mary Kay, hoping to score the top sales prize: a pink Cadillac.

The pressure on my mother never let up, even after she got a new husband. Still young when she was widowed, she was a looker, with twinkly green eyes (and a green trench coat to match), high cheekbones, a perfect bouffant, and stylish cat's-eye glasses. Her boobs were huge from having so many kids. When she got off work and settled into her fabric recliner chair, after tuning in to her police scanner she'd snap off her bra, which fascinated me. Once I tried it on and was shocked to find that each cup was about as wide as my whole body.

When I was three or four, she met Steve, an ex-navy man who wasn't daunted by her houseful of children. When they married, my sister Phyllis begged, "Ma, get the Pill or something. Six kids is enough." But for CIAs (Catholic Irish Americans), "rhythm" was the one form of birth control allowed. At Phyllis's wedding, my mother walked down the aisle pregnant, and she and my sister both had babies in 1971, just months apart.

My baby brother, John, was cute and so chubby-cheeked that I'd stuff his mouth with Oreos just to see how many would fit. He seemed to awaken some buried tenderness in my mother that the rest of us never got. Maybe John was more of a novelty, coming from a different father. I loved him, but I thought he was spoiled.

If Steve had any fatherly instincts, I never saw them. He was a drinker but, unlike Yapper, had a mean streak. Mostly, we tried to avoid him. He worked as janitor at the John Boyle O'Reilly School, contributing little family income. So money was a constant worry. Between her paying jobs, the housework, and keeping a half-assed eye on us kids, my mother always teetered on the edge of burnout.

• • •

It strikes me now that I barely knew my mother, though I lived with her into adulthood. I stayed because I was broke, working to get a toehold in the world. My mother's dependency was the trade-off. Once, when I bullshitted my way into a chef's job on a cruise ship, she wrote me a seven-page letter—basically a rant. How dare I just leave? Didn't I know how hard it was to have six kids and be abandoned by them all? Who would take her grocery shopping with her friends (meaning, who would drive them home after shopping, then stopping for a few martinis)? On and on . . . We didn't speak for months.

By then, Steve was gone. When I was about thirteen, she threw him out, probably for lying around drunk half the time, cradling a huge bottle of port, with his Irish music playing, in his wife-beater, shorts, and sandals with white socks. So she relied on me for everything. I was always telling friends, "I'll catch up with you later. I have to run to the druggie"—the corner store, to buy her lottery tickets or one of her three daily papers: the *Boston Herald*, the *Boston Globe*, and the *South Boston (Southie) Tribune*; "and then the deli," to get her favorite Land O'Lakes cheese, sliced off the block on Number 4, just the right thickness. Or I was off to D'Angelo's to pick up her favorite sub, Number 9—steak and cheese with mushrooms.

Christmas was a nightmare because I had to buy and wrap gifts for all my siblings, their spouses, and the grandkids, whose names and birthdays were recorded on a white card taped—and retaped, in yellowing layers—to the bottom of the wooden napkin holder on the kitchen table, her command post. Also on the table, which was draped with patterned vinyl to protect the fake wood, were stacks of the magazines she loved, like *Good Housekeeping* and *Reader's Digest*, interspersed with unopened bills; multiple half-used bottles of mauve-brown nail polish; and the syringes she used for her insulin, since she was diabetic.

But when I was a child, she was a whirlwind, sassy and capable—sewing, ironing the hand-me-downs we wore, sticking a bowl on our heads to cut our hair. Every couple months, she'd subject Beth and me to Toni perms, rolling our hair up on dozens of tiny rods to give us masses of curls. To this day, I gag when remembering the chemical stench of a Toni perm.

My mother was proud that instead of an apartment, we had a proper house, with a tiny fenced-in yard. Like all the row houses, it had a steel-topped sunken trash barrel out front that seemed to breed huge slugs, which freaked me out. To beautify the space, my mother planted roses and a lilac bush. If kids tried to pick the flowers, she'd poke her head out the window and shout, "You touch that and I'll boil you in oil!"

Other points of pride for her were the gleaming grandfather clock, which was the first thing you noticed coming into the house, and her hutch full of "Hummels," little statuettes that people used to collect. Only I think most of hers were the giveaway kind—like the little clay beer mug with a shamrock on it—that you'd get for spending a certain amount at Flanagan's Supermarket. Her favorites were elephants with the trunks pointing up, which she thought symbolized good luck. Every week Steve would dust her knickknacks—a hangover from his navy training, I guess—and shine the decorative white wrought-iron grating over our government-green front door as if it were made of brass.

My mother could be funny. Once I opened the fridge to find my face smiling back at me. She'd taped a picture to the rack to make me laugh. She could also be impatient and fierce. When I was in kindergarten, I was dawdling over breakfast one day and asked for a second bowl of cereal.

"Are you really hungry?" she asked, suspicious. I said yes.

"Well, you better be, because if you don't eat this, you're going to wear it."

Sure enough, I couldn't finish the second bowl, and she dumped what was left of it over my head. All day I was picking bits of Cheerios out of my hair. If this had happened later, I might have cut school, but kindergarten was the one grade I actually loved, before learning became a challenge for me. I still remember the day we put heavy cream in a mason jar and shook the hell out of it until it curdled. It turned into butter, which we ate on Saltines—a miracle!

Even that young, I had an interest in food, sparked by my mother's cooking. Though she made plain, down-to-earth meals, with heavy reliance on convenience products, she had particular tastes and added her own special creative touches. Like in her tuna-fish sandwich, which I loved, she'd use only StarKist white albacore in water and Cains mayonnaise, never Hellman's, thinned with splashes of milk and a secret ingredient, Vlasic pickle juice. She'd mash the mixture with two forks until it was creamy, spoon it onto Sunbeam, not Wonder Bread (which had too many holes), and top it with pickle slices. Before brown-bagging the sandwich, she'd double-seal it in clear waxed paper topped with Saran Wrap.

At school, I'd stick the bag between the cast-iron tubes of the radiator, both to warm it up and so I could enjoy the tuna-fish-pickle smell until it was time for lunch.

When I got home, I'd often find her in the kitchen, smoking a Benson & Hedges while reading the *Herald* or touching up her mauve-brown nails. "What's for dinner?" I'd ask.

"Shit on a shingle," she'd say. "You're gonna love it."

And I would. It might be her fantastic flank steak, or spaghetti with her delicious meatballs made of ground beef, garlic powder, dried onion flakes, herbs, Parmesan cheese, and—the magic touch—Saltines soaked in milk. If someone in the family got lucky at keno, she'd make a beef roast topped with sliced onions, seasoned simply with pepper and salt. My first hint of food attunement, as a child, was that I could tell just by the aroma when it was done.

Her pork chops, though tasty, were always fried rock hard. She let them sit in the pan, half submerged in fat, until it was time to serve them with a scoop of Mott's applesauce. It must have been years before I ever had a pork chop that was easy to cut.

On the side, she'd serve canned peas, but only the Le Sueur petite ones, which were sweet and packed in watery syrup. Even their silver cans looked classy. ("Can we have some of those 'leisure' peas?" I'd ask.) We'd have baked potatoes slathered with Land O'Lakes margarine, since no one ate butter back then, or instant mashed, out of a box, dressed up with sautéed onions.

I asked my mother once, "If you're taking the trouble to fry onions, why don't you fucking mash some real potatoes?"

"Barbara, honest to God," she said, snorting at such pointless effort. "Where do you come from?"

Today food is my language, the way I communicate with the world. So I wonder if, for her—a woman with too many kids, too little money, a foul-tempered, hard-drinking husband, too much stress overall—creative touches in the kitchen like pickle juice and sautéed onions were a way of expressing love.

Her recipes, her plants, her knickknacks, her scent (Emeraude cologne and powder, from a box with a fluffy puff), her sarcasm, her hard work—to me, these were the factors that defined her. I had no clue as to her personal dreams, her view of our life, her aspirations for her kids, or importantly, her feelings about me. I couldn't even tell you her favorite color.

Sometimes, in summer, I'd get a flash of a cozier family life. When Steve was sober and in the mood, he'd take my mother, John, and me on the ferry to Nantasket Beach in Hull. Paragon Park was there, with a giant Ferris wheel, a roller coaster, a water slide, the Kooky Kastle house of horrors, and other thrill rides. But what I loved best was the beach, cleaner and less crowded than our Southie Riviera, and the meal we'd share: fried scallops and clams, plus onion rings and French fries, thinly sliced and perfectly crisp, served in red-and-white-checked cardboard boats with crunchy coleslaw and zingy tartar sauce. We'd wash it down with tingly, real soda fountain Coca-Cola. As the sun began to set, we'd make our way to the dock for the boat trip back to Boston, sunburned, full, and sleepy; feeling a warm glimmer of closeness, of belonging, that soon passed.

• • •

Here's a more typical memory: When I was around five, Sterling Square got a new playground, with cement turtles to climb on.

But it didn't stay welcoming for long. Its benches were almost instantly tagged with graffiti. The sandbox was quickly polluted with sharp can tabs, bottle caps, and glints of broken glass. When it was sunny, all the steel equipment—the slides, the monkey bars, and the chain swings with rubber seats—got hot enough to sizzle your skin. The ground below them was peppered with cigarette butts, roaches burned to the nub, and here and there, crushed Miller High Life and Schlitz cans.

Having been pushed out of the house with the usual "Go play till the streetlights come on," I went to try out the grim new playground. Climbing on the jungle gym, I slipped and, whacking my windpipe on a bar, hurtled to the ground. For a while I lay on the littered cement, breathless, trying to swallow, petrified that I'd broken something in my throat and was choking to death. When the other kids saw I was alive, they started catcalling, "Hey, Big Bird! Good one!" I managed to get to my feet and head for home.

I found my mother standing on the cover of the hissing, piping hot radiator, a Benson & Hedges dangling from her lips. She had a fistful of newspapers, dipped in vinegar, that she was using to scrub the film of cigarette smoke from the windows. "Ma . . .," I wheezed, unable to explain the terrifying fall and my panicked belief that I was dying.

She threw me a glance, probably checking for blood. For a second I thought she'd climb down from the radiator, take me in her arms, cuddle me, kiss my forehead, and soothe me: "What a terrible spill. I'm sorry you're hurt. It's not serious, though, and I know you'll conquer those scary monkey bars tomorrow. To hell with those kids who laughed . . ."

Instead she turned back to her task. "Let me finish here," she said. "You're going to be fine. Just go lie down for a while."

Even if she had the inclination, she never had the emotional energy to be loving and giving. I now think that probably she wasn't just overwhelmed but also was depressed—a state of mind was that was barely acknowledged in Southie.

• • •

There's another indelible memory from that time that I label mentally as "Darkness." I say "indelible" though, for years, I could hardly force its images into consciousness. It's threaded through my psyche in ways that I struggle to understand.

The memory unfurled in my brain, like a film loop, back in July 2013, when the *Boston Globe* quoted testimony from the racketeering trial of Whitey Bulger. Under questioning about molesting an underage girl, Stephen "the Rifleman" Flemmi said, "You want to talk about pedophilia—right over there at that table." He pointed to Whitey.

Pedophilia. Though my experience didn't involve Whitey himself, the sight of his smug face sent a white-hot rage surging through my body. It was so intense that it seared the lamination off an incident that I mostly relived in disjointed sensations: terror crawling down my spine at the hiss of pipes, or the stench of old urine, or the cement mustiness of a basement; sudden, sharp, private pains; the flicker in my mind of gasping horror, confinement, and blindness.

I knew the details of the incident, of course, but I couldn't quite grasp the reality. It was like a crackling live wire, a rush of emotion and sensation that threatened to electrocute me. So whenever these feelings sparked, I'd clamp my mind down hard, walling them off. Each clampdown seemed to add a new layer of protection. But now that shell had fractured.

Here's what happened: I was seven years old, heading home for dinner along O'Callaghan Way. A passageway led off it to Old Harbor athletic courts, an area nicknamed Needle Park. My best friend Jane Mahoney lived on Needle Park, next door to Whitey Bulger's mother.

In the passageway, three guys were loitering who looked vaguely familiar. Were they friends of my older brothers? Friends of friends? "Hey," one of them called out, as if he knew me. "I've got a little puppy. You want to see it?"

"Yes." Of course I did.

I followed them into the passageway and through a door leading to the apartment-building basement. On the concrete stairs, the air had a clammy chill and the iron handrail was cold. Though normally brave, I was spooked by the dimness, the stinging smell of piss, the drip and hiss of pipes, and the rumbling of the boiler.

"Where's the puppy?" I asked.

"Over here, in the next room."

Then someone grabbed me from behind. A soft cloth—a bandanna? A rag?—was tied over my eyes. A deep fear, radiating from the core of my body to my arms and legs and the roots of my hair, numbed me.

Unable to see, too paralyzed with horror to cry out—not that anyone could have heard me—I remember the cold floor beneath me, the sense of being pulled apart, the thrust of fleshy objects inside me, a shocking awareness of undiscovered parts of my own body. I lost all sense of the passing of time.

Finally the prodding and poking stopped. I was dressed, roughly, and pulled to my feet. The blindfold was yanked off, and I fled up the stairs, too afraid to look back and lock eyes with my unknown attackers.

When I burst out of the passageway, the sky was dark. There was my friend Jane Mahoney. "Babs!" she said. "Your ma called our house. She's looking for you!"

I was in trouble, out after sundown, late for dinner.

"What are you up to?" Jane was saying. "Your shirt's on wrong. It's inside out."

Distraught, I took off running, unable to squeak out a word.

At home, my mother was cooking, distracted. She didn't notice my agitation or, at least, didn't ask why I was late or what was wrong. *Luckily,* I thought. Or was it lucky? Would I have told her what happened?

I don't think so.

I didn't have the words to explain it, for one thing. At seven, I didn't quite know that my experience was possible, anatomically. I had a faint sense that, according to the church, anything related to your "private parts" was sinful, but the details were sketchy. I felt deeply ashamed for reasons that I didn't understand.

Even today, picturing my child-self, I can hardly bring myself to connect that image with the word *rape*.

I also had no idea how my mother would react. There was a chance I'd catch hell for being naïve enough to think I'd get to see a puppy. Was I that dumb? I couldn't imagine that she'd sympathize. The prospect of her anger, on top of the violation I'd already endured, would have been devastating.

And what if she (or Steve, God forbid—I couldn't stand the thought of him knowing) got angry not at me but at the men? Violence was a constant current in our lives. There was a kid who bounced a basketball in Needle Park late at night, keeping the neighborhood awake. Even after Whitey's mother yelled at him to knock it off, he wouldn't stop. Finally Whitey came out and jabbed a knife into the basketball. Then he yanked it out, stabbed the kid, and rushed him to the hospital. No one found this surprising.

So, if there was a confrontation, anything could happen, I knew. Punishing my attackers, trying to even the score, was too frightening and dangerous to contemplate. So I was mired in helpless rage, mostly at myself, for being too paralyzed to save myself during the assault and, in the aftermath, still too powerless to fight back.

These were just some of the excruciating thoughts and emotions that flooded in, immobilizing me until I learned to quash them. So I told no one about the rape. It was a very heavy burden for a child to carry.

• • •

I kept that secret, that damage, locked inside until my forties, when the Bulger trial shook it loose. I ask myself now, how did I keep it at bay? At least part of the answer is: by outrunning it.

Since my teens, I've zigzagged from one adventure to the next, teaching myself to cook, traveling to train my palate and to discover the exotic world beyond the confines of Southie. Since I have a dose of ADD, I've always had—and like to have—a dozen possibilities percolating. My business has been something of a high-wire act without a net, taking gambles, thriving on the drama of creation. And working like a demon to the point of collapse, with unrelenting, tits-to-the-wall, full-throttle, thrusting momentum.

Even my pauses—for marriage, motherhood, and continued groping for understanding of myself as lover and as a woman—have been risk-filled and consuming.

Only now, in my second half century, have I had time—or, maybe, have allowed myself time—for the luxury of introspection and the effort to recover and make sense of memories.

But sometimes I think, *No wonder I work with flame, ice, and spirits; the clank of stainless steel and the hiss of steam.*

2

PISSAH

When I was a child, there were two things I could never resist—taking a dare and getting a laugh. Friends like Jane Mahoney loved to egg me on. Unlike me, Jane was a girly-girl with waist-length braids, not a bowl cut, and a wardrobe of dresses, not odd, plaid hand-me-downs. She always wore heels, even at age six or seven and even when we played "tennis," batting around balls in Needle Park, next to her house.

We also hung out on the grounds of Saint Mary's, her Catholic elementary school. We'd steal cigarettes from our mothers and huddle in a little shed there to smoke. If the nuns ever caught us, they'd chase us out with brooms. One day I showed up with a prize: an umbrella depicting characters from our favorite movie, *Mary Poppins*. We'd stage little shows in the passageways linking the project's apartment blocks, enjoying the echoes as we screamed, "Super-cali-fragilistic-expiali-docious!"

I wondered out loud, "With this umbrella, could I actually fly like Mary Poppins?"

"Of course!" Jane told me. "Of course you can!"

I climbed up on the roof of the shed, and she passed me the umbrella. "This doesn't seem high enough," I said, trying to picture myself soaring. The rest of our gang was watching, as hopeful as Jane that it was possible to fly. "Do it, do it . . .," they urged me.

Looking down at their expectant faces, there was no way I could chicken out. So I snapped open the umbrella. I stepped to the edge of the roof. Then I flung myself off it, into thin air.

Whoosh! I hit the ground in seconds, flat on my face. My teeth smashed through my lower lip.

Dazed and gushing blood, I staggered to my feet, fleeing before the others could see me cry. All the way home, I kept peering in the side mirrors of cars, to check on the bleeding. It was bad.

I'm sure I got stitches. I don't remember. But my main memory of the jump is my surge of courage at roof's edge—all fear banished by the thrill.

With that leap I gained a reputation (even to myself) as a badass kid who'd try anything. Though I craved excitement and lacked foresight, I had enough common sense and bad examples to steer clear of some Southie hazards, like heavy-duty drugs. Considering some of my antics, I guess I'm lucky to be alive. Maybe my father, Yapper—or some super dedicated guardian angel—really was watching over me.

• • •

A lot of people saw Whitey Bulger as Southie's guardian angel. He grew up in Old Harbor, in the corner row house where his mother still lived, next to Jane Mahoney's. He'd returned to Southie after nearly a decade in federal prison a year or so after I was born. During my childhood, he was slugging his way to the top of the Winter Hill Gang, the crime syndicate that ruled Boston by the 1970s. As it began knocking out the Italian and

Irish mob competition, so many corpses were dumped in the Dorchester neighborhood of Savin Hill that it got to be known as Stab and Kill Hill. Women's bodies—ex-girlfriends of Whitey and his crew—washed up on beaches or turned up in trunks brutally dismembered, with their toenails ripped off. Whispered stories of such grisly murders passed into legend, but Whitey himself, whom we called Charlie or Uncle Charlie (instead of James, his real name), remained sort of a folk hero.

One reason for his aura was glory reflected from his brother Bill, a respected, popular state senator for some twenty years and after that president of the University of Massachusetts. (The tale of two kids, born from the same womb, winding up totally different was familiar in Southie, and even in my own family.) That respectable air was heightened by the common belief that Whitey preyed only on the rich or fellow mobsters, not on regular people. Sure, every day we saw drug dealing and petty racketeering like loan-sharking and illegal gambling. But people thought Whitey kept a lid on person-to-person crimes, like stick-ups and break-ins—that he kept the projects safe.

Certainly, he was everywhere—charismatic, good-looking, and well dressed. Brothers and fathers I knew were rumored to work for his gang. Whitey was the godfather to many Southie children, including some of my friends. When we were old enough to sneak into bars with fake IDs, he'd often buy us all a round of drinks. Still, even as little kids, we knew to keep our distance.

Once Whitey pulled up in his car when my brother John and I were out walking, with our dog, Shatzi, snuffling along behind us. "Hey, kids!" he yelled, waving an arm out the window. We froze until we saw what he was brandishing. "You gotta have a leash," he said sternly, thrusting one at John, then going on his way.

Another time, when Jane and I were playing on the tennis courts, Whitey came barreling out of his mother's house.

"Quick," he hissed at Jane and, grabbing us, shoved us down behind a car. Minutes later, three black limousines appeared, and bullets raked his mother's yard. It must have been some kind of threat in the ongoing gang wars.

We crouched there till Whitey decided that the danger had passed and let us go. We'd been scared stiff but quickly recognized the moment for what it was: a good story. Just a high-drama blast of business as usual in Southie.

* * *

Jane and I were inseparable during elementary school, though she went to Saint Mary's and I attended John Boyle O'Reilly, where her mother, Florence, was a lunchroom monitor. Florence was tiny and thin and a Nervous Nellie, but very kind. She also made a kick-ass fried baloney sandwich, so I was always angling for an invitation to eat at Jane's.

The entire Mahoney family was musical. Jane's brothers played in bands, and her mother and aunt Millie gave performances, doing dance numbers to show tunes at local social clubs. I used to love going with them to the Polish American Club, which was right around the corner from Saint Mary's. We'd get to play the jukebox, dance, and order Cokes with maraschino cherries and my favorite square ice cubes, with a little dip in the middle where the soda pooled and you could sip it. To me, that was the height of glamour.

I also loved watching the women hanging out there, smoking and popping Schlitz cans like nobody's business. These were the mothers of Southie. There were a few fathers around, or step-fathers like Steve, who didn't count, but a lot of the dads who weren't off working were cruel or drunk. So kids didn't often interact with them. Instead, it was the women who ruled the projects.

Many, like my own mother, were hardworking and proud. If

they lived in apartments, their hallways were swept and gleaming; in row houses, the yards were groomed. Though they were poor, their families never wanted for anything that could be borrowed, handed down, or bought on layaway by pinching a few dollars out of each paycheck. Though plenty had more kids than they could supervise, any of those mothers would take care of you and give you the back of a hand if you got out of line.

They were tough. Once, my teenage brother Kenny stayed out all night without bothering to call. The next day, my mother called her friend Peggy Mahoney (no relation to Jane), threw on her green trench coat over her housecoat, and set out with Peggy to find him. I tagged along. They spotted him sprawling in someone's car, smoking a joint and drinking a beer. The fact that he was with his friends didn't faze my mother.

Marching up to his window, she reached into the car and snatched the beer out of his hand. As he wheeled to face her, she smacked the half-full can right into his mouth, knocking out his teeth. That was scary. Today we'd consider it abuse. But back then it was hard-ass-Southie-mother-style discipline, fierce and swift—and typical.

My mother, being older than some of the other parents, was often stricter. But because she was funny and could drive, she was considered the local "cool mom"—a reputation boosted by the fact that, since she was stretched so thin, I had a lot of freedom, with loose curfews and little supervision. Constantly in and out of my friends' houses, I was taken under a lot of different mothers' wings. It was those mothers—not Whitey—whom I came to admire as Southie's true guardian angels, the ones who really kept the projects safe.

* * *

Like everyone in Southie, I had a fairly well-known extended family. Not so much on my mother's side, since she had only two siblings: Buddy and Maureen. After serving in World War II, Buddy had a terrible car crash, suffering such severe head injuries that he spent the rest of his life in Veterans Administration assisted living. He would visit us on Saturday afternoons and sit there just smiling, perfectly quiet. He was in his own world. My aunt Maureen is still very much alive, with four children and many grandchildren. But my mother remained close to the Lynches, Yapper's family, who were very well liked and well respected in Southie. There were a lot of them, so I had a lot of cousins who I didn't really start keeping track of until I was in my teens.

Being many years younger than my own siblings, I didn't have all that much contact with them. My baby brother, John, was mostly a curiosity to me until we were both young adults. My oldest sister and brother, Phyllis and Paul, seemed to belong to a different generation. Phyllis had actually gone to high school with some of my friends' mothers; and her best friend, Eileen O'Sullivan, was my godmother.

Paul and his girlfriend, Mary Ellen (soon to become his wife), used to babysit for Beth and me, even before John was born. We'd always beg to comb Mary Ellen's hair, which was beautiful, long, and blond. I can hardly remember Paul's hair color because it turned white very early on. For years, he's looked like the Southie version of Steve Martin.

Paul was a sheet metal worker back then, before buying into the Quiet Man pub. He'd been injured somehow and was on crutches forever. Bratty kid that I was, I would hear the bell of the pizza truck, clanging as it drove through the projects, and demand that he get me some. Kids would compete to ring the bell, alerting customers, in exchange for a free slice. Being a good-natured brother, Paul hobbled out to the truck to buy it.

Until Paul moved out, he shared the basement with my brothers Gerald (Jazz) and Kenny, seven and five years older than me, respectively. The basement was a semifinished space with dark paneling and a huge old soapstone utility sink that always smelled like beer from the six-packs the guys would smuggle in. In one wall was a door that opened onto a tunnellike pipe leading to my friend Patty Sullivan's house next door. All the houses in each row were connected by these pipes, which became our secret clubhouses.

I loved that little hideaway and was fascinated by my brothers' underground lair. Kenny was a serious Boy Scout, who taught me to tie knots, among other skills. Thumbing through his set of Boy Scout manuals, I discovered his private hoard of precious trinkets—and later, pot—stuffed in hollows he'd carved into the pages. I'd check now and then to see what new treasures he had stashed. When I got caught rifling through their stuff, my brothers would threaten me with "knuckle sandwiches," shaking their fists, or drive me out of the basement with "noogies," knuckles twisted on top of my head.

The worst was when a water bug—a winged beetle resembling a huge cockroach—crawled out of some damp cranny. Kenny, especially, hated them and, if he saw one, which he often did, he'd tear ass out of the basement, with me right behind him.

Music was always wafting up the stairs: songs by the Beatles or my brothers' favorites, the Moody Blues and Van Morrison. I think I could still sing "Moondance" from memory. Both my brothers played in bands and were always practicing their cover versions. If I was lucky, they'd let me and a friend or two come down to listen and dance.

Jazz and Kenny hung out with a big crew called the Wall Nuts, named for the place where about thirty of them gathered almost every night. It was a long brick wall lined with cement benches that ran along the Needle Park athletic courts. All the Wall Nuts went by nicknames: Jane Mahoney's brother Walter was Wazz, someone else was Yazz, a guy named Danny was Red, and so on. Every year they'd throw a huge party in Needle Park that was like a battle of the bands, with all the neighborhood groups playing. It was the highlight of the summer, though my strongest impression, as a child, was everyone staggering around trashed. But I was so proud of my rock-star brothers.

My sister Beth, a couple years older than me, hung with the Wall Nuts but also with some older, druggier Old Colony gangs. Our sisterhood was complicated. To begin with, we shared a bedroom. My brothers had their own private world in the basement, but our room was upstairs, just off the small landing where the telephone rested on a desk full of batteries, old pens, and other junk. The room next to ours belonged to my little brother, John, the only member of the family who had his own space. Across the landing was the tiny bathroom, with a bar of Irish Spring soap always perched on the ledge of the tub. Next to the bathroom was the light yellow bedroom that my mother shared with Steve.

Beth and I shared a closet and each had our own twin bed, but every other inch of that little room was disputed turf. We fought constantly. One day we were tussling—punching, cursing, yanking each other's hair—with such fury that we could barely hear my mother yelling, "Stop it! Cut it out!" I was never a girly doll lover, but I did have one: a Mrs. Beasley doll, from the TV show *Family Affair,* about two feet tall with a plastic head, little granny glasses, and a stuffed cloth body. When you pulled a cord, she would say things like, "Long ago, I was a little girl just like you," or "If you were a little smaller, I could rock you to sleep."

I think I was choking Beth when my mother grabbed the closest thing to hand—Mrs. Beasley—and started walloping the shit out of us, to drive us apart. After one fierce whack, Mrs. Beasley's head broke off and went flying. It wasn't until I heard her voice box die—*"Lonngg aaggo"*—that I came to my senses and let go of Beth. Poor Mrs. Beasley. I was crushed. Wouldn't you know it, today those Mrs. Beasley dolls sell on eBay for several hundred dollars. They're collector's items.

Though I mostly hated Beth, I did have a typical younger-sister crush on her. She looked like a model, taller than me with Major League breasts and, in her Levi's cutoffs, legs that seemed to stretch forever. She used to accuse me of stealing her clothes, which was crazy, since they'd never fit me. I was (definitely in my own mind and probably in fact) a lot stumpier.

Beth had long black hair and blue eyes, which were much more dramatic than my own sparrow-brown and hazel-green. She had a sense of style, always wearing boots, big hoop earrings, and a kerchief on her head, like a pirate. She looked tough and beautiful, listened to Carole King albums, and always walked around with a camera, snapping photos and acting cool. When I grew up, I promised myself, I would be her.

Besides sharing a bedroom, Beth and I shared a moped. One day some kid was harassing Beth, and Kenny went after him, beating him up. To clinch the punishment, he took the kid's moped and told him never to come back for it. So it became ours. One of our big adventures was riding the moped to the first McDonald's branch in Boston.

Most of the time, though, Beth had no use for a tag-along little sister. I should have been suspicious the day she asked to come shopping with her at Downtown Crossing. But she seemed to be in a rare good mood, and I was flattered by her attention.

I thought we were going to hit the big department stores, but Beth sent me into Louis Boston, famous for its super exclusive and super expensive clothes. "Just tell them that your shopping bag broke," she said. "Say you need a big one for all your stuff."

I guess she thought that they'd believe me and take pity on a kid. She was right.

When I came out with the bag, Beth took it and steered me to the Paine Furniture Building. I couldn't imagine what we were doing there. "Just go along with what I say," she told me.

In the showroom, Beth spotted a clerk and said, "Can you help us? My little sister is so dizzy that she's about to faint. Would you get us glass of water?"

I tried to look woozy as the clerk hurried off to get me a drink. I finished the water, and then Beth said, "Thank you. I'd better get her home." She hustled me out. When we made it around the corner, she pulled something out of the back of her pants and shoved it into the Louis Boston bag. It was a small Oriental rug.

What fucking nerve! On one level I was impressed. My own shoplifting years were still ahead of me, so I could hardly process stealing an expensive rug. I couldn't guess why Beth would want it.

But on another level, I was pissed. Beth had taken advantage of my little-sister admiration to make me a stooge. I could have gotten busted, which didn't scare me, but she hadn't even clued me in to her plan. She'd never planned on having a sisterly adventure or on cutting me in on the proceeds of the theft. She'd just fucking flat-out used me.

We grabbed a cab back to Southie. On Old Colony Avenue, we both jumped out and tore ass in opposite directions—a classic scheme to beat the fare. I later heard through the grapevine that Beth sold the rug at Aces High, a well-known dive where you could bet on anything—from team sports to horse and dog races—and score any drug you wanted. But Beth refused even to discuss our caper.

A day or so later, I took Shatzi out for walk. It was mid-March, around the time of my birthday, but the air was unusually warm and springlike. The sun felt good on my face, and I was starting to get excited about playing outside after spending the winter cooped up. I headed across Columbus Park to Carson Beach. The water would be icy cold, but I longed to stick my hands in it. My mother's saying was running through my head, "Salt water cures everything."

Walking down the beach, Shatzi and I approached the bathhouse, which was still closed for the winter. That made it the perfect hangout for kids cutting school, close to but out of sight of the projects. I was surprised to see our moped there, propped in a half-assed way against the wall, with its kickstand sticking out and the seat flipped open. Beth used to keep pot in that compartment, either in nickel bags or prerolled joints.

I started circling the bathhouse to look for her, kicking a path for Shatzi though the litter and broken glass. As I came up on her, she was hunched over, with her sleeves rolled up and a needle in her hand. She was zoned out, in such a stupor that she didn't even see me.

So that's what she did with rug money . . ., I thought. I was shocked.

Since my mother was diabetic, I was no stranger to needles, though I was scared to watch her inject herself. I had seen every kind of drunk—happy ones, sloppy ones, angry ones—and observed my brothers and their friends in what I'd come to recognize as the mellow glow of pot. But seeing Beth like that freaked me out.

Maybe I was shocked because I'd idolized Beth (underneath my bitter resentment). Maybe it was the violence of the act of stabbing herself to get high. At that point, I didn't have a real grasp of the heavier drugs and their effects, even though they were starting to show up in the projects, but I'd probably heard scary, exaggerated stories about addiction and inevitable death.

I clearly recall feeling sick with terror—literally, ready to puke. I didn't dare say a word to Beth, for fear that whatever spell she was under might engulf me too. I ran home, dragging Shatzi. When I got there, not wanting to rat out Beth, I told no one what I saw. Anyway, my feelings were so overwhelming and raw that I never could have expressed them.

In time, Beth's drug use got out of control. Then it was no longer just my horrible secret but a drama that we all lived with—and Beth struggled with—for years to come. I made a new promise to myself: no way would I become Beth when I grew up.

● ● ●

My loose but close-knit gang of friends seemed more like my real family. In the winter, we'd ride the bus to the ice rink at Castle Island, the last stop. All of us had cool skates, like my CCM clear blades, hot "off the truck"—that is, stolen and sold cheap. Since we had no other equipment, we played Southie hockey, our own invention, with broomsticks and pimple balls. The game involved hitting the pimple ball, made of hard rubber with a spiky pimpled surface, in the air, as well as batting it over the ice. Naturally, between slipping and get smacked by flying pimple balls, we always came home bruised and battered.

Summer meant Carson Beach, where everyone greased up with iodine and baby oil to bake in the sun. If there was sunscreen back then, we didn't know or care. The goal was a mahogany tan, which was hard to achieve with white, delicate, easily fried Irish skin. It always fascinated me to see pregnant women digging holes in the sand for their bellies so they could roll over and tan their backs.

But what really grabbed my attention, as I roasted on the beach in my orange bathing suit, was the little snack shack that we called the Pickle. Rumor had it that the Pickle belonged to Whitey Bulger, who took a cut of the profits and used it to retail drugs. What I cared about was the food—your basic beach fare like hamburgers, with or without cheese and pickles, hot dogs, French fries, and Cokes.

Running a joint like the Pickle—how exciting that would be! I could pretty much live at the beach, for one thing, and for another, I could cook whatever I wanted. Even before the AA pesto party, I was always trying out recipes. Once, a bunch of us had a sleepover, and I made pancakes for breakfast. I mean

PANCAKES—with so much batter that I could have fed half of Old Harbor. I just kept pulling them off the stove and stacking them up, all over the kitchen. Other than the volume, they were pretty damn good.

So I had a vivid fantasy of the Pickle, not with a walk-up counter but with an outdoor café and waitresses. I'd be in command of the tiny but gleaming kitchen, wearing a long apron, waving a burger flipper. Or I'd be sliding a tantalizing pizza from the fiery oven onto the counter, driving everyone crazy with the smell. I even imagined myself doing cleanup at closing time, polishing stovetops, sweeping the floor, and chopping vegetables for the next day. When your dream includes shit work, you know it's serious.

I told everyone on the beach, "You know, someday I'd love to have a little restaurant here . . ."

● ● ●

When we reached junior high, Jane Mahoney enrolled at Monsignor Ryan Memorial, a school outside the neighborhood. We drifted apart, but other friends in my ever-growing crew were just as eager to encourage and join me in troublemaking. We all liked to joyride by hopping on the back bumper of Dizzo's ice cream truck. One day, the exasperated driver sped up, to shake us off. Hanging on for dear life, I thought, *No fucking way! I can't last.* I let go and hit the street.

The last thing I remember was the screech of brakes and the huge crash as two cars behind us collided, trying to avoid hitting me. I blacked out, and I woke up in the emergency room, in terrible pain. My stepfather, Steve, was there, looking pissed that he'd been dragged in. It turned out that I'd fractured both legs, which didn't faze me. What killed me was that I wouldn't be able to ride my new bike for months and months.

That close call didn't teach me anything. One day, after fooling around downtown, my friends and I happened to get off the T, Boston's subway, at Broadway, a stop ahead of our usual station. We took the escalator up to the street and there, just outside the station door, we saw an MBTA bus idling with the door open. There was no driver inside.

"Hey, I could drive this bus home," I said, half-joking.

"Yeah!" said my friends, all gung ho. It never occurred to anyone to point out, "You're thirteen years old, Barbara. You don't know how to drive."

We climbed onto the bus, and I got behind the wheel, which was bigger than I was. I couldn't reach the floor, never mind the pedals, with my feet. But I did figure out that you had to pull a stick, probably the emergency brake, to get underway. So, with one friend helping me turn the heavy steering wheel and another on the floor working the gas and brake pedals, we managed to start rolling.

"Ahhhhhhh!" we were screaming. The bus was moving slowly—straight ahead, luckily—but gaining speed. I don't know how far we traveled—it felt like blocks and blocks—before we'd had a big enough dose of danger. We stopped the bus with a sickening lurch, then jumped off and hauled ass back to the projects. All the way home, we were practically foaming at the mouth we were laughing so hard.

*   *   *

When I asked friends to share reminiscences for this book, every single one of them piped up with memories of times when I was, as one of them called me, "a wicked pissah." I have a full-body laugh, which has led to some embarrassing moments. I'm sure that they doubted I'd have the nerve to include their stories, but obviously I still can't back off a dare.

Joanie: All my friends lived in the projects, but my family lived in a private house nearby. One day Barbara, Mary, and I were sitting on the shag rug in my parlor, playing the board game Pay Day. Pay Day was like Monopoly, except it was about making money instead of buying property. We were cracking ourselves up, goofing on each other, saying, "It's Pay Day, Barbara, Pay Day! Woo woo!" And then it happened.

Tina: My story takes place in a pizzeria, either Papa Gino's or Billy's, I can't remember. Barbara and I were seated across the table from Karen, a friend who used to mimic Alfalfa from *The Little Rascals*. She'd wet a chunk of her hair with Coca-Cola so it would dry like his, standing straight up. We were laughing like crazy as she did her Alfalfa voice. Then, all of sudden, it felt like my leg was on fire, and I said, "Jesus, Barbara! What the hell . . . ?"

Cheryl: One day, I was downstairs in my house, talking to my grandmother on the phone, while Barbara, who was up in my room, decided to try on my doctor's pants. Doctor's scrub clothes were the fashion at the time, and my pink ones were especially cool. But I'm a lot taller and thinner than Barbara. I kept switching conversations, saying "Nana, hold on," while yelling up the stairs, "Barbara, they'll never fit you." Barbara somehow made it down the stairs with the pants halfway up. "Take them off," I insisted. "They're gonna rip." Barbara started laughing and suddenly my pants turned dark pink. I was screaming, "Oh my God!"

Mary: How about my poor mother? We had a pullout couch that three or four of us would pile onto for sleepovers. In the morning

Barbara would say, "Gerry, can I have some coffee?" First of all, no kid back then dared to call a mother by her first name, and secondly, we were too young for coffee. But my mother would give her a little, to indulge her. Barbara would take a sip, then let it drool out the side of her mouth, to make us laugh. "Barbara . . .," my mother would warn. "I love you, Gerry," Barbara would say, hamming it up. "I love you . . ." That would snap my mother to attention. "Barbara, stop it right now." She knew what would happen if Barbara started laughing. "You're not peeing in my kitchen." Part of the reason that my mother—and everyone else—loved Barbara was her humor and the way she laughed.

• • •

I guess I have a weak bladder, but more than that, I could never contain my high spirits (or, until I got older, my temper). I'm relating these memories not as teenage gross-out humor (or to meet a dare) but to show the deep, close, and comfortable bonds that we project rats shared, as well as our crazy exuberance— such wild laughter, all the time, that it would make me famous as a "pissah."

We didn't have much in the way of material comforts or cushioning from the harshness of the world, but we definitely had—and we still have—each other.

3

THE MAGIC PAN

I've always worked, from the time I was twelve years old. My first job was tidying up and cooking for the priests at Saint Monica's rectory, across the street from my house. Father Sullivan, the oldest priest, was in his eighties. His bedroom always seemed so sad to me, with its bare hard floors and almost colorless beige walls. The only furniture was a nondescript bureau, topped with a picture of the Virgin Mary, a small night table that held his Bible, and a very hard, narrow bed made up so tight that I bet you couldn't slide a finger between the blanket and sheet. It looked ready to pop. There was a distinct smell to the room: of wool, mothballs, and old age.

Father Clifford, in his sixties, was the rock star of my mother's set. Dapper and nice-looking, he'd slip in and out of a charming brogue. When he was saying Mass, my mother and her pals would go every single morning. If one of them didn't show, Father Clifford would pay a call to see if she was okay. He knew what his flock wanted. Father Clifford scared me because he seemed high-strung, as if his Irish temper might flare up any minute.

The priest most popular with us young people was forty-something Father Quinn, who had real kindness and spunk. His bedroom had personality, being the only one with a rug, which was dark shag. The rug was usually strewn with the covers of the opera albums he had loaded on his stereo. He loved to blast them, and I enjoyed listening.

The rectory kitchen had the same linoleum floor as all the government-issue apartment kitchens in the projects. It had a large refrigerator and enormous stand-alone freezer, crammed with huge icy steaks and giant slabs of fish, mostly bluefish. God, I hated that bluefish, which was the oiliest, smelliest fish I'd ever seen, with vile-looking gray flesh. It must have fallen off the truck or been donated because it's hard to imagine that any fish store could sell it. Old Father Sullivan loved it, though, so I had to cook it, when I could hardly bear to touch it. After that, I avoided bluefish for decades until a friend insisted that I try it freshly caught, grilled with lime and salt. Then I could see its appeal. But I still couldn't shake the trauma of those frozen monsters.

Besides cooking and light housework, my jobs were to answer the door to parishioners too troubled to wait till Saturday, when confessions were heard, to spill their guts to the priests; and—best of all—I had to sort out the daily collection take. I was supposed to put the checks in one pile and the cash, organized by bill denominations, in the other. A little for me, a little for them, is how that went.

I saw that less as stealing from the church (probably a mortal sin) than as payback. Since I went to public school, I had to take catechism classes, which bored me to no end. If you fucked off in catechism class, talked in church, or seemed guilty of any of a number of other religious infractions, you'd be disciplined in a

ends in-
, aimed
he YES
ay, then
o New
Father
;—how
plenty
topped
e aisle.

scuffed
next to
. That
advan-
ich on
there
uoyed
nd the
were

they
augh-
head
g out
ne of
ne to
skier,

t the

assed

discomfort and public humiliation.
n, the sacrament when young Cath-
the church, for some reason all the
were put on punishment. The whole
altar, arms outstretched, and stay like
hem. If any arms drooped, the priest
inter, flick them back up.

think up a punishment like that? Of
I found it hysterical to see all the guys
then it happened to me. I was guilty
hilarious when you're twelve or thir-
Mass when you shake hands with your
ay, "Peace be with you," I'd gob into my
person who grabbed my hand (usually
lady who'd turn me in).

so weapons called lungies or deucies
ers to lob them). I'd hock up whatever
and, and fling it at kids I didn't like or at
ys, stuck serving the priest saying Mass,
That's how I wound up kneeling on the

, if I pinched just a little cash from the
ere lucky. After all, I could have gobbed

, I had some genuine feeling. "Now, Bar-
to see you at Mass sometime," he used

Mass, I'd sneak around the corner to Jolly
ip with crunchy nuts and real coffee with
rather than my mother's powdered Nes-

urch might cave in if you came, he'd add."
ure me, "But we'd be willing to risk it."

Father Quinn was the one who got me and my fr
volved in the Youth Enrichment Services (YES) progran
at exposing project rats to new experiences like skiing. '
office outfitted us with rental skis, which took a whole o
we gathered at Saint Monica's at 5:00 a.m. to travel
Hampshire on a broken-down jalopy of a bus. Of course
Quinn had no idea that we'd been up all night drinkin
else could we get up that early?—and had brought alon;
of contraband. On one trip, when the bus suddenly
short, cans of beer broke free and came rolling down tl
My friend Tina took the rap for that.

When we got to the lodge, they'd pull our clunky,
YES skis from the belly of the bus and line them all up
the sleek, polished, pricy-looking skis of the real clientel
was one of the very few times in my life that I ever felt "di:
taged" or "less than." In the projects, we were all pretty m
equal economic footing; and in Boston, where, of course
were richer people, we were still on our home turf and l
by Southie pride. But skis were such foreign equipment, :
New Hampshire landscape felt as alien as the moon. W
definitely out of place.

No doubt the ski lodge owners would agree. I'm sur
hated the sight of us scrambling off the bus, shrieking and
ing, drunk and high. We'd skip the wimpy bunny trails an
for the killer slopes, which we'd hurtle down, quickly wipi
and collapsing, colliding with each other. Once I fell, and
my skis popped off and went sailing down the hill. "Want
get that for you?" a little kid offered, clearly a much better
though he was half my age.

"No," I blurted. I think I threw my pole at him. "Just g
fuck away from me!"

Kid, I apologize, whoever you are. I was just so embarr
and frustrated.

But losing a ski was nothing compared with crashing into a tree, as one of my friends did. She broke a couple limbs and had to be carried off the slopes on a stretcher. The rest of us found that hysterical because we were tripping on what we called the "laughing pill," mescaline. Skiing was a hell of an adventure.

● ● ●

Besides the rectory gig, I had a patchwork of other jobs. Like most of Southie, I often tested products at Gillette, our local manufacturer. To test disposable razors, you'd go into a steam room that would soften the hair on your legs or face as your shower would at home. Then you'd shave and be quizzed on how the razor felt on your skin, how closely it cut, blah, blah, blah. We also got to test the Bic pens and lighters, which I especially liked because you got to keep them. My girlfriends and I called ourselves the Bic Chicks.

I also worked at the Soda Shack, an ice cream and sub shop owned by Mary's brother. Steak-and-cheese subs were its specialty. I'd glug some oil onto the flattop, then tear open a bag of presliced beef and dump it onto the puddle of oil, along with onions, peppers, and mushrooms. When everything was browned and smelled delicious, I'd melt some Land O'Lakes cheese on top and scoop the nice, hot, greasy pile onto a grilled roll. Those subs were classic and irresistible.

The Soda Shack was across the street from the Rabbit Inn, a bar that, just a few years before, had been a battleground in what was known as the Boston busing crisis. In the mid-1970s, with racial tensions running high, the Boston Tactical Patrol Force (TPF) was a heavy-handed presence in Southie, though many of the cops were local guys. One night during a scuffle, a guy threw a brick through a cop-car window and ran into the bar, where his pals shielded him from arrest. The next night, to retaliate, the TPF raided the Rabbit Inn, trashing the place and busting heads.

The brutality of the raid was just one more blow to a community that already felt attacked from all sides.

So the Rabbit Inn crowd that refueled at the Soda Shack included antibusing activists amid the usual hardworking union guys, petty mobsters, local politicians, and daytime boozers. Besides subs, they all loved the black-and-white frappes. In Boston, a milkshake is milk shaken with syrup until frothy (not with syrup stirred in, which would make it mere chocolate or whatever flavor milk). Adding a scoop of chocolate (black) and/or vanilla (white) ice cream to a milkshake makes it a frappe.

A lot of the Rabbit Inn guys liked to make a meal of their frappe by adding raw eggs. "Lynchie," they'd say, "I need my protein today. Give me three [or four or five] yolks."

Nasty!

• • •

I didn't just work, because I was still in school, which I found unbearable. I badly wanted to learn. I loved to read and write, and I was curious about everything. But I couldn't pay attention long enough, it seemed, for abstract information to sink in. I'd have a flash of comprehension that would evaporate—*poof!*—and I'd struggle mightily to recall enough facts to recover it. It was a losing battle. Being "learning disabled" wasn't a thing back then, and neither was having ADD.

I wasn't stupid, though, and I was resourceful. I cheated my way through school every which way, from bullying kids into doing my homework to using the scheme I concocted for French class, which now strikes me as pure genius. Somehow I got the answer key to the big exam, so I came in early that day to grab the seat by the window, in the front row. I wrote the test answers in pencil on the blackboard, so they'd be invisible to the teacher and the class, but when the sunlight hit the letters, I could read them. I can't even guess how the fuck I figured that out. That, in a nutshell, is the story of my education: using low-down cunning or, if necessary, my fists to overcome limitations I couldn't understand.

When I pulled the French class scheme, I was in ninth grade, attending South Boston Heights Academy. It was an all-white private school set up specifically to save public-school kids from being bused to Roxbury. For the first time in my life, I had to wear a uniform—a black-and-blue plaid skirt with a white blouse and a string tie—which seemed like a fun alternative to the hand-me-downs I despised. It was harder to adjust to the small class size, which meant closer supervision than we had in public school. Pranks I used to get away with were suddenly major offenses, like (on a dare) putting thumbtacks on the seat of the goofy student who carried a briefcase, or stringing a fishing line trip wire between the classroom door and the teacher's chair. I was also busted smoking in the bathroom. For each of these shenanigans, I was suspended.

One of my teachers, Brenda Sporacco, reached out to my friend Mary and me. Along with another faculty member, she would take us on excursions, like to historic Faneuil Hall, where the Declaration of Independence was first read, though the part we liked better was its newly developed urban mall. She must have thought we had promise.

Even so, I wasn't long for South Boston Heights Academy. Between my suspensions and my poor grades—my schemes didn't save me—I didn't seem to be private school material. That is, I showed too little payoff for my mother to keep scraping up tuition fees. After a year, I was back in public school and thrust into the busing furor.

The theory behind busing was that when schools were segregated by race, black students got an inferior education, so busing would let black kids attend some of the better white schools. That might have been true in the rest of the city, but

South Boston and Roxbury high schools were both so poor and disadvantaged that there was little difference between them. As well-known reporter Michael Patrick MacDonald, author of *All Souls: A Family Story from Southie,* wrote in an essay, "Busing and Whitey Bulger,"

> White South Boston High School had the highest number of students on welfare in any school, citywide . . . Southie's three large housing projects and the "'Lower End,'" . . . collectively held the highest concentration of white poverty in the United States, with 73 percent single-parent female-headed households and upwards of 40 percent unemployment rate among adult men. . . . Former Boston NAACP president Ken Guskett has recently said that, during the battle for desegregation, while white students citywide received more funding per student ($450) than black students ($250 at the black schools in Roxbury)—"the South Boston kids got less than Roxbury."

So poor black kids were being bused not to a better school— like in a rich neighborhood or in the suburbs—but to one that was more underfunded and even shittier. Obviously no one, black or white, attending either school was likely to get a decent education.

There was huge resentment of Judge W. Arthur Garrity Jr., who handed down the busing decision, and Senator Ted Kennedy, who backed him, because both lived in a lily-white world and would never enroll their kids in public schools. My mother joined some of the antibusing motorcades—lines of cars, sometimes a couple hundred, driving from Southie to Garrity's home in exclusive Wellesley, flashing their lights and honking their horns all the way. White students were encouraged to boycott school, rather than be bused, and many of those who were old enough simply dropped out. One of them was my sister Beth, who was supposed be bused to English High School but just decided, "Fuck it."

As Michael Patrick MacDonald wrote, "A generation was lost to that chaos."

Busing polarized the black and white communities in Boston more than ever. Growing up, I had friends from Columbia Point, the mostly black section of the projects, but once busing started, that carefree association grew to be impossible. One night, the local TV news showed our neighbors, the Doyles, being evicted for nonpayment of rent. One of the guys clearing out their stuff happened to be black, which drove Mrs. Doyle wild. She attacked him, and the cops swooped in, followed by a news crew. As the cops dragged her off, Mrs. Doyle was screaming the N-word, which was broadcast to the world.

That image shows how ugly race relations had become in Southie.

I can still picture myself on that first day of school waiting for the hated bus. My hair was ratted into a sky-high bouffant, shellacked with Aqua Net (I kept a can in my bag for touch-ups). I had a Southie dot on my wrist—a little tattoo proclaiming neighborhood pride that the rest of the city saw as a provocative emblem of defiance. My Claddagh ring, with its traditional Irish design of two hands clasping a heart topped by crown, was on my right hand, heart pointing outward, to show I was single. I was wearing a Nefertiti-head necklace, the height of fashion in Southie for some reason. Though I was scared shitless—of leaving the neighborhood, of being mugged—I was like a billboard reading, "Fuck you, I'm Irish."

I was headed to Madison Park High School in Roxbury. The violence had peaked by then, but I was nervous. Once I got to school, I was relieved to find that black and white students pretty much stuck to their own groups. Still, there were inevitable clashes (and exaggerated stories of clashes) in a highly charged atmosphere of racial fear on both sides. I did my best to look and act tough, but the day came when I too got jumped. Three black girls came at me in the bathroom, and after some shoving and slapping, they took what little cash I had, along with my Nefertiti necklace.

But I made a place for myself. Since I was hardcore Southie, some of my teachers assumed—or, to be fair, I implied—that I was connected and could place illegal bets for them. I'd collect their money to give to my "bookie," then pocket the cash. Winning was so unlikely that I wasn't worried about getting caught. Even if I were, how could teachers admit to using a kid to gamble illegally? Luckily, I never had to find out.

One time I was even honored as hero of the school. One day during a break I was out smoking a joint with my friend Maureen, who'd been bused from Dorchester. When the bell rang, we tried to hightail back to the building but were too late. The doors were closed, so they wouldn't let us into class and, instead, escorted us to the principal's office. Since I had nothing to lose, I started bullshitting: "You wouldn't believe what just happened! We were joking around, and Maureen was laughing. She had a pen in her mouth, so the cap came off and got stuck in her throat." Maureen was playing along. "So I remembered seeing those posters on the Heimlich maneuver. I tried it, and the cap came flying out. Thank God!"

Amazingly, the principal believed this utter fucking lie, and at an assembly, I was called up on stage, in front of the whole school, and presented with an award. It was almost impossible to keep a straight face.

I used to hang out in the office of the guidance counselor, Mr. Gilardi, and complain, "You know, school and me—it's just not working out." I mean, they had me studying Gaelic—when the hell would I ever use that, even if I could grasp it? Luckily it struck Gilardi that I might do well in something more vocational and less academic. That's how I wound up in home economics with Susan Logozzo.

It was proof that there is such a thing as destiny. A lot of kids, black and white, felt scarred by busing—and its effects persist in the city today—but for me it was the best thing that ever happened. Susan Logozzo saved my life, maybe literally, and has since remained a mentor and friend.

● ● ●

Susan inspired me with possibilities I never knew existed, like the time she took me to a restaurant in Back Bay called the Magic Pan. Back Bay itself was beautiful, with Victorian brownstones that you don't find anywhere else in Boston, and I'd never seen anything like the elegant boutiques on Newbury Street, its commercial strip.

The Magic Pan fit right into the sophisticated setting, I thought. I didn't know it was a chain restaurant out of San Francisco that perfected the art of making crepes by machine. I'd heard of crepes, vaguely, but this was my first glimpse—I hadn't quite grasped why you'd eat them. Now I knew: they were incredible, light as air yet substantial enough to support any filling, from spinach and mushrooms or creamy chicken to strawberries and cream, chocolate, or in the most glamorous version, crêpes suzette—caramelized butter and sugar, topped with orange liqueur that could be set on fire!

To someone coming from a world of steak-and-cheese subs and black-and-white frappes, where pesto was exotic (though earthy enough to understand), crepes were otherworldly. To experience their delicacy was like hearing a new food language for the first time.

● ● ●

I'd always had strong instincts about food and was always trying out recipes. But I didn't have a framework of knowledge to organize my discoveries and build on them. In her class, Susan gave me that, and more. She was not only a great teacher but also a great role model.

She was in her late thirties, around the same age as many of my friends' mothers (younger than my own), but Susan couldn't have been more different. She was from Connecticut, gracious and well spoken, with no rough Southie edges; and beautiful enough that she'd modeled wedding gowns. In a school that felt chaotic, with a constant tinge of violence in the air, she was like the eye of the hurricane, calm and centered. Her classroom was an island of peace.

She recognized something in me and accepted me in a way that no adult ever had. The second youngest of seven children, with a working mother, I'd never had focused, positive attention. Adult scrutiny, by my teens, made me want to squirm. But Susan wasn't trying to discipline or impose anything on me. She seemed be drawing out and channeling and expanding qualities I already had, which empowered me tremendously.

It thrilled me to learn kitchen arts, like knife skills. Once, I'd seen a recipe in *Good Housekeeping* for a stir-fry with twenty-two ingredients, most of which had to be julienned. It was so much work—why go to all that trouble, I wondered—but I tried it, cutting matchsticks like in the pictures. It was hard labor using my mother's cheap, dull knife set from Flanagan's, but it came out so well that even she seemed to like it. Now, with Susan's guidance, I was learning the right way to chop and slice and dice, processes that seemed to flow naturally into my hands.

In class, we made *pâte à choux* (a light dough used for filled pastries like éclairs), and then at home I crafted it into swan boats, with piped-in Jell-O instant pudding. What a sense of accomplishment that gave me. I struggled with written recipes (and with paying attention), but kept plugging. Once I made pizza dough and forgot about it until it rose and overflowed the bowl onto the refrigerator shelves. "I'm gonna kill you," my mother said. She had no patience for my experiments, having accused me (half-kidding) of trying to poison her by making a grilled cheese sandwich with provolone. Even years later, when I had become an award-winning chef, her praise was grudging. "That's great," she said. "If you like that kind of food."

Students in Susan's class would alternate weeks cooking in the home ec kitchen and waiting tables, serving the teachers our creations. I soon managed to weasel out of waitress duty and just cook. When the clean plates came back from the faculty table, I felt excited and proud. It was the first time I had ever felt recognized and honored in school.

Home ec was supposed to be a one-year program. But Susan knew that, as soon as her class ended in late morning, I'd skip out and walk through the projects to Cardinal Cushing, the Catholic school that many of my friends attended, to meet them at recess. Some afternoons, I'd head over to Northeastern University to shoot pool and maybe drop in on the pastry class that Susan taught there. So she went to Mr. Gilardi and said, "No way will this kid stay in school if she doesn't have home ec." He agreed. I think I was the only student ever to be enrolled in home ec for multiple terms. It did keep me in high school (though I never graduated) and out of the infinite range of troubles awaiting a bored dropout on the streets. And it gave my life shape, a purpose.

• • •

When I wasn't in school or working, my universe revolved around my friends. A huge pack of us—thirty or so kids—used to hang out on Patterson Way, smoking, drinking, and doing whatever. The cops would drive by constantly, just to show us that they were watching and to keep us in line. We even got to know a couple of them, whom we called Spick and Nose. Usually, they'd take away our beers and drive off laughing.

Now and then, though, something would set them off and they'd start rounding us up, loading us into squad cars and paddy wagons. Squad car doors couldn't be opened from the inside, so I'd go from car to car, freeing my friends and driving Spick and Nose wild. There were just so many of us that they couldn't keep track. One night I got caught, wearing a flaming orange sweatshirt, but managed to escape. I couldn't stay out of the action, though, so they soon spotted my neon top and chased me for blocks, shouting, "If it's last thing we ever do, we'll get you!"

But they never did.

By day, especially in the summer, we had a lot of freedom because by then some of us could drive. We loved to go to Quincy to jump into the deep, water-filled quarries, despite the rumors that they were full of bodies from gang killings. One day when Mary was driving us to the quarries, Kerri Foley, a girl who was picked on since she was a bit younger and shy, got left behind. She looked so forlorn. Then the next day, when we were all heading to the beach, Kerri rushed to catch up with us. "You can't come. You weren't invited," someone told her. Teenage girls are cliquish, but that was wrong.

"I invited Kerri, so she's coming," I announced. We were best friends from then on.

We were a good fit, because Kerri was much more levelheaded than I was. The only child of a single mother, she'd grown up with more attention and rules. But otherwise we had a lot in common. Her father, who was Bill Bulger's brother-in-law, had left when she was born. So she knew him only as I knew Yapper, from stories and pictures. Once, we spotted her father on the train, which was surreal, but we didn't go near him.

I became Kerri's protector. I was in a bar one night (with a fake ID) drinking Pearl Harbors—a deadly concoction of vodka, green Midori, and pineapple juice—when I saw Kerri's boyfriend, Donald, with another girl. So I threw a drink at the girl, not realizing that she came from the D. Projects, which had a long-standing beef with Old Colony and Old Harbor. When we took it outside, she beat the hell out of me before I could wrestle free. I was proud of my long, painted nails in those days, which broke off in the fight and somehow got snarled in my teased bouffant. My hair was such a rat's nest from the struggle that I had to go to the beauty shop to get it combed out.

"What happened to you?" the hairdresser asked as she cut the shards of fingernails out of my hair. As I started to tell her, I noticed the girl from the D Projects glaring at me from a nearby chair. "Holy shit!" I said and stopped midstory, tearing out of there to avoid another brawl.

But then Kerri caught Donald with yet another girl. One day Kerri found him in bed with someone else. Furious, she grabbed the nearest object to hurl at him, which turned out to be a can of Hershey's syrup. "Chocolate syrup?" I said, laughing, when she told me. "That's the best you could do?"

• • •

I hate to think what I would have thrown at him. Everything I did in those teenage years, which seemed perfectly natural then, now sounds extreme. Sometimes simple curiosity got the best of me. Once Mary and I were coming down from the roof of her building, where we'd been smoking. As she continued down the stairs, I paused at the third-floor landing, suddenly conscious of the curtains on the window there. I couldn't tell what they were made of, so I flicked at them with my lighter. They burst into flame. "Mary!" I yelled. I ran to get her, and the two of us watched the flames sputter out for a minute, before running away so we wouldn't get caught.

Excitement seeking was always a strong motive for me, compounded by poor teenage judgment. One day, a bunch of my friends were hanging out in Old Colony when a cabbie, who had picked up a pie from Billy's Pizzeria and stashed it in his back seat, somehow got into a fight with Joey, a neighborhood guy. Joey beat him up, grabbed his keys, and hid the taxi in the courtyard by Mary's house, where they hung out the wash. All this had happened before I got off the school bus from Roxbury and bumped into Joey. "Hey, hold these for me," he said, sticking a set of keys in my hand. I shoved them into my pocket.

After dinner, when I came outside, everyone was buzzing about the fight and the hidden taxi. *I bet these keys are for that cab*, I thought.

Sure enough, when I tried them, the taxi started right up. Tina got into the passenger's seat to help me navigate, and another friend, Suzy, climbed in back. My first move was grazing a tree and knocking off the side mirror. But as we started down the street, I got cockier and started taking corners in lurching, wide, fast turns that sent Suzy, who was thin and tiny, bouncing all over. We were all shrieking with laughter.

We approached the Tynan Elementary School, which had a short flight of wide steps in front, leading to an open courtyard. We tried to drive up them, but the cab resisted, making terrible *GRRRRing* mechanical sounds, so we turned in to the courtyard and bumped down them. "Fucking pepperoni pizza!" I heard from the back seat. When Tina and I looked back, there was cheese hanging from the ceiling and Suzy was covered in grease and pepperoni.

For the finale, we turned down Patterson Way, where our friends were gathered. "Hey, I'm driving!" I was shouting. That's when I lost control of the cab but managed to stop it so we could jump out. I have no idea what became of the taxi after that. Joey never came back to get the keys because he was arrested for something else.

• • •

Stealing in Southie was considered less a criminal act than a fact of life, and often necessary. My mother always said, "You have champagne tastes on a welfare budget." She was right. Usually I shopped at Filene's Basement like everyone else, hiding the best clothes until the automatic markdowns reached rock bottom. But I'd inherited my mother's love of magazines, and sometimes, despite all my jobs, the only way to get the fashionable clothes I saw in their pages was to shoplift. Some of my friends, who were equally clothes-crazy and broke, were more squeamish. So during the week, Tina and I took orders: "Can you get me a pair of Perry Ellis pleated pants, size seven?" "I need some Girbaud jeans, the kind with the little ticket, in black . . ." Then we'd go downtown, liberate the desired items in time for the weekend, and sell them cheap.

A lot of guys in the projects would casually boost cars for transportation. I used to babysit for my sister Phyllis, who'd let me bring a girlfriend for company but insisted that I was not allowed to party at her house. My friends considered Phyllis's rule to be just a suggestion, not an order, so a bunch of them came to visit, parking in the driveway. When Phyllis and her husband, Bob, got home, they were pissed. "Damn it," Bob said. "Move the fucking car."

That got everyone scrambling and asking, "Shit, where's the screwdriver?"

They'd stolen the car, so they now had to hot-wire it again to start it. I think Phyllis and Bob cared less about the car theft than the fact that I'd disobeyed and had boys over.

We'd steal steaks from Flanagan's to grill in the park. We'd go out to eat and come up with crazy schemes to avoid paying, sometimes even when we had money. We pulled this stunt so often that we even had a name for it: Chew and Screw.

One of our favorite targets was Ocean Kai, a Chinese restaurant and bar. We loved to go there after tanning on someone's roof, with our reflectors made of album covers wrapped in tinfoil. We'd have a few rounds of mai tais and pupu platters, then ask for the check. An easy scheme was simply to pretend to go to the bathroom and slip out the door. A more advanced move was to have everyone put her share of the money on the table, where the server could see it, then as we left, snatch the pile of cash to redistribute when we got outside.

One night, the Ocean Kai people got fed up and four kitchen workers chased us down the street, waving machetes. I was holding the money, so I turned around and said, "Hey, we were just joking, we forgot to pay," and handed it over. Now that I'm a restaurant owner, I can only hope that I've done enough good deeds to beat that Chew and Screw karma.

● ● ●

Since we were too young to drink legally, many of our wilder schemes involved getting alcohol. When the liquor delivery truck pulled up to the Soda Shack, we'd wait for the driver to go inside, then open the back panel and quickly hand out cases of beer and booze, relay style. With the goods safely stashed in someone's car, we'd book before the driver could bust us.

It was pretty easy for us to get beer, but one day I insisted that we try something new, a kind of liqueur. For that we had to go to the "packy," or package store, which is what they call liquor stores in Boston, and find a "runner," an older person who would front for us to buy booze.

We convinced a guy with strong foreign accent to help us, and gave him all the money we had. The liqueur was expensive. But the heavy bag he handed us before getting into his car contained seven quarts of orange juice, not liqueur. Evidently he had a change of heart or realized suddenly that he was breaking the law. So there we were, with no money left, stuck with nothing but juice to enliven our Friday night.

Everyone was mad at me until Pat, the older brother of another friend, came along. Somehow he convinced the packy owner to exchange the orange juice for the liqueur I'd been promoting. I poured it into little cups and passed them around. "Jesus, Barbara, this is God-awful," someone said. Another friend agreed. "This shit is disgusting. I can't stand it. " They didn't even want to try to get drunk on it.

After all the trouble we'd gone to—not to mention the cost—I couldn't admit that I too found the drink vile, with a taste that could make you gag. I'd blown all my friends' cash, as well as my own, on one of my quests for new, exotic flavors. But by now, my friends were getting used to my missions. Instead of asking, "Where did you come from?" they just shook their heads, resigned to a sober evening, and said, "That's Barbara."

At local bars, the fake IDs we carried were mostly a formality, since people knew us. At one point, my friends and I all used the same phony name: Joanne Lynch. At places that checked IDs at the door, like our favorite bar in Faneuil Hall, we couldn't possibly get in together as a whole crew of Joanne Lynches. So one of us would slip in, flashing the ID, and after ten or fifteen minutes, the next one would try it, and so on. Bouncers never checked the name closely enough to remember.

To look older, I started wearing a long black coat with a fake fur collar, which I found at the Morgan Memorial thrift shop. It seemed to work, and just putting it on made me feel grown-up and sophisticated. I considered myself an adult, anyway, since I had a job and no parental supervision. I felt entitled to go out drinking, the time-honored Southie weekend ritual.

I tried the coat strategy one night at Triple O's, showing off the fur collar to Chuck the bouncer. "Oh Chuckie, you can see we're old enough, me in my fur and my friends . . ."

"Just get in here out of the snow," he said. A blizzard was brewing.

It was snowing even harder when we left Triple O's for Street Lights, in search of a new selection of guys. We called the bar Street Fights, since so many broke out there, a few involving Tina, so sometimes she was barred. But we thought it probable that with my coat setting a different, classier tone, they'd let Tina in, along with the rest of us.

The wind was picking up, and we could hardly see in the blowing snow. Suddenly a huge shape came looming out of the darkness. It was a bus. We stepped back onto the sidewalk as it pulled in front of us, up to the bus stop.

Then an impulse grabbed me. On a night when I was feeling very adult, parading in my coat, I had an overwhelming flashback to childhood. The bus rumbled back to life, its red taillights glowing, and began to creep forward. As it did, I hooked my hands over the bumper and skied along behind it, in pure innocent exhilaration, my grown-up coat billowing behind me like a black sail. Looking back, that moment seems like a snapshot of adolescence, the veneer of adulthood growing more solid, day by day, but barely able to contain the inner child.

● ● ●

Boyfriends were changing stars in my constellation of friends. John, a sweet blond guy, proposed to me in high school. He even gave me a ring. But I wasn't ready. I had a lot more scheming and playing to do and too much curiosity about the world beyond Southie to settle down.

Then Mary started feeling and acting queasy enough to draw my mother's attention. "Oh no!" she said. "I bet Mary has diabetes." Being diabetic herself, she was hyperalert to symptoms in others. She kept after me, "Mary better get checked. Diabetes can sneak up on you, and it's serious."

My mother was so relieved when she learned that Mary was not diabetic but pregnant, even if out of wedlock. Mary married the baby's father, Brian, the love of her life, and they went on to have four children.

When I was eighteen, I started dating a guy from Old Colony. He and his brother Billy were in a circle of guys, including Bubba McCormick, who dated my closest friends. Kerri was especially close to Bubba; and Cheryl and Joanie, who were in Catholic school, had taken the guys to their junior and senior proms. We were all closely intertwined and fresh out of high school.

One night, the cops chased us off Patterson Way and then out of the park, so we were hanging out, drinking, near Saint Monica's Church. A guy from Billy's Pizzeria found us there and invited us to a party in Dorchester. Having somewhere to go besides the street corner sounded great, but Kerri and Cheryl and I were iffy. The two of them were already out past their curfews, and for some reason, I was in trouble with my mother. I was practically in the car when I decided not to go.

My boyfriend offered to walk me home, which meant we'd get a chance to make out. His brother Billy, Bubba, and four other kids, including two younger teenagers, Keith Miller and John Baldwin, piled into the car.

A couple hours later, I got a call. The car, speeding the wrong way down the street, had crashed head-on into an MBTA bus. Twelve riders on the bus were injured, including the driver, but the car was demolished, its left side totally sheared off. Two passengers still clung to life but our friends Billy and Bubba, and the younger guys Keith and John, were dead. They'd been killed instantly in the crash, some of them decapitated.

The horror reverberated through the projects. Since the guys came from big families, the radius of pain was wide. Everyone loved Billy. Bubba had a scholarship to Boston College. The two younger ones probably didn't even drink much but were tagging along. They'd all held such promise. It took months for me to acknowledge how close I'd come to being in that car and to feel grateful, again, for the protection of Yapper, a guardian angel, or plain dumb luck.

I went to all four funerals in a state of shock, too numb even to grieve.

There's a custom in Southie called a Time, which is different from a wake. When a person dies, someone throws a party with food, music, and often raffled-off prizes, charging admission to give some money to the family. I don't remember the Times for the four lost guys, but funds were raised to construct a monument that still stands at the corner of Babe Ruth Park Drive and Columbia Road, near Carson Beach. It lists their names and ages, along with a poem.

It doesn't mention that they weren't innocent victims. They were driving drunk, a danger that we're much more attuned to today. They hurt a lot of other people and could have killed them, but instead paid with their own lives. Nowadays I can't see anyone erecting a monument to kids who were killed that way.

But in Southie back then, young men (and women too) were constantly being consumed by the streets—by drugs and booze, by criminal activity, by suicide. So to have four of our own die in such a grisly, violent way that had no connection to illegal substances or brutality or despair was inconceivable. It was an unimaginable tragedy.

What did we learn from it? Not a fucking thing. None of us stopped drinking or taking drugs. A tragedy that seems so unreal doesn't even teach you how to cry.

But it was a kind of marker for me, a bright line separating an adolescence of cutting class in high school and hanging out on Patterson Way from my own real adult life, which I was eager to begin.

4

BUILD MY WORLD

What set the course of my real adult life, as it turned out, were three jobs I had in my teens and early twenties. The first was at the St. Botolph Club, an exclusive private gathering place for Boston's cultural elite—authors, journalists, publishers, academics, painters, and sculptors—as well as prominent arts lovers. Founded in the 1880s, it had hosted famous three-named members like Henry Cabot Lodge, John Singer Sargent, and William Dean Howells, along with double-namers like Charles Eliot, president of Harvard. Its twentieth-century members were like updated versions—the same mix of Boston Brahmins and creative types, except that after 1988 when they were first allowed in, a few women were among them.

The St. Botolph clubhouse on Commonwealth Avenue is a terra-cotta-colored mansion with white trim and two banks of grand bow windows. Inside are a music room, where they hold concerts and monthly art shows; a library with a fireplace and big leather chairs; and eleven chambers for overnight guests.

Valuable oil paintings hang everywhere. The spaces with the most buzz are its main and smaller private dining rooms, where lavish lunches and dinners are served every weekday, paired with vintages chosen by its wine committee. It's an oasis of old-school gentility.

For thirty years, Mario Bonello was the reigning chef at St. Botolph. He was old school too, coming out of the Escoffier tradition, a turn-of-the-twentieth-century modernization of classic French techniques. With just two other cooks, Paul, also French-trained, and Gino, plus a single dishwasher, Mario could juggle a full dining room plus two or three private parties in a single evening. He was a dynamo.

Mario had a fierce temper but also a dedication to elegance. He gave everyone who worked for him a sense of dignity, showing by attitude and example that it was noble to create and serve meals well. At the end of service each night, he'd sit at the small bar near the club's reception desk and enjoy a scotch on the rocks in a beautiful cut-crystal glass. Coming from a plastic-cup world, I found that so inspiring. Today a huge portrait of Mario, five feet tall and bald—the soul of the club—hangs behind that bar.

The club's waitstaff was solid Southie: my mother and her gal pals, including Peggy Mahoney, her best friend; Peggy Harrigan, Franny Bellmore, Dot White, and Nancy Henderson. Since there was no tipping at the club—the members ran tabs instead of paying on the spot—the gals worked as a team, all decked out in the same white shoes with sheer white L'eggs pantyhose and polyester uniforms with two front pockets, one for order pads and the other for smokes. Their pay was decent, steady, and increased with seniority. My mother, who'd anchored the lunch crew since before I was born, was probably a top earner.

When I was fourteen, she wangled me a job at the club making beds and cleaning rooms. After a couple years, I graduated to waiting tables—and nearly flamed out. My very first week, there was a party for Rhodes Scholars on the second floor. I'd been told to load dinner salads onto trays five at a time, then send them upstairs on the old dumbwaiter. But as I set them up, I saw that eight salad plates fit just fine on each tray. So, what the hell? I packed up two trays of eight, stuck them in the dumbwaiter, and pressed "2."

I was on the steps, racing up to the finishing kitchen to meet the dumbwaiter, when I heard a huge *CRASH!* Peggy Mahoney came bounding up after me. "Stay here!" she said. "Don't come downstairs. Mario's gonna kill you."

By overloading the dumbwaiter, I'd sent sixteen brand-new fine china plates, decorated with the St. Botolph crest of mermaids and crowns, plunging down to the basement, smashing; and scattering Mario's Boston lettuce greens with his famous Italian dressing. *Holy shit!*

I stayed out of Mario's way until the end of my shift, when I had to return to the main kitchen. When he caught sight of me, Mario flushed bright red, all five feet of him quivering. "Why you . . . you dumb fuck, you fucking . . .," he choked out.

"You better run," said my mother, and I did.

It took a couple weeks for me to work up the nerve to show my face at the club. Mario had a short fuse, but thank God, his rage quickly burned off. He hired me back.

As a waitress, I wasn't supposed to interact with the guests. I took their orders, delivered their meals, and refilled their glasses—nothing more. That was fine with me. For one thing, I felt too shy to chat up the hotshots, and for another, it gave me downtime to hang out in the kitchen and watch Mario, a real chef, in action. His menu was a conservative club version of fine dining at the time: chicken cordon bleu, Dover sole filleted tableside, lamb with Kelly-green mint jelly, beef tenderloin. My mother loved his homemade marinara sauce, often served at staff meals before shifts. She and her friends found some of his other creations disgusting, like jellied consommé and squab, which is actually just pigeon. Those were the dishes that most fascinated me.

The most mysterious and glamorous dish of all was sweetbreads, which Mario dusted with flour then sautéed with pearl onions and served in a Madeira-laced sauce of cream, mushrooms, and ham. I'd bring them to the table under a bell-shaped glass cloche. When I lifted the cloche to serve them, the scent of Madeira would waft out, and everyone at the table would *oooh* and *aahh*. God, that thrilled me. I'd dazzled my Southie friends with pesto, but the club members were so worldly. Some were definitely famous. Their reactions to Mario's creations showed me that cooking was about more than feeding people. It was artistry.

So I loved it when, now and then, Mario and Paul would stage fancy Escoffier-style dinners for members. Every detail mattered—the food, the presentation, and the service. Servers had to wear white gloves. There would be one server per guest, and our movements were choreographed. We'd enter the dining room in a procession, carrying trays, and in a unified motion, lower them onto stands. We'd serve each dish (always from the right) at the same time. It was like a ballet. Between courses, I would take notes, so I could absorb all the elements that defined an elegant meal.

Watching Mario convinced me that I wanted to become a chef. I started to bug him about it. "I want to cook!" I'd say. He'd always give me the same answer, "You're too young to know what you want." I think he was also getting exasperated by my scrutiny and constant questions like, "Wow! Why did you do that?" and "What are you making now?" But I never let up, coming at him from different angles to ask, "How do I get started as a chef?" Finally he swatted me off. "Why don't you just call up Julia Child and ask her?" he suggested.

Julia Child. For years I'd seen her at the club, often clutching a St. Botolph coffee cup. I didn't know what she was drinking, but it wasn't coffee. She loved little goldfish crackers, so at the bar we'd always keep bowls of them, freshly stocked. Growing up, I'd never watched her show. My family wasn't big on public television. But like everyone in Boston, I knew she was a celebrity.

Could she really tell me how to become a chef? I didn't know if Mario was serious. And what would I say to her? "I'm a waitress, but I worked in a sub shop and took home ec, and I love to cook and . . ." Then what?

Still, at home I checked the phone book and was amazed to find a Julia Child listed in Cambridge, with a phone number. I dialed it, shaking, and got an answer.

"Helloooo?" That voice—it was her, all right.

"Oh shit!" I blurted, slamming down the phone. It took a minute before I realized what I'd done and started laughing, still in shock.

Christ, I thought. *I just crank-called Julia Child!*

•　•　•

It would take more than a phone call—and a few crazy jobs—to get me out of my white waitress oxfords and into chef's clogs.

•　•　•

On weekends, I was a cocktail waitress at the Bayside Club, the tavern where, for decades, Senator Bill Bulger hosted his annual Saint Patrick's Day breakfast. Hundreds of people would cram into its upper room—some even crawling up the fire escapes—to sing Irish songs, tell stories and jokes, and "slag," or roast, politicians. Anyone running for office—wannabe governors, senators, and even national candidates like Al Gore and George W. Bush—would show up to match wits and test their ability to withstand ridicule. US presidents, including Ronald Reagan and

Bill Clinton, would phone in on the Bayside hotline. Today other politicos host the event at the more antiseptic Boston Convention Center, in much-watered-down form.

But on a regular Saturday night, the Bayside Club was a popular destination. It had a good deejay and sometimes live bands like Cat Tunes, a Southie favorite. It was also favored as a "last call" stop for anyone who hadn't managed to hook up earlier in the night. By 1:00 a.m., drunk-ass- and double-parked cars jammed the street, as hopefuls dropped in to check out the chances of getting laid. "After two, anything will do," we used to say.

My friend George, who hung out in the downtown clubs, would bring in his crew at last call and scream out, "Lynchie!" They'd order at least a case of beer in multiple Buds, Miller High Lifes, and Schlitzes, with chasers of vodka and grapefruit juice. "Make sure the juice is freshly squeezed, Lynchie," George would say, grabbing my (post-Aqua Net) ponytail.

"Yeah, right—and fucking let go," I'd demand. On the way to place their orders, I'd get the nod from another waitress, who'd mouth "One." That was the number of the bathroom stall where a last-call nightcap of coke awaited me. I'd nip in with a penne noodle tucked in my apron pocket. I'd never snort good coke through a rolled-up dirty dollar bill.

Kerri Foley also worked weekends as a cocktail waitress at Scotch 'n Sirloin, a more upscale joint on the border of the Italian (Mafia-ruled) North End and Irish Charlestown. Since most of her customers were horny older men, she had to show cleavage in a knockoff Diane von Furstenberg wrap dress, hemmed way above her knees. The manager also ordered her to drop ten pounds so her five-feet-one frame would look more willowy. Thinking that could mean better tips, Kerri decided to try jogging to lose weight.

Every day she'd do five or six laps in Columbus Park, and I'd trot along behind her. On weekdays, the park was deserted and seemed like an unsafe place for a woman alone. I'd felt like Kerri's protector since the first time I stuck up for her. So there I was, Kool menthol dangling from my mouth, huffing and puffing, trying to keep pace. Now and then, I'd have to pause, gasping, to say, "Jesus, Kerri, you're killing me." But I was determined to guard her, to keep her from harm. Knuckles Lynch to the rescue.

Kerri says that she also kept me safe, since I was so impulsive and craved excitement. One of my favorite partners in crime was our friend Joanna. Her mother, Pat, who was even more permissive than mine, didn't seem to notice us young teenagers drinking in her house. We loved that but also questioned her mental state, since she had the habit of talking to herself. Her moods would shift in the blink of an eye. One minute, she'd call you "Lovey" and the next she'd be saying, "You prick . . ." We'd roll our eyes and ask each other, "Is she cuckoo?"

Once I stole two live goldfish from Woolworths, slipping them out in separate plastic bags. When I showed them to Tina, we laughed like crazy. "What'll you name them?" she asked. In honor of Pat, I called them Lovey and Prick.

Joanna and I loved road trips. When I was in my late teens, gangs of kids—not just from Southie, but also Dorchester and Charlestown—would take the bus or hitchhike to Falmouth, on Cape Cod, where there was a motel/club called the Brothers Four. It was right on the ocean and had a pool. Every weekend in the summer, they'd have a deejay playing music, as well as dance contests, water games, and general partying.

Since we couldn't afford to stay there, we'd cram into a few rooms at a dirt-cheap place nearby and sneak over the Brothers Four's treacherous, high picket fence to join the action. We'd start our mornings poolside, slathered in baby oil and iodine to get our tans on, sucking down cold draft beers or soda water in blue plastic cups, doctored with vodka from our secret stash. By the afternoon, we were blasted.

When we got a little older, our adventures grew more ambitious. In the mid-1980s, we went to Bermuda four or five times on People Express. It was a no-frills, discount airline that didn't require reservations or prepayment. You could just show up, hop on the plane, and pay by credit card while in the air. Credit reporting services must have been less effective back then because it was a cinch, even for young thieves like us, to beat that system.

George, who at the time was dating Joanna, came up with a genius scheme. We'd go down to Faneuil Hall, which had become a tourist trap, to look for people eating (or better yet, drinking) with their bags stowed on the floor under their tables or barstools. It was the easiest thing in the world to nudge a bag with your foot till you could grab it and snatch the credit cards. We'd board the plane, pay with the stolen cards, and ditch them when we got to Bermuda.

Once there, as we did on the Cape, the sixteen or so of us would cram into a few hotel rooms and then proceed to live by our wits. We'd rent mopeds to get around, siphoning gas to fill their tanks. We'd hit a liquor store, where I'd pretend to faint—shades of me and Beth at Paine Furniture—while the guys shoved booze bottles down their pants. The way we pushed our luck, it's shocking that we never got caught.

Our shenanigans on these trips always mortified Kerri, our one sensible friend. Joanna and I got so drunk and crazy that, more than once, Kerri stormed out, refusing to share a room with us. "You guys are too nuts," she'd say. "I can't stand it."

* * *

Kerri was my only friend who, at that point, had plans to go to college. She wasn't that keen on the idea, she recalls, and wanted to have a baby and settle down like Mary and other friends who, like me, were a few years older. "Absolutely not," Diane, her single mother said, hammering home the drawbacks so hard that Kerri was forty-two before she finally had a kid. "You are going to college."

Before Kerri left for school, we decided to blow our tip money in Atlantic City. We'd seen an ad in the paper for a quickie trip, catching a plane at seven in the morning, gambling all day, and returning that night. After takeoff, our tour guide, who seemed creepy, announced that we were holding a lottery. He told us all to write our seat numbers on $5 bills, which he'd collect and then draw one at random, to see who won the pot.

Incredibly, I won! It was a big jet, so there was at least $500 in the pot, plenty for the two of us to gamble with. The plane was full of Q-tips, our name for graying senior citizens. They were pissed. "I'm sure he has a crush on that young girl," one said loudly. "He let her win." I suspected she was right, especially after the guy told Kerri and me that he'd gotten us a hotel room so we could "freshen up." "Great," I said, shrugging it off. But Kerri was disgusted.

In the casino, I had a lucky star over my head. We hit the blackjack table, and right away, I started winning big. The chips mounted up, and when I cashed them in, I had $1,800, which would be like $13,000 today. It was a fortune.

"Never go back to the same table where you won," the cashier warned me. "I know," I told him, but I ignored the advice, and still kept winning.

Since we had the hotel room, I wanted to stay overnight, but Kerri put her foot down. "No fucking way," she said. "We're out of here."

As we headed back to the plane, the tour guide made his move, claiming that he'd rigged the lottery because he found me "really cute," so how about if we got together—blah, blah, blah. Kerri shut him down. When we got back to Southie at midnight, I wanted to head straight to the Bayside Club to brag about my triumph. "No," Kerri said, "you just want to score some coke." I had to admit there was truth to that.

Kerri really did become my protector by putting the brakes on me now and then.

A week or so later, Kerri's mother and I drove her to Salem State University, which was twenty miles and a galaxy away. Kerri was trying not to cry, and was so scared that her skin got blotchy. When we met her fellow students, she cackled nervously. "Where do you go to school?" they asked me, and I shoveled a heap of bullshit. I knew I'd never fit into the college scene. But Kerri might—I had faith in her. As a going-away present, I gave her a big chunk of my blackjack winnings.

With the rest of the cash, I went to Saugus, Massachusetts, right off Route 1, and bought my very first car. I was inspired by my brother Kenny, who swore by BMWs and drove a white Model 2002, which I loved. I got the same model but older, an adorable, boxy, green used 1974 Model 2002 coupe. Never mind that I didn't have a driver's license—to me, that was just a formality.

The car was the prize, a life changer. With mobility came freedom—to go anywhere, to do anything I wanted. That was intoxicating. But just as exhilarating was the fact that, for the first time in my life, I owned something. I'd bought it, not boosted it, so it was mine, and only mine. It didn't have to be shared and could be used at will. I didn't have to answer to anyone. Though I'd been self-sufficient for years, that act of possession made me feel absolutely adult, in full command of my life.

Driving home from Saugus, I felt like Supergirl. When I glanced down at the steering wheel, just seeing the letters BMW on its hub shot me a surge of strength. "BMW," I repeated, like a mantra. "BMW." I recognized what the letters signified, for me, honoring the way the car could change my future: Build My World.

• • •

Though I continued to waitress part-time, I needed a real job, with benefits. Since I never graduated from high school, my prospects were limited. Finally I landed an administrative job with Port Terminals Company, Inc., a dry-goods warehouse. In my four years there, I worked my way up from customer service representative to traffic manager, responsible for ensuring that products arriving by ship from canning plants or wherever made it onto the right trucks to fill orders. I'd compile lists for the teamsters—"Throw on five pallets of Such-and-Such canned tuna . . .," and handle the paperwork to insure the load.

Yes, it was boring as hell but I liked the responsibility. I learned a lot about importing and exporting, and I enjoyed working alongside my friends Mary and Cheryl. This was the second job that would change my life: first, because I left it—forcing me to focus on what I really wanted—and second, because of the friendship I later developed with the warehouse owner, David Petri.

Sometimes I'd visit Kerri at college, and once even went along on a student outing to Montreal. I was a great mimic, and one of my bar tricks was using a foreign accent to pick up guys. My friends found it hilarious and still talk about the time I got stuck speaking in an Irish brogue for twenty-four hours. I started putting on an accent in a Montreal bar, probably using one of my standard lines, like, "Hello, are you Swedish too?" and Kerri didn't laugh. Instead, she shut me up by saying, "You sound stupid talking like that."

I don't know if I'd embarrassed her, exactly, or if she was worried that her college friends would make fun and insult me. We were both out of our depth, but felt so far beyond these kids just getting their first taste of freedom, when we'd been running wild for years. Yet they knew things we didn't. Kerri had a roommate whose parents were together, and the father still did everything—calling her, helping her with homework, you name it. That shocked Kerri, who assumed, as I did, that fathers were absent, distant, or forbidding, and showed her "just how small my world was," as she said. But she was adjusting her vision.

On a trip home, she came to meet me at the warehouse. She'd never been inside. I don't know if the place really looked that grim or if she was seeing it through the lens of her new expectations, but she flipped. "Oh my God," she said. "You work with Q-tips. No one here is young."

"So what?" I said.

"And there are no windows. How can you take it?"

She wanted me to go to Cancún with her during a school break. I asked for a week off, and they turned me down. "So just quit," Kerri urged me. "You've been stuck in a cubicle for years. What do you have to lose?"

I could see her point. Our roles had reversed somehow. I, the daredevil who'd always dragged Kerri into crazy schemes, had been drifting, lulled by a little security; and levelheaded Kerri, who usually yanked me away from the edge, was shoving me toward it. So I took the leap. Since Filene's department store had a travel agency, I charged the whole trip to Cancún on my credit card, figuring that when I got back, I'd find a new job.

• • •

With a jazzed-up résumé, which now read *Madison Park High, Special Studies in English—Business Law 1 & 2, Graduated with Honors,* I got a job answering phones at the John Hancock Mutual Life Insurance Company. It was deadly. "Thank you for calling JHMLI. How may I direct your call?" I said dozens of times a day.

Once, I picked up to hear a familiar voice. Kerri's: "How's it going?"

"I should fucking kill you," I told her. "The warehouse was okay, but this job blows."

She calmed me down with the news that a friend of a relative, a Southie guy, was opening a restaurant that summer on Martha's Vineyard. He needed staff. The next day I quit John Hancock, we packed up the BMW, and we moved to Vineyard Haven, the gateway village to the island, where the ferry docked. The owner hired us instantly, Kerri as a waitress and me as a cook.

The restaurant was right on Main Street, with a huge, second-floor prep kitchen. I couldn't wait to try it out. At the Soda Shack, I'd just heated sub fillings on the flattop, but here I could actually make food. The owner, however, wanted a fast-food operation, where my only hands-on work was opening cans, defrosting, warming up, and slapping food onto plates. "I hate making this shit," I complained. Worse, I had to work back-to-back twelve-hour days. After dumping my umpteenth industrial-size can of soup into the kettle, I begged the owner, "Just let me try making some real chowder. I can do it." He refused.

I was pissed that Kerri took his side. "Barbara, you don't really know how to cook," she insisted. "Sure, you did it for the priests and took home ec, but that's not the same as actual restaurant cooking."

Where did you come from? I wanted to ask. Nothing in my Southie upbringing taught me to care about or respect legitimate credentials. Buying goods cheaply "off the truck," drinking with fake IDs, shoplifting to order, and traveling on stolen cards were perfectly normal, if illegal, activities. If you beat the system and got away with it, you were proud.

In fact, I was already looking for a new job, claiming not only to have graduated high school with honors but also to have attended Johnson & Wales, the famous restaurant college in Providence, Rhode Island. My résumé now carried the statement: *Over the past five years, I have worked at the St. Botolph Club and Restaurant, a five-star restaurant in the heart of Boston. I started as a line cook and worked my way to sous-chef and proceeded to executive chef.*

I concluded, *References available on request*. Thank God nobody checked them.

I finally got a nibble from the owner of the *Aegean Princess*, a ship that did dinner-and-dancing cruises from the Vineyard to Nantucket every night. He wanted to hire me as server but I held out for a cook's position. I now realized that I had to quit fucking around in warehouse and waitress jobs. I'd already wasted four years, and if cooking was my calling—I believed it was—it was time to get cracking. So I was thrilled when I got called to meet the head chef of the ship, who said he would train me a few days later, before the first cruise.

I quit the fast-food job in July, the height of the tourist season. The restaurant owner was so outraged that he stormed the decrepit apartment that Kerri and I shared, which had birds infesting its ceiling. "You can't just quit!" he shouted. "Oh yes, I can," I said. I was pressing a shirt, and as he threatened to kick my ass, I picked up the hot iron, saying, "I'm going to smash this in your face if you don't get out of here." He left in a hurry.

But I got karmic payback for leaving him in the lurch. Right before the cruise—and before teaching me how to cook for 150 high-paying guests in the tiny galley kitchen of a heaving ship—the head chef quit. The owner was more annoyed than worried. "You can handle it, right?" he said. "You've got the experience."

"Sure," I told him, thinking, *Now I'm royally fucked*.

I called Mario Bonello and Susan Logozzo in a panic. They helped me recognize that, luckily, the menu was really basic: chowder and salad to start, a choice of lobster or beef tenderloin as the entrée, baked potato and corn on the cob as sides, and a couple of simple desserts. I pored over cookbooks to get a sense of the techniques and kept checking back to get tips: *Mario, in the chowder, what the fuck is béchamel?* and *How do you make zamboni?* Guessing what I meant, Mario sent me his favorite zabaglione recipe, while Susan talked me through the pastry for strawberry shortcake, the alternate dessert. Steaming the lobsters seemed straightforward, but the beef was terrifying. I'd seen the tenderloins, which were whole and had to be trimmed of fat and their silvery skin, then cut into individual steaks. I'd never performed these tasks or, for that matter, ever cooked a pricy steak to order. A friend of a friend set me up to shadow a chef at a steakhouse called the Beef Tender. He saved my life, teaching me not only how to butcher but also how to how to broil a mess of steaks all at once to the desired doneness. That was my first experience of a salamander, the kind of ultrapowerful commercial broiler that I'd be using on the ship.

Just hours after leaving the Beef Tender, I reported for chef duty. I butchered my tenderloins and kept checking on the lobsters, barely stirring in their stack of plastic crates. I'd be steaming them in special built-in drawers, not in a pot of water on the stove. Imagine what would happen to a boiling pot if the ship hit a wave. The doors of those drawers and of the salamander were secured tightly with bungee cords to keep the steaks and lobsters from going flying if the sea got rough.

Whenever the owner looked in on me, I flashed him what I hoped was a convincing smile to hide my terror. Luckily, though the captain was a veteran, everyone else on the boat—the bartenders, the waitstaff—was also new, so they couldn't tell that I was floundering. I did look organized, with my baked potatoes keeping warm and my corn cob halves all arranged in the pan, as the 150 guests enjoyed sunset cocktails on the deck.

When the cymbals starting crashing in the band's rendition of Neil Diamond's "Coming to America," the headwaiter popped by the kitchen. It was showtime! The next few hours were a blur—of clattering dishes, shouted orders, and above all, heat: scalding steam and the radiant blast of the salamander. I was dripping with sweat and grease, my skin slashed and pocked with cuts and burns that I never even felt. Pure adrenaline was pumping through my veins.

Finally, incredibly, it was over. I was crashing from spent energy, but even through my exhaustion, the joy and satisfaction swelling inside me were profound. Never before or since have I experienced such an overwhelming sense of achievement. But it also struck me that, along the way, the process of cooking—its movements and rhythms—felt perfectly natural and instinctual, like something I was born to do. Maybe, as I kidded my mother when she asked, *"Where did you come from?"* I really was her secret love child with Mario Bonello.

• • •

None of my friends, and especially not Kerri, took my job on the cruise ship seriously. Kerri and I squabbled constantly, sometimes over my hookups, including one with a guy who lived in a tent, and sometimes over bullshit. One day, when we were exploring Edgartown, one of the Vineyard's most picturesque spots, I noticed a small white shack sitting on a pier. "Can you just see that as a little olive shop?" I said, the image sketching in my mind. "We could get all these olives, then mix them in a tub with herbs and spices and sell them."

"What the fuck?" was Kerri's answer. "No one likes olives."

"Are you kidding? Let's ask people right now. We'll see how many like them and how many don't. You know, like take a poll."

"I'm not doing that," Kerri said. "People hate olives and the idea is stupid."

"Okay, Miss Nancy Negative."

Years later, Kerri confessed, "I should have listened. We could have made a killing on those olives." She remains one of my most treasured old friends. But back then, she was sure my dinner boat story was just another pile of horseshit. "You are not the chef on that ship!" she kept saying, and I would laugh. She thought that I was exaggerating, if not flat-out lying, and that she had to keep me in line.

Then, one day, when we were short-staffed, I begged her to cover a server shift. When she got to the boat, there I was, giving orders. I was probably scolding the waitstaff for doing "whippets," sucking the nitrous oxide out of the whipped cream canisters to get high. Because, when I went to top the strawberry shortcake, what came out of the nozzle was a puddling white mess.

Kerri stood there, staring, as if she couldn't believe her eyes. All she could say was, "Holy shit."

But that's exactly how I felt too. The *Aegean Princess* job, my third life changer, was like a neon sign flashing: *This is your vocation*. Holy shit.

5

THE FOOD OF ITALY

After Labor Day, the *Aegean Princess* was headed to Florida to spend the winter as a charter boat. I decided to stick with the ship and try working as a charter chef.

I didn't have another job lined up or even a place to live—I couldn't go home because my mother and I weren't yet speaking after her letter accusing me of abandonment—and Kerri was going back to college.

The two-week sail was brutal because we hit a tropical storm belt off the Carolinas. Once we reached Fort Lauderdale, our home port, I was upset to find that my job had changed from head chef to general crew member, meaning that I had to scrub down the ship between rentals and wear a flunky's uniform of white shorts, a shirt with epaulettes, and Sperry Top-Siders.

Without a car, I was stuck on the boat, so at one point, I flew to Boston, planning to drive back down in my little green Beamer. I'd never passed driver's ed, I didn't have a license, and I had no concept of the distance between Florida and Massachusetts. When I asked my brother Kenny for advice on the long drive, he told me to pick up a can of Fix-A-Flat—how to use it, I couldn't guess—and also, "If you want to speed, stay right behind a truck. That way, you'll be hard to catch."

I made it to Florida, but living there was something else. I hated Fort Lauderdale, with its seasonless weather, and the boring boat culture, which was mostly about boozing and having sex with people who were cheating on people you knew. A friend introduced me to Coconut Grove, a part of Miami with an urban vibe, which reinforced how claustrophobic I felt in my tiny, incestuous, alcoholic world. Not only did I miss city life, I was a deckhand instead of a chef. So what was the point of being there?

It was time to head back to Boston and start over.

• • •

Again, I called Mario for advice. "You gotta work someplace," he told me, meaning that I needed a real apprenticeship. He set me up to interview at a place called Harvest in Cambridge, not mentioning that it was one of the hottest restaurants in town.

From the time it opened in the mid-1970s, Harvest had attracted both Harvard big shots and foodies on the emerging Boston scene. Ben and Jane Thompson, its owners, had a mission: to serve cutting-edge food inspired by French nouvelle cuisine—clean, inventive preparations with top-quality ingredients—instead of the snooty, formal French food that chefs like Mario produced. The Thompsons gave their chefs free rein to create whatever they wanted. So it's no wonder that so many famous ones passed through Harvest—Lydia Shire (Biba, Pignoli, Scampo), Sara Moulton (chef of the executive dining room at *Gourmet* magazine and on-air food editor of *Good Morning America*), Chris Schlesinger (the East Coast Grill, the Blue Room, the Back Eddy), Jim Burke (James), Bob Kinkead (Kinkead's, Ancora), Frank McClelland

(L'Espalier, Sel de la Terre), and Scott Bryan (most recently, the Milling Room in New York City), just to name a few.

Both Thompsons were prominent designers. Jane was a hero to me for breaking into urban planning and industrial design back in the 1960s, when women were not welcome. Ben, who taught architecture at Harvard, had founded Design Research, a store ahead of its time in scaling fine furnishings for average homes. Because of their passion, Harvest's decor was 1970s cheerful-chic, with a big horseshoe bar always jammed with professors and a back dining room with vibrant yellow walls and banquettes covered in splashy, colorful Marimekko prints. It felt fresh, upbeat, and welcoming. Paul and Julia Child, who were close friends with the Thompsons, lived right up the street and often ate at Harvest.

I was hired as garde-manger, or pantry chef, in charge of cold foods like salads and appetizers. The executive chef at the time was Chris Hood, and the menu (which I'd saved) featured entrées like grilled Atlantic swordfish with mascarpone dumplings and basil cream, and baked red snapper with pineapple-cashew salsa—a big change from Mario's sweetbreads under a bell. The dishes I prepared included a timbale of trout with yellow tomato coulis, a four-liver pâté (chicken, duck, squab, and pork) with mustard made from scratch, a salad of young greens with blackberries and champagne vinaigrette, and a seven-leaf salad with a "cornucopia of mushrooms" and tomato vinaigrette.

But my favorite thing to make—in fact, what I loved most on the menu, of all the delicious possibilities—was Harvest's signature Irish soda bread with caraway seeds and currants. We'd put it on the table with butter, and there was rarely a crumb left in the breadbasket. I think it might be my favorite bread of all time.

I started hanging out with other young restaurant people. One night, at somebody's party, I was talking about Harvest and working on the ship to a guy who turned out to be the sous-chef at Michela's, another Cambridge hotspot. "Wow," he said. "We're starting a café and looking for a cook. You'd be great for it."

I'd only been at Harvest a few months. So I didn't take the guy seriously until I started getting phone calls every day, asking when I was coming to Michela's to meet the chef, Todd English. I'd never heard of Todd but thought I should check it out.

In the late 1980s, the East Cambridge waterfront was undergoing a huge revitalization, so streets were barricaded and torn up. I didn't know my way around Cambridge that well to begin with, so on the day of the appointment, I got hopelessly lost. When I finally arrived, two hours late, they stuck me in the atrium area to wait for Todd. A young, tall, handsome guy in whites came by, and I started bitching about how tough it was to find the place. "Who the fuck in their right mind would put a restaurant here?"

"Aren't you a sassy one?" the big guy said. "I thought you weren't coming."

It was Todd. I had no idea that he was just a little older than me. But he liked my attitude enough to give me the job.

Todd got started in professional kitchens at age fifteen, graduated with honors from the Culinary Institute of America (CIA) at twenty, then worked under Jean-Jacques Rachou at La Côte Basque in New York. Along the way, he met Michela Larson, a legendary Boston restaurateur who was opening a place serving sophisticated Northern Italian food. Because she liked Todd's creative vibe, she sent him to Italy to apprentice. There he developed the *nuova cucina* cooking style he would perfect at Michela's when, at age twenty-five, he became executive chef. The reviews of his food were over the moon. He was a rock star.

Todd was fierce in the kitchen—a screamer—and so manic that he scared me. Since I had almost no professional experience—just the ship and a few months at Harvest—I hadn't yet developed much discipline. "Get organized, Lynchie," he'd say. "Get your shit together, or I'm going to fucking roast you in this fucking oven!"

Once, when he was jammed on the line, he burst into the walk-in, where I was distractedly looking for something, and shouted "Move, damn it!" before picking me up and dumping me off to the side, out of his way. He'd bellow, "What the fuck, Lynchie, haven't you ever heard of salt and pepper?" He'd tell people in the kitchen, "She sucks! She plates like a dyke!"— whatever that means. Today, I laugh at that, thinking, *Hmmm, did Todd know something I didn't?*

Todd was even harder on the managers. I once saw him fling a pound of butter at someone who'd pissed him off. The butter was soft, so it was just a blob of grease, splattering the guy's coat and tie, not a deadly weapon. Todd was a young hothead, and always frantic.

But he didn't fire me and he did put me in charge of the café, which was in the restaurant's atrium, separate from the main dining room, and had a more casual, sexy vibe. It had nightclub lighting, a live piano player to set the mood, and an inventive menu cheaper than in the main dining room, with entrées topping out at $8.95. These are late-1980s dollars, don't forget, and our prices did edge up over time. In the beginning the bargain alone attracted diners, but pretty soon, according to the write-ups, they were coming for the food.

My food! Under Todd's supervision, I was allowed to riff, trying flavor combinations that excited me. I had a tiny work space, with a proper Hobart commercial oven behind me, which was way better than a ship's galley. This was serious cooking now, the miracle of creation; and I was super energized, percolating with ideas. Early on, I got interested in clay-dish baking and developed entrées to make in that Hobart oven, like pasta shells with mascarpone and Gorgonzola cheese, and lamb marinated overnight in yogurt and juniper berries, then roasted, served with very crispy golden potatoes, fresh rosemary, and a red-wine reduction sauce. Both were fucking delicious—and big hits.

Before the exhilaration, though, there was terror. It was shocking that I was in charge of anything at a prestigious Cambridge restaurant. I never went to cooking school, I brazened my way through the *Aegean Princess* gig, and my apprenticeship consisted only of peeking over Mario's shoulder, then spending a few months at Harvest before working the line under Todd. Todd wasn't technique-driven, luckily, so my poor skills weren't a problem. He'd never peel a tomato or beautifully *brunoise* (mince) vegetables, but just shove things into the Robot Coupe. He was a big man, with huge hands and a huge personality, who made food with huge flavors. Somehow he recognized me, female and a foot shorter, as a kindred spirit.

But I was self-conscious about my inexperience, especially with Italian food. I didn't grow up with that flavor palette, learn about it in home ec, or experience it much at the St. Botolph Club or Harvest. It was like a language that Todd spoke and I didn't but had to learn. So every day, on my T commute to and from Michela's, I kept working my way through the book I'd heard was the Bible, *The Food of Italy* by Waverley Root. Organized by region, it covered history, traditions, and legends about food, along with recipes. It was a whopper, more than seven hundred pages long.

For a dyslexic like me, reading and taking in that many pages was torture. Still, I was fascinated by the subject—and determined. I had to go through the book a couple times until I got it down. It was a steep and frightening learning curve.

• • •

Once I got my bearings at Michela's, I made friends, like Annie Copps, a cook who was also Michela's assistant, and Marianne Dijaro, a student at Emerson College, who was the general manager. The three of us, along with Marianne's cousin Chrissy, who were all around the same age, decided to get a place together. We wound up renting the second floor of a house that Susan Logozzo owned in Charlestown.

What a party house that was! Marianne, who is Puerto Rican, was model-gorgeous, and so was Chrissy, who was very tall, with long, graceful hands. So there were always a lot of guys around. Marianne's drink was Cuba Libres, and Sundays were often "Puerto Rican days," when we'd all eat fried food her grandmother sent over, along with rice and beans. My Southie friends would come by, but since I worked most nights, it was often easier to connect with restaurant friends, who worked the same brutal schedules.

Even so, I got a steady boyfriend—I'll call him "P"—a Southie guy who was an encyclopedia salesman and always on the road. I'd joke that I was going to marry either a doctor or an astronaut because he'd never be around and would give me space. A major reason that P and I stayed together for nine years, no doubt, was his constant absence.

Annie would join me as a cook when Todd opened his own restaurant, then go on to become a food writer, magazine editor, radio-show host, popular network-TV talking head, and even the producer of a few PBS television series with Todd and with Julia Child. In interviews, she's said that when she pictures me back then, my nose is always stuck in *The Food of Italy*. That's how hell-bent I was on mastering it.

I finally got a chance to see firsthand what Root was writing about thanks to Sara Jenkins, another friend from Michela's. Sara was the café's garde-manger, handling the antipasti and salads to go with my hot entrées. So we were a team, with stations right next to each other. Sara had a tremendous sense of humor, which helped us all cope when Todd got nuts. A photography student at the Rhode Island School of Design, she was taking a break from school to refine her cooking skills—which were already pretty great—in a professional kitchen.

She spoke Italian better than I spoke English. That amazed me, and so did her stories of growing up in Tuscany, where their neighbors had no running water. Her father was Loren Jenkins, a famous journalist, and her mother was Nancy Harmon Jenkins, the reigning expert on Mediterranean food and the author of some cookbooks that I loved. No wonder Sara was like a walking fucking pamphlet on Italian culture.

After work, Sara and I would sip glass after glass of great red wine and she'd talk about harvest festivals, the tang of fresh-pressed olive oil right out of the spigot, and the scent of herbs crushed underfoot. Her descriptions of the dishes she'd eaten were so poetic that they put me in a trance, and I'd beg, "Tell me more." Then I'd have to laugh because Sara always got two red triangles at the corners of her lips when she was drinking wine. "You look like a vampire," I'd tell her. "Oh yeah," she'd say. "Well, your teeth look stained with blood."

When Sara invited me to visit her in Tuscany, I got chills. I had to go. Todd had left Michela's, and his replacement, Terry Endow, didn't want to give me two weeks off. When he heard why I was asking, he gave in, but insisted, "I'll give you one week—that's it." I grabbed it.

But how could I afford the trip? I wasn't even making a living wage. I pulled every pitiful cent from my account at the South Boston Savings Bank and borrowed some cash from my brother Kenny. Then a kind friend stepped up and loaned me a credit card. Saved! Every hurdle that followed seemed minor, like getting a passport—what the hell was that? Finally I was on the plane, heart and mind racing, on the verge of my greatest adventure yet.

• • •

I landed in Milan, where it shocked me that no one spoke English. *Shit,* I thought, *even the fucking signs are in a foreign language.* By drawing pictures, I managed to get directions from the airport to what seemed like the biggest train station in the world. Thousands of people were milling around, loudspeakers were blasting incomprehensible announcements. Dazed from the flight, I was overwhelmed.

I was supposed to meet my escort, Sara's brother Nicolai, who'd also worked at Michela's, at the ticket window for the train that would get us to their tiny village, Teverina, in Cortona. Sara had told me what to ask for, and I wrote down what I'd heard: "Lacusa." But when I went from one ticket window to the next, presenting my scrap of paper, the clerks rattled in Italian and shooed me away. Not wanting to seem dumb by asking Sara how to spell the word—which turned out to be La Chiusa—I had totally fucked myself.

When I say *totally,* I mean it. Never having traveled abroad, I had no idea how to change money, make a phone call, or check the bags I was dragging along—nothing. All I had in my pocket was twenty lire, which I spent on Kinder eggs, so I could eat the chocolate shells and keep busy trying to assemble the intricate toys encapsulated inside. I must have downed a couple dozen of them. Hours passed. It was early evening when, like the sun breaking through storm clouds, I heard a few words of English. Thank God.

I spilled my whole sorry story to the British girl, who suggested that I stow my bags in a locker and spend the night in a youth hostel run by nuns. I could try again in the morning. That made sense. But she also wanted me to sneak into a rock concert with her. "Mötley fucking Crüe?" I said, horrified, thinking, *Back home, we beat up metalheads.* But I was sticking with her, no matter what.

Just then, out of the corner of my eye, I caught a glimpse of messy hair and round, Harry Potter–ish glasses. Nicolai! "What the hell, Barbara?" he said. "I've been looking for you all day!"

I was so glad to see him that, once we were on the train, we practically got it on, right there in public, while the worldly Italians ignored us. I felt that I owed him.

What I'll never forget about that train ride are the stops where we bought bowls of *tortellini en brodo*—little handmade, stuffed rings of pasta, swimming in delicious broth, with Parmesan shaved on top—which I'd read about but never eaten. Then, when we got off the train, the taxi driver who picked us up invited us to lunch the next day. His wife was a local culinary star and had even written a cookbook. He told us to bring fennel flowers gathered from the roadside so she could use their pollen in her special *tacchino*, or turkey. To a budding chef like me, the meal we enjoyed in their very modest home was utterly humbling in its depth of flavor. Italy was like a paradise, where preparing food and eating were celebrations of life for everyone, from train station kiosk cooks and poor village housewives, on up the social ladder.

●　●　●

Teverina was as magical as Sara had made it sound. All these years later, I still remember its smell: wood smoke tinged with the pungent scent of sage and rosemary bushes. The farm where Sara spent much of her childhood was down a twisted road, in a little valley that was shrouded in fog early in the morning but bright and clear by ten. It was planted with olives, interspersed with fig and chestnut trees. Made of stone, with cement floors that were swept with hand-tied brooms, the farmhouse had huge hearths in the kitchen, dining area, and living room, where cooking and heating fires had burned for generations. The enormous window overlooking the farm was shielded with heavy wooden shutters. Outside was a huge stone patio, where we

ate our simple but delicious meals and drank the fragrant local wine.

The farm's caretakers were Bruno and Mita Antolini, who owned a neighboring plot of land. When I first saw Bruno, he was standing on a pile of charred wood that he used to cure tobacco, his cash crop. He was wearing his uniform: one of the Ralph Lauren suits handed down by Sara's father. Besides tobacco, Bruno and Mita raised food crops and livestock to use and sell. They were totally self-sufficient.

Mita, whom Sara called her adoptive grandmother, was the one I longed to meet. I almost felt that I knew her from Sara's stories. When she invited me into her kitchen to watch her cook, I wanted to cross myself, as if I were entering a sacred space.

A huge leg of home-cured prosciutto rested on a stand on the kitchen table. In the massive fireplace, a cast-iron pot dangled on a hook over the embers, emitting the delicious smell of white beans and rosemary stewing slowly in Chianti. For lunch, Mita served one of her own rabbits, which she sold at the village farmers' market and delivered live to customers in bowling bags.

After lunch, she took me outside to see large drums of tomato sauce bubbling gently over a wood fire, picking up the smoky scent, until it was ready to be jarred for the coming year. Then we picked and scrubbed potatoes to roast in her wood-burning oven. When they were done, Mita peeled them, putting the flesh through a ricer and letting it cool. Making a well in the cooled potatoes, she cracked an egg and added flour by the handful, as needed, plus a pinch of salt, until she'd formed the perfect dough. She rolled the dough into logs, then swiftly chopped them into bite-size pieces, which she passed over a grooved wooden board. These were her handmade gnocchi—the most intensely flavored, pillowy, and delicate that I've ever eaten.

The next day, Mita taught me to make her Bolognese sauce.

There was no beef in it—just pork, veal, and lamb ground together, a lot of fresh sage, and her secret ingredient, chicken livers. That's the Bolognese I serve in my restaurants. It can never be the same of course, without Mita's fire-roasted tomato sauce and the aromatic olive oil pressed from her own trees.

While the sauce was cooking, she brought in an apron full of chestnuts she'd gathered and showed me how to slit them on the flat side. We soaked the chestnuts in water, so they wouldn't burn, while we stoked the hearth with olive branches. Then we roasted them in the fireplace. When they were done and cool enough to handle, we peeled them and plunged them a tub of vin santo, a sherrylike wine made from dried grapes, where they sat until it was time to eat.

Mita was tiny—not much more than four feet tall—and hunched over from a life of hard labor. She was probably fifty-something at the time I met her, wiry and strong. Even so, I couldn't believe it when I saw her lift a huge slab of slate and heave it into the fireplace. As it heated, she showed me a hunk of dough she called *cha-chi,* which I took to mean focaccia. After punching it down, she flattened the dough into a rectangle and made indentations by poking it all over with her fingertips. She slathered olive oil and salt over the indented surface.

By then the slate was hot on one side. I would have been scared to touch it. But Mita reached right into the fireplace and flipped it over, as if were weightless. God, she was tough. She slapped the indented side of the *cha-chi* onto the slate, and it began to crackle and puff up. I felt almost drunk on the smell of sizzling dough and olive oil. Then she pulled out the *cha-chi* and dressed the other side with olive oil and sprigs of rosemary, just cut from a bush, before plopping that side onto the slate.

When the dough was golden and crusty on both sides, she let it cool then scrubbed it with a clove of garlic. She topped it with thin slices of incredible prosciutto, earthy and sweet, from her

well-fed pigs. That, along with the chestnuts cured in vin santo, was our lunch. It was a soulful, profoundly flavorful meal.

Those two days with Mita were like a master class in Italian cooking. But there was so much more to see—and hear, touch, smell, and taste. I wanted to absorb Italy through all five senses. A few of Sara's art-student friends from the Rhode Island School of Design were also visiting, but I was too antsy to hang out with them. When Sara had some errands to run, I went along.

One of her tasks was photographing a cemetery for Faith Willinger, an expert on Italian food and culture who was one of Sara's mother's friends, to use in some project. That fascinated me, since I'd heard of Faith, who introduced fennel pollen to America. But even shopping for items we needed on the farm was exciting.

The Jenkins car was an old Fiat Cinquecento. To get up the hill from Sara's house, it often needed a push-start, that is, to get rolling in neutral gear until the engine caught. I couldn't drive a stick so Sara got behind the wheel, while I, much smaller and many pounds lighter, had to push.

What a sight we must have been, me huffing and puffing, straining under the heft of car and passenger, while Sara, with her lit cigarette sticking out the window, shouted, "Faster, faster." Finally I heard a *vroom* and had to jump into the moving car like a stuntwoman, screaming with laughter.

At the top of the hill, just past the gas station, was a wild-boar butchery. It was just a storefront, like a bodega, where the hunters who stalked their prey all night in the valley would bring the boars they shot to be dressed and sold. Boar carcasses hung from the ceiling. The butcher would whack off whatever cut you wanted to buy—say, a leg, to make prosciutto. I wasn't horrified by the sight but fascinated. It seemed fitting, closer to the natural order in the world, to be intimately connected to the source of food. That recognition later inspired me to start a butcher shop of my own.

I was utterly charmed by the old boar butcher, who insisted that we drink shots of vin santo before going on our way. Our next stop was the village market, where we planned to hit every stall. Among other things, I was looking for tools like Mita's grooved gnocchi board.

But the minute we got out of the car, we were practically mugged by an amazing smell. It was a *porchetta* truck. A guy had rigged the bed of his truck with some kind of oven to slow-roast a pig that was encrusted with fennel pollen and salt. "Oh my God," I said. "We've got to try this." The guy cut off some thick, succulent slices and stuck them in a bulky roll for each of us. We ate them while walking around the stands. Today Sara has a restaurant specializing in *porchetta*, and hers is amazing, but for me, that guy in the truck will always define it.

Sara had really come to the market to get the local wine. We bought two huge jugs, one white and one red that at home we'd decant into regular-size bottles, using a funnel. Sara's mother had an entire wine pantry, but this would be the household's "school night" or everyday wine. Before heading back, Sara and I each got another *porchetta* sandwich for the road.

As the week sped by, I was almost in sensory overload, trying to process everything I'd seen, tasted, and even breathed. Though I couldn't speak the language, in just a week, I'd tuned in to entirely new frequencies of tastes, smells, sights, and sounds. My connection to Italy was so visceral and intense that I felt I'd discovered my true spiritual home.

But, too soon, I had to leave. Nicolai and Sara drove me to Milan, where I'd spend the night in a hotel and catch an early-morning flight. As we said good-bye, I gave them my leftover lire, saying, "You'll need these sooner than I will."

But the next morning, I overslept and missed my plane. Again, I had no clue what to do. I tried to change the ticket, which involved paying extra money, but the name on my borrowed credit card was different from the one on my passport. *Jesus, fucked again*, I thought. Clearly, Milan was out to get me, coming and going.

I was escorted to the American embassy under threat of arrest. They must have confirmed that I hadn't stolen the credit card because they allowed me to call the States. I needed cash wired so I could buy a new plane ticket under my name.

But when I reached my mother, she was ready to leave me stranded. "Jesus, Barbara," she said. "None of us have that kind of money. You're shit out of luck."

That convinced me that my siblings wouldn't sympathize either or be able to help. Susan Logozzo was the only other person I could think of who might bail me out. Thank God, she wired the money right away. Her faith in me, at that point in my life, was as important as getting out of Italy.

When I landed in Boston, I was like an astronaut coming off a moonwalk. My mind was still flooded with exotic images and, especially, smells, like wood smoke and damp black earth, fumes of vin santo, tomato sauce bubbling, pork roasting, *cha-chi* grilling on a hot slate, and more. I'd not only experienced the customs of another culture but also had stepped back in time to see how people had been cooking for hundreds, if not thousands, of years. It was a hell of a sensation to be connected so directly to human history. I felt like an expanded, larger-than-life version of myself. "Killing a rabbit?" one of my friends joked. "Could a South Boston girl do that?" Yeah, I might have made that claim. Whether I'd killed a rabbit myself or had just watched Mita do the deed, I had changed, becoming a new, Technicolor version of myself.

● ● ●

Terry was pissed that I was gone a couple extra days, sure that I was lying about missing the plane. But I applied what I'd learned in that week away—practicing what I called the crazy, amazing simplicity of Italian cooking—in the café. To experiment with cuisines of different Italian regions, I came up with the idea of changing menus to provide an eight-week armchair tour. Terry went for it and supervised my dishes. My menu for Veneto, in the north, offered, for example, the classic risotto *risi e bisi* and also *fegato di vitello* or calves' liver. For the island of Sardinia, I focused on seafood dishes like saffron risotto with clams, oysters, and squid, and tuna baked in seaweed with grilled leeks. For Lombardy, the entrées included an unusual *pizzoccheri di teglio*—a buckwheat lasagna with potatoes and cabbage—as well as *tacchino alla milanese*, or breaded turkey scaloppine. The tour, along with my other menu innovations, was a huge success, and I started getting my picture, alongside Michela herself, in places like *Boston* magazine. The café attracted a lot of well- or soon-to-be-well-known regulars, including Jeffrey and Cheryl Katz, who over the years have been the designers and architects for all my restaurants.

All thanks to Waverley Root and *The Food of Italy.*

6

CHARLESTOWN

Todd English had put Michela's on the map. So it was a big up-heaval when he and his wife, Olivia, a fellow CIA graduate who ran the dining room, left to start their own restaurant. Michela was hurt, but probably not surprised. Even if Todd weren't so driven and intense, he caught fire as a chef so fast that no one could have contained him. The café was flourishing, but in the main dining room, he'd created such huge expectations that he was a hard act to follow.

Olives, Todd's first restaurant, was a tiny fifty-seater in Charlestown near his home. Today, because of its beautiful redbrick townhouses, Charlestown is super gentrified, but back then, it was mostly Irish and mob-infested, known as the home of gangs that rivaled Whitey Bulger's. Todd's first investor, Jack Sidell, was leery about the location. He told *Boston* magazine, "The only thing in Charlestown are bank robbers."

But Olivia, especially, believed in the neighborhood—and in Todd's magic—and that faith paid off. Right away, there were hour-long lines out front. Of course, at Michela's, we were closely watching these developments. Todd had an agreement with Michela, which he honored, not to poach staff for a certain period. So I stayed in Cambridge for two years, happily, and even recruited Kerri as a waitress at Michela's when she graduated from college.

During that time, my roommate Marianne decided to move to Spain. Rather than try to replace her, Annie and I decided to give up our apartment. My mother's diabetes was getting worse and she needed someone around. Also, since running the café at one of Boston's best restaurants didn't pay much, it would let me save money. Kerri and I figured we could drive back and forth to work together from our mothers' homes in the projects.

But I remained fascinated by Todd, convinced that he had a lot to teach me. I was remembering his boldness and creativity, I guess, and forgetting the pain. I interviewed a few times with Paul O'Connell, his sous-chef, but nothing came of it. So, one afternoon, I rode the T out to Charlestown, on the chance that I might run into Todd himself and see whether he had room for me.

I could hear the music blasting as I approached the restaurant: Black Box, "Strike It Up." (Later "Everybody, Everybody" by Black Box would become our theme song.) Looking through the window, I could see Todd on the line rocking out and prepping. When he caught sight of me, he unlocked the door. "Lynchie!" he said. "What's up?"

Quite a lot, I told him. I described my trip to Tuscany: the train station tortellini, the turkey with fennel pollen, the *porchetta* truck, Sara's house with the three huge hearths, Mita's gnocchi and Bolognese, her *cha-chi* baking on the slate, and her tomato sauce simmering on the wood fire. He smiled. "Wow," he said, "you got the bite."

I had. Italy had bitten him hard too. That's why I wanted to work for him, I explained, and why I was ready to leave Michela's.

Todd wasn't ultrasure of my cooking skills, though he'd put me in charge of Michela's café. "But I'll work my ass off," I told him. "You know that."

"Okay," he said. "I'll give you a shot."

The pay was shit—$6 an hour, as I recall—and the commute would suck, two trains plus a long walk. "Just say your prayers that you made the right decision," my mother said. She thought I was crazy to give up what looked like security at Michela's. But even more, she was scared that I might be getting ahead in a world that she didn't understand. "My kids are all the same," she kept telling me. "Don't think you're special. You're not better."

* * *

There were times when I questioned the wisdom of my decision too. If I thought Todd was manic at Michela's, he was a fucking whirling dervish in his own shop. The James Beard Foundation named him a Rising Star Chef, which made him feel even more scrutinized and driven to shine. Every night, he'd throw new specials at us, pushing us, testing our nerve. But the food at Olives, often prepared in the incredible wood-burning oven or on the wood-fire grill, was brilliant, with Todd's signature big, bold flavors. He was also getting famous for his huge portions—what *New York* magazine once called his "artful, Hungry Man" cuisine. I felt so lucky to be there.

Yet I also stood out in the small kitchen staff at Olives. Not as much as the line cook who liked the Grateful Dead, instead of high-octane rock, but a lot. Everyone else had strong training—cooking school and line work at major restaurants—which made me feel incompetent and weird. Along the way, they'd picked up a certain polish that I thought, by comparison, made me look uncouth. Feeling gawky and shy about my background, I even hated to accept when Paul would offer me a ride home. I'd say, "Just drop me at Dot [Dorchester] Avenue" or at some station on

Red Line, rather than reveal that I lived in the projects. (My blue eye shadow, which took me a while to give up, might have been a tip-off.) It took a few months for my insecurity to let up.

Luckily, Annie Copps soon came to Olives as garde-manger. Her hilarity cranked up the craziness in the kitchen, which was as cramped and frantic as a MASH unit. Even Todd's temper didn't dampen her nerve. Once, he bellowed, "Fucking Annie, I need those olive tarts NOW!" She shot back, "I've got your fucking tarts right here, Todd!" yanking up her shirt to flash her tits. *God, what a huge bra,* I thought. It was even bigger than my mother's, after all those kids. It made Annie's defiance even funnier.

When I first started, I was assigned to the pasta station, in a little alcove; Paul O'Connell worked the grill; and Todd worked the brick oven in the middle, with an eagle eye on us all. Periodically he'd come over and check my pasta, saying, "Thinner! It has to be thinner," or, "Come on! That sauce needs more seasoning." Too scared to ask him in advance what he expected, I took all my cues from Paul.

I actually had a nightmare of royally fucking up on a brown-butter sauce with sage. In my dream, I dressed butternut squash tortellini, painstakingly handmade, with the screwed-up sauce, then had to shitcan the whole mess. But when I tried to start over, searching the freezer for new sheet trays of tortellini, it was all gone. What a horror! I shook at the thought of Todd's rage. I had that vivid nightmare over and over, and even today now and then it still haunts me.

One night I did have a pasta catastrophe. I came to work wearing big earrings—bad idea—and took them off, stowing them in a little cubbyhole above my station. One of our offerings that night was pasta with clam sauce, which included some shells for visual appeal. Todd was in the dining room, meeting the guests, when one of them held up an earring he'd found in his food. Todd went batshit.

He came storming into the kitchen, shouting, "What the fuck! Whose is this?"

I tried to looked puzzled instead of terrified as he backed me into the alcove. "Uh, I don't know," I stammered.

"You don't know? You're the only fucking female in this kitchen. You damn fucking well know that this earring is yours!"

I tried to apologize, but he snatched up a bowl of pasta I had sauced and slopped it onto me. "Make another one," he roared and stomped off.

Before I could, I had to claw off gobs of pasta, wash the sauce from my face and my hair, and change my clothes.

But, again, he didn't fire me. In fact I moved up to the middle of the line when Marc Orfaly, a chef who'd graduated culinary school then cut his teeth at Davio's, a Northern Italian steakhouse, was hired and put on pasta. That meant working the brick oven, which was scary. Todd was so tall and strong that he could easily move platters in and out of it. Since I'm short, reaching in to grab the cast-iron, double-handled paella pans was tough and left me with burns up and down my arms.

One of my other tasks was to do Todd's *mise en place*—that is to chop, dice, mince, or whatever, and arrange the ingredients Todd needed for his stage of the cooking process. Mostly, these were garnishes that took painstaking effort to prepare, like his favorite, julienned scallions. But every time he'd swoop in to put his finishing touches on a dish, he'd wipe out all my hard work. His hands were so huge that a pinch for him was like a tablespoon for someone else. So he was always going, "Come on! Prep me!" Since one of our most popular entrées, fig and Gorgonzola tart with prosciutto, was topped with scallions, I went crazy trying to keep up.

All night long, Todd would bitch about our work on the line, which shook me. Once, after he returned from some trip and saw me working with confidence and speed, he said, "What happened to you? You're great. You can cook!" All I could think was, *Yeah, I can, when you're not fucking breathing down my neck.*

Many local celebrities came to Olives, and one night, we had the queen herself, Julia Child. Paul was on the grill. I was working the middle, and Marc Orfaly was on pasta, as usual, with Todd frantically running around. Back then, Marc was such a cherub, with his baby face, dark curly hair, and red lips. After dinner, Julia came back to the kitchen to greet Todd. "The food was delicious," she told him. "And, Todd—I'm so glad to see that you have two women on the line."

While I laughed my ass off, Marc pouted, with his lips pouched out, looking even more feminine. "You're gorgeous, baby girl," I kept teasing, never letting him forget. In those days, women were scarce in high-end restaurant kitchens. When present, we women were underdogs, which I didn't always mind because, when I did well, the guys were shocked. (Today, of course, I have zero tolerance for sexism.) But Marc became a friend, and I talked Kerri into dating him. They would later marry, have a beautiful daughter, and start their own restaurant, Pigalle.

Another famous chef who dropped into Olives when I was cooking on the line was Lydia Shire. She'd been honored with a James Beard Award as Best Chef: Northeast for her restaurant, Biba, on the Boston Common. She wore clogs and, instead of a standard executive chef coat, a funny one with flowers. She told me, "Sweetie, at my age"—her forties—"I can do whatever I want." I admired her so much.

And I admired Todd, who taught me some valuable lessons, like to how make great pasta and risotto. Some of his dishes were pure genius, like his Parmesan pudding with fresh pea sauce, his beautiful roasted lamb ribs in mustard, and his crispy duck, just to name a few. For the duck, he'd dress it with his special spice mix, then roast it in the oven low and slow, for several hours. Then he'd pull it out of the fat and chill it, before returning it to the duck fat to crisp it up. Maybe it was a heart attack in a pan, but it was spectacular. Watching Todd create sparked my own imagination.

But working at Olives also taught me how not to run a restaurant. Todd and Olivia wouldn't take reservations, and they were determined to do at least three seatings a night—a crushing pace for the staff. Lines would form out front before the doors opened—people sitting in lawn chairs, for God's sake—pressuring us to cook fast, to keep the dishes coming. Talk about stress! Every time I saw that line, I almost puked.

To me, that focus on the number of guests, rather than the quality of the experience they were paying for, seemed cold. After inventing such beautiful dishes and working hard to prepare them perfectly, I thought diners should get to savor them—not to hog a table forever, of course, but not to feel they had to gulp them down because of the line outside. That felt to me like the opposite of hospitality.

But the customers kept on coming. Pretty soon, Todd would have to move to a bigger space down the street at 10 City Square.

● ● ●

Before that happened, I accepted a gig that should have scared the shit out of me. Sara Jenkins was getting married in Tuscany. A few months before, she asked me if I'd cook for her wedding. "Sure," I said. Lisa Kerr, an artistic friend, made me a hand-bound journal (the first of many I'd fill with food thoughts over the years). So I started jotting notes on the textured paper: *Actual date September 27, 1992 . . . Expecting about 75 people. So far it is undecided if it will be a buffet or a sitdown. I think for sure she and her father want porchetta roasted on a spit, which I'll be very happy with . . . Must start collecting recipes for myself . . .*

I was so psyched, flattered to be asked, and ready to jump in with both feet. I'd never staged a banquet for seventy-five people, but what the hell? Half the excitement was the risk, the breath-taking, heart-stopping challenge. *I'll figure it out,* I thought. *I always have . . .*

Then I got a call from Sara's intimidating mother, Nancy Harmon Jenkins, wanting to nail down plans. For the first time, it struck me who I was cooking for: probably a bunch of her famous culinary friends, along with the Tuscan neighbors. I was a young, untrained American chef who would be making Italian food for authorities on Italian food and—even worse—for Italians.

I started to break out in hives. "Uh, Nancy, I'm sorry, but I can't do it." I lied. "Todd won't give me the time off to come to Italy."

"It's too late to back out now," she said. "You tell Todd if he doesn't let you go, he'll never see another good write-up."

Holy shit. I didn't know if she was kidding. Luckily Todd didn't put up a fight.

This time I flew into Rome, instead of Milan, which made sense because it was closer to Teverina. After my first, fish-out-of-water trip, I found it easier to navigate Italy. I managed to connect with Ernesto, a nice young Italian guy I'd met in my travels, who toured me around Rome on his motorcycle. I'd also hoped to meet up with Marianne, who'd moved to Spain, but it didn't work out. I'd been counting on having her help me cook for the wedding.

I arrived in Teverina wild with ideas. When you're a young chef, you want to cook everything; and this was a part of the world where I could get any ingredient, common or exotic, fresh from the fields or farms. Nancy had to rein me in. Not only was I overambitious, but I couldn't even guess where to find some of the fascinating items described by Waverley Root.

One was a *rosticino,* a traditional device in Abruzzo, where they love lamb. It's a box containing a sharp grid, like a giant

French-fry cutter. You stick in a hunk of lamb, insert skewers through holes in the top of the box, then press down on the grid to slice the lamb into perfect kebabs, ready for grilling.

But lamb wasn't on our menu. I learned that there was a budget for the wedding when Nancy took me grocery shopping. We each had a list—mine with ingredients, and hers with numbers that we couldn't exceed. With my limited experience of the world, I had no clue that even people who seemed glamorous, like Loren and Nancy Jenkins, then in the throes of a divorce, watched their spending like the rest of us.

We settled on a menu of roasted rabbit with sage and creamy polenta, roasted chicken with rosemary and garlic and roasted potatoes, roasted pork loin with fig sauce, and my special lasagna, featuring about twenty layers of very thin pasta interleaved with béchamel and Mita's Bolognese ragù. I'd start with a huge antipasti spread and finish with a beautiful fruit tart with almond cream, berries, and fresh figs.

It was simple food, inspired by the resources at hand, like open cooking fires and the sage and rosemary bushes and fig trees growing everywhere. I felt like someone with new, hot crush writing a love note to Tuscany.

Even our shopping trip was an adventure. I'd never spent time with Nancy, who knew everyone in Teverina and the surrounding area, Cortona. She took me to her favorite shops, where I picked out eight plump-looking chickens and some handsome pink pork roasts about seven inches across, capped with plenty of fat. I'd expected to buy rabbits, but Mita insisted that I use hers, which she would skin and dress.

Our final stop was an ironworks, to order a couple of *Toscana rosticcerias*, which were revolving spits for the pork. You'd wind them like a watch to rotate the meat, and when the spring ran down, a bell rang to alert you to give the crank another turn. The spits were on legs, so they could stand over embers, with a drip pan beneath the meat to catch the juices. Since they were custom made, they took a couple of days.

Back at the house, I must have prepped for forty-eight hours straight. I think I was up all night making pasta and hand-cranking it through the machine. There were no electrical appliances of any kind in the Jenkins home—no dishwasher—and no gas line. So I had to parboil my pasta, make my béchamel, and everything else on the rustic wood stove, which was basically a cooktop with burners over a firebox. Using that sucker was an education in itself.

I got a shock when the birds were delivered, beautifully wrapped and tied with string. The chickens were whole—heads and feet on—and fully feathered. I fired up a Marlboro, thinking, *What the fuck?* I'd never plucked a chicken.

After Nancy explained, I loosened the feathers by blanching the birds, then pulled them out. With the long matches used to light the hearth, I singed off the strays. I cleaned the chickens, keeping the livers for the Bolognese sauce, and made a super gelatinous stock with the feet and cockscombs. It reduced to an incredible golden jus to serve with the chicken.

Meanwhile, guests were dropping by. Sara kept poking her head in the kitchen to ask, "How are you doing? Do you need help?" I kept hearing famous names, some of which I recognized, like Faith Willinger, and others I couldn't place, like Burton Anderson, who happened to be the world's greatest expert on Italian wines. I felt totally out of place among such well-known figures and just as alien to Sara's college friends, who'd wander in, often a little buzzed, to try to lend a hand. "Thanks, I don't really want anyone else in here," I insisted. I was most comfortable hidden in the kitchen, spared the obligation to chitchat, and I was busy—happily lost in the rhythms of my work.

On the day of the wedding, I set up my spits in the fireplace and put the pork, doctored with fennel pollen, rosemary, garlic, and salt, on to roast over a low, slow fire. The whole time it was cooking, I basted it with juices from the drip pan. Early that morning, Mita had fired up her wood-burning bread oven then let it cool to the perfect temperature to roast the rabbits. I used their livers to make a kick-ass pâte, to be served on crostini.

The wedding dinner for seventy or so people was held on a terrace outdoors, under an arbor entwined with grapevines. Olive trees, along with tree-size bushes of rosemary and sage, perfumed the air. Local musicians, playing folk instruments, provided the entertainment. It was a magical, incredibly romantic setting.

Everyone seemed delighted with the food. The chicken and rabbit were perfect, the pork was irresistibly succulent, and the lasagna came out light as lace. But the biggest hit was the fig sauce I made for the pork, which was simple but sensually delicious: red wine reduced with cinnamon, sugar, and rosemary, with the figs thrown in at the very end. The townspeople who were there, mingling with the bigwigs, were crazy for it and kept calling out, *"Fichi, fichi,"* to ask for more.

By dessert, I was throbbing with exhaustion but also overcome by waves of triumph, both feelings boosted by all the wine I had sloshing around inside. Someone handed me a pipe with the flowery incense smell of opium. A toke or two, and I was gone. I woke up in the bed that Sara and her groom were trying to climb into for their wedding night. All I could say was, "No, no, I don't want to go to Rome right now . . ." I was *sooo* high.

We spent the next day recovering, eating leftovers. Then, the following day, when Nancy took me out for a thank-you lunch, I learned the truth about "Lacusa," the destination I'd misspelled on my first trip to visit Sara. It *was* a landmark, La Chiusa, an ancient olive mill that had been converted into a guesthouse, with a restaurant considered to be the best in Tuscany.

Nancy introduced me to the chef, Dania Masotti, who was

stuffing quail while wearing an elegant designer outfit topped with an apron. I couldn't imagine her working with Todd English in that getup, dodging hurled butter and bowls of pasta. In fact, I couldn't imagine myself ever staying clean enough in the kitchen to dress that way.

But what impressed me even more were the women patrolling the dining room wearing sandwich boards, which they used for hand rolling fat spaghetti-shaped noodles called *pici*. *Pici* were made from an eggless flour-and-water dough, cut into strips, which a woman would roll at your table between her hands and her board until they were about half as thick as a pencil. As each noodle grew long, she'd gather up the rolled length into one hand while continuing to roll the rest of the strip with the other.

Today, a demonstration like this might seem touristy-tacky, but back then it was a good show, an interesting technique to observe. After rolling out the strips of pasta to amazing lengths, the woman would take the batch to the kitchen, boil it, and bring it back dressed in a simple tomato sauce. It was incredibly satisfying, toothsome, and delicious.

Nancy had been so supportive. I had to admit that she'd taken a leap of faith by having me cook on such a momentous family occasion, with all those famous guests. Sara had given me the chance to showcase my skills outside the enormous shadow that Todd English cast creatively, temperamentally, and even physically. What a huge honor! Thank God I hadn't fucked up.

Because of the wedding dinner, a bunch of influential food people now knew my name. But, more important to me, that dinner proved that I was talented enough to cook for anyone. This was no steam-table steak-tips, keg-of-beer affair at Florian Hall in Southie. I'd planned and executed a whole Tuscan banquet, with my own two hands, guided by my own instincts, that was good enough to impress both professional critics and Italians, who'd invented the cuisine. I was also proud of the way I'd jumped up to do it—fuck-the-consequences fearless. I was hot shit. I'd earned the right to call myself a chef.

But I still felt tongue-tied around Nancy. I had periodic flare-ups of awareness that my Southie accent, constant f-bombing, and cultural ignorance marked me as a project rat. I wasn't ashamed of who I was, but I didn't want to be a curiosity.

So, when it was time to go home, I was unnerved that Nancy, who was flying somewhere else, took the train with me to Rome. I squirmed the whole ride, practically flinching whenever she started talking. I managed to get by on grunts and smiles until we reached the airport and were on the shuttle bus to the terminal. Disco music was blaring over the loudspeaker. "I don't understand this," Nancy said. "Italians love beautiful music, like opera." Then she addressed me directly, looking right at me. "Why can't they play some beautiful opera?" she asked.

I'd been bottled up so long, out of shyness, that I couldn't hold back. "I don't know," I blurted out. "Why don't you ask them?"

Awkward. When I got off the shuttle, heart pounding, I almost took off running.

Maybe I wasn't as hot shit as I thought. But pretty soon I could call myself a chef.

● ● ●

Before leaving for Italy, I'd written in my journal, *Well, I feel like another chapter of my life is about to begin. I will no longer be cooking at Olives but running the show down at Figs. I have no idea what to expect . . . Haven't seen my raise yet. Must talk to Todd when I get back . . .*

Todd had made the move from what we now called Baby Olives to the new Olives at 10 City Square, which had double the number of seats. The transition wasn't smooth. The electrical system was messed up at first, so we couldn't use the new kitchen, but there were private events that couldn't be postponed. One was a party for the Italian consulate spearheaded by chef Lidia Bastianich. As a makeshift kitchen, Todd rented three generator-powered trailers. Waiters would run the hot dishes from the trailers to the guests waiting in the restaurant.

What a shit show. Lidia Bastianich was pissed. "I can't cook risotto in a trailer," she said. "I can't believe this."

But the party was a success, and afterward we all celebrated at Baby Olives. I recall being dazzled by the sight of Jean-Louis Palladin, the brilliant mentor of a whole generation of French chefs in America, including Daniel Boulud and Eric Ripert. He was a rock star, sitting there with his long, dark hair, smoking. Sadly he would die just a few years later, in his fifties, of lung cancer.

Since there was time left on the lease for the Baby Olives space, Todd planned to turn it into a more casual pizza and pasta restaurant called Figs. The wood-burning oven was already there. To develop the concept, he asked me to collaborate— offering me my first major creative job as sous-chef of Figs. He even put me in charge of ordering everything, from food to china, glassware, and silver. It was a hands-on education in running a restaurant.

Todd and I both had been thinking hard about pizza and pasta after our time in Italy, observing traditional cooking methods. Now we set off on a field trip to check out some classic American pizza shops, like Frank Pepe Pizzeria Napoletana and Sally's Apizza in New Haven, Connecticut. Founded early in the twentieth century, both had cult followings because of their coal-fired, brick pizza ovens.

Todd and Olivia rode in the front seats of the car, while I was stuck in the back with Oliver, their cranky toddler. His mood didn't improve when we hit Pepe's, as it was called, and faced a twenty-minute line. The place was always packed.

But Pepe's famous clam pie was worth the wait. The crust was thin, blistered around the edges, charred, and crisp, with no hint of sogginess. It crunched when you bit into it. The clams were so fresh—briny and plump—resting on a light bed of olive oil and cheese, with the scent of garlic and oregano wafting off it. We couldn't stop eating slice after slice. "This is what we want to master," Todd said, jotting notes in a little journal labeled, *DON'T LOSE IT: THE ART OF MAKING PIZZA.*

When we could pry ourselves up from the table, we went back to inspect the brick oven. The front was yellow subway tile, blackened in spots by the fiery coal. For protection from the heat, the cooks slid in the pizzas on peels (paddles) that looked at least ten feet long. As the pies hit the oven, I noticed something intriguing: a billowing rush of steam. *That dough must be sopping wet,* I thought. *Maybe that's the secret?*

Back in Boston, I worked to perfect the dough. After a lot of experimentation, I hit the jackpot: a formula of 60 percent water to 30 percent flour plus 10 percent semolina. I kept the dough in a wooden box at room temperature, instead of in the fridge, to relax it and make it stretchy. Then I started developing toppings. One of our popular pies, with white clams, credited the inspiration we found at Pepe's. I billed it as "the best fresh-shucked littleneck pie east of New Haven."

Todd's fig and Gorgonzola tart with prosciutto was a highlight of the original Olives menu. So we echoed it in pizza, right down to the julienned scallions, adding zip with a sprinkle of rosemary. I kept trying new ideas: fried calamari on spicy red sauce, pancetta and corn in the summer, slow confit red onion with caramelized leeks and scallions, and more.

On the pasta side, some of my hits were rigatoni with spicy sausage and white beans, and butternut squash tortellini with brown butter and sage. Mark Ladner manned the pasta station. He had a shaky hand, so I couldn't resist giving him shit, like, "I hope you don't aim with that hand when you piss." Mark went on to a major career, becoming the executive chef and the partner of Lidia and Joe Bastianich and Mario Batali at Del Posto in New York.

Every night, I'd create a big selection of antipasti and set them out in bowls on the counter. We also baked our own bread, which Todd hoped someday to expand into a wholesale sideline. When Figs first opened, for some reason, we had to cut bread on the meat slicer. Once, while slicing bread, I was distracted by a kid in the kitchen, and the next thing I knew, people were tying a tourniquet on my arm—the wrong one, because, with all the blood, they couldn't tell which hand I'd cut.

In the ambulance, someone radioing the hospital described me as "an amputee—but she doesn't know it yet." I was flying so high on morphine that even those words couldn't freak me out. My thumb was hanging off, nearly severed. It took thirty stitches to close the gash. Luckily, I didn't lose more than a piece of my palm. Todd rushed to meet me at the hospital, which touched me, though in my drug euphoria, I was also thinking, *Woo-hoo! I'm getting Saturday night off!*

• • •

Figs was an instant success. I started getting write-ups like one in the *Herald* jokingly addressed to Boston's mayor, Raymond Flynn, whom Bill Clinton had appointed US ambassador to the Vatican. It asked "Ray" what he'd do in Italy when "the suitcases of Bumble Bee and Jif are gone . . . when you *truly* realize that you are 3,500 miles away from a Sully's dog ('Hold the onions!') . . . when nobody passes the ketchup." Peter Gelzinis, the writer, suggested that Ray bring me along because, "You need a chef you can trust"—to bridge the gap between bland Irish-American and fine Italian cuisine. I was Ray's "destiny," Gelzinis said, because "the echo of the most sublime pizza I've ever experienced continues to bounce off my taste buds."

Of course, the article thrilled everyone in Southie, but I

gulped thinking of Todd's reaction—terrified that he'd flip at sharing the spotlight. Fortunately, he took all my press in stride as great publicity for him and his restaurants. He was very excited when Figs and I won Best Pizza honors in *Boston* magazine.

Bruce Ployer, a manager of the steakhouse Grill 23, gave a party for the Best of Boston winners at his triple-decker house. I was making hors d'oeuvres in the third-floor kitchen and got tired of running down to serve them. So I rigged up a basket on a rope that I could lower to the guests and stay upstairs, smoking, drinking red wine, and screwing around. Cat Silirie, who'd been the sommelier at Grill 23, tasted some of the food. "Who's cooking this stuff?" she asked, and followed the rope up to the kitchen to find out.

She was one of few women in the wine business back then, and very young. At nineteen or twenty, she'd come to Boston from Boca Raton, Florida, looking for culture—opera, art, food, and wine. Michael Fahey, a respected sommelier at Grill 23, had taken her under his wing, and when he left, she got his job, until recently when she was hired away. Like everyone else in the restaurant business, she'd checked out Olives and spotted me— the rare woman—on the line.

We hung out together for the rest of the party, laughing and dancing to the reggae band. After that she came into Figs a lot, sometimes with her new boss, Patrick Bowe, from Rocco's, a 180-seat restaurant, with a wacky fusion menu, that drew the theater-going crowd. I believe Bowe was also angling to buy Harvest from the Thompsons.

Cat would sit at the bar, and we'd shoot the shit. That's how I learned that Burton Anderson was a god in the world of wine. "I can't believe you cooked for him," she said. "And for Nancy Harmon Jenkins." Her enthusiasm got me thrilled, all over again, about the wedding dinner. Besides my Best of Boston pizza, Cat loved my antipasti, especially the *porchetta*, the tuna crostini, and the gorgeous array of olives, she recalls.

Clearly we were on the same wavelength. We were both in our twenties (Cat was a few years younger); both self-taught, from unusual backgrounds; both trying to make it in male-ruled fields. We liked the same food. Cat confided that the Rocco's menu was hard to pair with wines. It was just too eclectic— Korean *bibimbap* next to Chinese duck-and-scallion pancakes next to old-school spaghetti with meatballs—and was confusing to diners. A change was probably in the wind. "Would you consider coming to Rocco's?" she asked.

"No, no," I said. "I'm happy here. I'd never leave Figs."

• • •

Actually, I wasn't that happy. Todd wasn't around much, for one thing. He'd opened a restaurant called Isola on Martha's Vineyard in partnership with Cam Neely of the Boston Bruins, Glenn Close, and Michael J. Fox. Olivia had moved to the Vineyard for the summer to run it, while Todd went back and forth.

I went to Isola to help on the line at one point, when Olivia was very pregnant with their second child. On the ferry, rocking with the waves, she said, "Oh my God, I think I'm having this baby." That scared me to death. But we made it to the house, where she filled the bathtub with cold water and just soaked a while. I didn't understand what was going on—how hot and miserable she must have been. Being too young when my brother John was born, and too wild when my friends were having kids, I'd never been that close to a pregnant woman.

Isola wasn't doing well and would eventually fail. So Todd was not only distracted but also seemed financially overextended.

Then, too, while I loved what we were building at Figs, it soon came to seem limited. The place was so small—just fifty seats—and so casual. You can do a lot with antipasti and pizza and pasta, but I wanted a bigger canvas—whole meals, with elements designed to work together. Meals with an appetizer and a dessert—with a beginning and an end. So, when Cat and Patrick Bowe kept dangling carrots, like the idea of taking Rocco's in a new, nonfusion, all-Italian direction, I started nibbling.

Finally Patrick Bowe made me an irresistible offer: I'd be the executive chef, charged with reimagining Rocco's. It could be more than a pretheater option, he thought. "I want you and Cat to take the lead, in terms of food and wine pairings, and make Rocco's a destination restaurant."

Did I want the job? Hell, yes, I did. The fact that I'd be getting a 20 percent raise was just the cherry on top.

• • •

But I had to tell Todd. He still scared the shit out of me, though I weathered his rages better than most people. The next afternoon, when he came into Figs, I was sitting at the bar writing out my menu, which in Todd English fashion, changed nightly. I stood up to deliver the news.

"Todd, I need to talk to you," I said. My mouth felt full of sand. "I'm giving my notice."

"What?" He towered over me.

"I got hired as executive chef at Rocco's."

"What the fuck, Lynchie, you fucking, goddamn—why the fuck?"

"I want to cook more. I want the challenge. I want meals with a beginning and an end . . ."

"You should have fucking told me you were bored."

My mind was racing. *Right, like you would have listened. Fuck you . . .*

Todd was sucking down Coke from a glass bottle. He drew back and whipped it, barely missing me. It smashed into the brick oven, gushing Coke over the loaves of baking bread.

I ran out one door of the restaurant. Todd ran out the other. We practically collided outside. I was bawling.

"Todd, you're like my big brother." I sobbed. "Can't you fucking be happy for me?"

"You're right," he said. Then he repeated, "You're right," too enraged to say more.

•   •   •

At least Todd didn't say, "You have no idea what it means to be an executive chef," or "You don't know what the fuck you're doing." If he had, he would have been right.

•   •   •

7/11/93: My Last Day at Figs, I wrote in my journal.

Then Rocco's: I want it to be the best restaurant. I want its simplicity to shine through.

7

MISS KITTY'S SALON

I knew how to perform my first executive duty at Rocco's—cleaning a grease trap the size of Chicago, clogged with what looked like years of foul-smelling slime. The kitchen was god-awful, with yellow walls that were sickeningly splattered and stained. Its fluorescent lights gave me a headache and made the food look weird and unappetizing. It was too depressing to spend an hour there, never mind a workday.

So I called Sheldon Friedman, a friend who worked at the Ritz. "I'll owe you big-time if you help me paint this place," I told him. "What would it take?" He laughed, and we settled on dinner and a couple of six packs.

With the walls clean and white, I set to work on the menu. The first order of business was shitcanning Rocco's marinara sauce. The cooks would dump giant cans of cheap tomatoes into a pot, add herbs and sugar, and let it simmer all day. At night they'd shove whatever sludge was left in the pot into the walk-in and, the next morning, plunk it down on a burner to stew again. *Not in my restaurant,* I vowed.

But when I met with the staff, I hit a white wall of resistance. They were tired of changes, having just made a shift from eclectic fusion to Italian food. All the cooks were men, mostly older, who resented being bossed by a woman in her twenties. Clearly, my initiation would be tough.

Fuck that, I thought, and got to work. I replaced littleneck chowder, a weird offering at an Italian restaurant, with a *tortellini en brodo* featuring fish broth and pasta rings stuffed with salt cod; or for clam lovers, littlenecks roasted with spicy tomatoes and balsamic, served on fried polenta. My other popular starters included celery root and Gorgonzola soup, with grated apple and fresh oregano, and a white bean soup with lamb broth, roasted garlic, and herb croutons.

The risottos I added included a substantial one with spicy sausage, fontina cheese, and sautéed greens; and a lighter one made with seafood-leek broth, grilled lobster, and julienned zucchini.

I remade that menu from top to bottom. If I had to pick one dish from that time that makes me proud, I think it would be my smoked trout tartlet. I cooked down red lentils with heavy cream, garlic, and leeks, baked the mixture in a tart shell, and topped the tart with smoked trout and three dollops of asparagus puree. The combination was so unexpected, yet harmonious.

I'd just started making these changes when I got a call from Mireille Guiliano, the spokesperson for Veuve Clicquot champagne and CEO of Clicquot, Inc. A major player on the restaurant scene, she is even more famous as the author of *French Women Don't Get Fat.* Mireille knew Cat from the wine world and had heard of me from Olives and Figs. Maybe she was also intrigued by the thought of two very young women, as executive chef and sommelier, reinventing a restaurant.

She wanted to host a luncheon at Rocco's for Boston's top

women in food. "Of course," I said, again not grasping the event's significance. I was just glad that I was drumming up business so soon. I'd been at Rocco's only a couple of weeks.

I began to sketch out a menu. Cat voted for tuna crostini, one of her favorite antipasti at Figs, which I decided to make with a lemony aioli, fried capers, and lemon zest. I'd follow that with an open-faced lasagna, light but luxurious enough to seem sinful, with braised rabbit and truffle or olive béchamel. These ideas inspired me so much that I got pissed when Mireille objected. "Rabbit doesn't go with champagne," she said.

"Bullshit," I told Cat. "I'm not changing the menu for that." I don't know where I got the nerve, since Cat and I were both fascinated and intimidated by Mireille. She seemed stressed and, we assumed, snobbish, because of her connection to a high-end French champagne. Once I got to know her, I found Mireille warm and generous (supporting programs for underprivileged kids and flying Sarah Hearn, my assistant, to Provence to recipe-test her books). But at the time, my insecurity made me a little arrogant.

As it turned out, Mireille accepted my menu. The big challenge was getting my sullen, foot-dragging staff to pull their weight.

By the day of the luncheon, I was out of bravado. I was too shy to come out of the kitchen and meet Mireille's guests, though I knew a few, like Michela Larson and Olivia English. Julia Child, Lydia Shire, Fiona Hamersley (wife of Gordon and partner in the hotspot Hamersley's Bistro), Jody Adams, then executive chef at Michela's—every female culinary star in town was there. When I poked my head out now and then, they seemed to be enjoying the food, which pleased Mireille. I was amazed that she actually seemed to like me.

But the next day, when Todd called to say that Olivia had found the food amazing, I actually blubbered with joy. By the time I started at Rocco's, we'd made up, and Todd congratulated me and wished me well. Now, though, to hear him—such a fierce mentor—praise my food was like getting a benediction from the pope himself.

The lunch gave me a psychic boost that helped me whip my kitchen into shape. Calling a staff meeting, I announced, "The fucking bad attitude around here has got to change. You've had a chance to adjust to me. If you're not happy working here, walk out now."

A few people did—and good riddance. I could rebuild on the foundation of an incredible crew: Cat, of course, who'd become a trusted friend; Kim Krause, a great general manager; a fine line cook named Bao; and Maria Cavaleri, also from Southie, a strong pastry chef.

One of the people I hired to round out the team was a sous-chef from Morocco named Aziz. It was thanks to Aziz that I became close friends with Kevin Tyo. Kevin owned a Dorchester restaurant, 224 Boston Street, where I ate now and then. He knew that I cooked, so one day, out of the blue, he called my mother's house and left a message: "I'm having a nervous breakdown. I'm closing my restaurant because my chef just quit."

Though I barely knew Kevin, I called back right away. "Don't shut down," I said. "I'll help you find a chef." I got him through a couple of nights and then decided Kevin needed Aziz more than I did. Aziz jumped at the chance for a promotion, so it was a win-win.

From then on, Kevin and I were—and to this day are—best friends. I even asked him to be my daughter's godfather because he loves children and may be one of the kindest people I've ever met.

• • •

Meanwhile, at Rocco's, I faced an enormous challenge. The place was huge—180 seats—and open for lunch and dinner, plus

brunch on weekends. After 7:00 p.m. when the theater crowd, our most reliable clientele, cleared out, we had to attract second-seating customers who'd never had Rocco's on their radar—and lots of them. Even 100 seats, approximately half our capacity, would be hard to fill. Covering 180 seats requires a big staff, who would just be standing around costing money, if few new customers showed up. We had to work with a skeleton crew until the size of our second seating got predictable. Luckily, if there was one thing I knew how to do after working with Todd, it was busting out food.

Managing staff and building a steady, predictable following were just two of my responsibilities as executive chef. At the same time, I had to stay creative and keep coming up with new dishes. As part of her work as a sommelier, Cat traveled a lot, tasting and picking out wines, so I'd always debrief her as if she were a spy and I were her handler. "What did you eat in Sicily? How about Liguria? Tell me about the pork in Emilia-Romagna . . ." I drew a lot of inspiration from her stories. We were coming to be seen as a team, two sides of the same coin—head and tails, food and wine, Barbara and Cat.

Within six months, Rocco's was starting to turn around. I still cherish a letter that Barbara Krakow, one of the most prestigious art dealers in Boston, wrote to Patrick and Jane Bowe, who passed it on with big, red exclamation points. It reads, in part: "Barbara Lynch is an amazing creative chef whose incredible food will rush your restaurant to the top of everyone's list . . . I was so impressed that I ate there Friday night, Saturday night, and Tuesday night . . ."

Someone coming to eat your food three nights in one week— you don't get higher praise than that!

Cat and I accomplished what Patrick hoped—built a second seating and made Rocco's a dinner destination. We were so successful that when he bought Harvest from Jane Thompson,

Patrick dispatched the two of us to get it up and running. For a while, we were working two jobs, though not drawing double paychecks, of course.

Then, for some reason, Patrick started stressing about food and wine costs. As a very rough guide, to make money a restaurant has to take in about three and a half to four times what it spends on food. Wine costs and profits are computed separately, but ideally wine will bring in at least half again as much as the gross food income. Patrick had other ideas, though, and he was literally shaking as he led me to the front table, by the window, for a serious chat.

"Your costs are too high," he told me. "You've got to cut your food budget way back"—to a figure that is unheard of in the industry. *What the fuck?*

He added that, if Cat didn't cut her wine costs, he didn't know what he was going to do.

I was outraged. Didn't he give a shit about our second seating—a brand-new income stream—and our raves from both diners and the press? To shrink the pool of ingredients needed to create inventive dishes—or worse, to compromise the quality of those ingredients—was crazy. We'd lose that following. Why the hell had we worked so hard to give Rocco's a new life? Of course, a restaurant is a business that has to make a profit. But to get some more bathwater, Patrick was throwing out the baby.

"You've got the wrong fucking chef," I told him. "Go get some fast-food flunky."

I stomped out, then told Cat what Patrick said, including the bit about her wine costs.

So we quit on the spot, the two of us.

We left together and went to sit in Park Square. "Someday," I said, "I swear to God that I'm going to own a restaurant. It will be all about education—surprising people with flavors that go together. The staff will get educated too—giving them pride and a chance to learn about food. And when I open my own place, it will be with you."

I smashed a bottle and, with a sharp edge, we each cut a finger, then pressed the cuts together. We pledged: "Blood sisters forever."

• • •

In the meantime, I needed a job. As it happened, there was a slot at Pomodoro, a tiny but wildly popular place in the Italian North End. Excellent chefs often cycled through it between gigs because its owner, Siobhan Carew, paid cash.

Siobhan is a real character. Raised on a farm in Ireland, she made her way to Boston in her teens. One night at a pub, she met Matt Murphy, a mason, immediately married him at city hall, and had three daughters. She'd planned to become a teacher, but to save child-care costs, started waitressing at night, when Matt could watch the kids. Waitressing at Michela's awakened her love of food.

Siobhan was working at the Daily Catch in the North End when a tiny storefront next door became vacant. A local guy loaned her $38,000 to open an itty-bitty twenty-four-seat restaurant, in exchange for a 10 percent stake (probably the only way an Irish gal could get a foothold in the neighborhood). Later, they fought over the bookkeeping and wound up in court—and someone tossed a pipe bomb through the restaurant window. Was that a coincidence or a message (classic North End–style persuasion)? I'd left by then and no one was hurt, thank God.

Siobhan didn't cook, but she had a genuine vision—never to stockpile food but to bring in the freshest and best organic ingredients every single day. Being an Irish farm girl, she thought American food tasted plastic; and besides, the space was too small for a refrigerator. It was even too tiny to have a restroom, so diners would dash across the street to the café where Siobhan would also send them for coffee and dessert. (The staff peed in the alley.) There wasn't room for an espresso machine in a kitchen where, to prep, the chef had to balance the cutting board on the stove burners or the cash register.

But the food was great, drawing on the best Italian markets, and Siobhan was a charming hostess/waitress. Every night, there was a line down the block of diners waiting to get in. When the line got long, she'd say, "Drop the calamari"—that is, plunge a batch into the deep fryer. Then Siobhan would walk up and down the line, chatting up guests and passing out samples of calamari, often accompanied by generous pours of our cooking wine (not the good stuff).

It was brilliant marketing. Pomodoro felt authentic in an area where the restaurants were mostly touristy and clichéd. Reviewers said eating there was like having dinner in an Italian home—one with a super gifted cook—and as I learned one night, even the local wiseguys agreed.

Bobby Luisi, a bookie and leg-breaker, was one of the so-called Steak-Tip Boys. He called Siobhan to say he was coming for dinner, bringing friends who wanted fried clams. "We don't serve fried clams," I pointed out.

"We do tonight," she said, "so you better get shucking or I'll box your ears."

That's what I was doing when a big white Caddy pulled up. Four huge men got out, and I remember being surprised that they were all wearing brand-new, sparkling white sneakers. This was before high-end sneakers—the kind that guys might kill each other to steal—were in fashion. The guys sat down, tucked their napkins under their chins, and watched me work in the open kitchen.

"You better make some tartar sauce too," Siobhan had told me. The tartar sauce I knew came in a jar. It was delicious, but who knew what the hell was in it, never mind how to make it out of Italian pantry staples. "So, just throw in capers or something," she'd instructed.

The meal was a success, I guess, but it freaked me out to see mobsters just sit there and eat. Whitey Bulger drank, surrounded by henchmen, in his own pubs, not out in public. I kept flashing on scenes from *The Godfather,* guys busting through the door with machine guns blasting. As it turned out, my vision was prophetic. It seemed like days later that Luisi, his son Roman, his nephew, and a friend were all shot to death in the crowded 99 Restaurant and Pub, just across the Charlestown Bridge from the North End. The funerals were held in Old Saint Stephen's Church on the Paul Revere Mall where Rose Fitzgerald Kennedy, JFK's mother, had been christened. "Don't ask me to cook for that wake," I told Siobhan.

She could be tough. One day I called in sick after working seven days a week, back to back, for a long stretch. I was so burned out and exhausted that all I could do was flop on the couch with mug of tea. My mother was lounging nearby on her recliner, either listening to the police band and or watching TV. The phone rang, and I heard her ask, "Do you want Big Barbara or Little Barbara?"

I shook my head to say no, I'm not talking to anyone, but she ignored me. "Yes, Barbara's right here, Siobhan."

"So, you're alive, Chef," Siobhan said. "Get your fucking ass in here now or I'll box your ears."

But her intense commitment was paying off. Siobhan would open a couple more equally beloved branches of Pomodoro, as well a pub with good Irish food, named for her husband. Twenty years later, those restaurants are going strong. She definitely has the knack.

Like any serious restaurateur, Siobhan researched trends, which in those pre-Internet days, especially, meant going on-site to scope out the competition. At one point, when I'd convinced P, the encyclopedia salesman, to go to Paris—I'd longed to see it—she begged me to take along her husband, Matt, to check out the scene. By then, he was no longer working as a mason but cooking under Stan Frankenthaler at the restaurant Salamander in Cambridge.

P and I had plenty of breakups and makeups, and that trip showcased our differences. Here we were, in the most romantic city in the world and—at Siobhan's urging—on a mission to eat, drink, and collect menus from its most fabulous restaurants. High on our list was Alain Passard's L'Arpège, winner of multiple Michelin stars, which today is ranked the twelfth-best restaurant in the world. There was also Lucas Carton, then run by Alain Senderens, a three-Michelin-star chef and a pioneer of nouvelle cuisine. Lucas Carton describes itself as a "chrysalis," with a "luminous cocoon" for a ceiling—fascinating to imagine and amazing to see—and takes pride in its antique mirrors inset with butterflies. What a place. After a four- or five-hour meal there, we planned to meet P at Willi's Wine Bar, a Paris institution open twenty-four hours a day, where we could get any wine that met its standard of "greatness and individuality" by the glass.

Who could resist? Well, P could and did. Not only did he refuse to eat with Matt and me, but when he met us at Willi's Wine Bar, he threw a fit. Matt was bent over the menu as if he were reading but he was actually snoozing. I guess the scene looked too cozy because it made P jealous. Yet, what was he doing all those hours when Matt and I were out exploring Paris? I never got a good reason when I begged, "Come on, P, why won't you come out to eat?" I couldn't understand it, and it drove me crazy with suspicion. He cast an oppressive shadow on a fabulous trip.

It's not like P hated travel. Being a top encyclopedia salesman, he was often treated to junkets, including a trip to Ireland. Since he loved Irish history and the band U2, that was major. Once, when he won a big award, I went with him to Chicago. I really wanted to take him to Charlie Trotter's flagship, then considered one of America's best restaurants. But his idea of fun was joining his sales colleagues—all tricked out in big company rings and cufflinks—at a huge, commercial, imitation Maryland crab shack, where you got mallets to smash the crabs.

It's possible that, in Paris, P was too cheap to splurge on meals. Unlike me, he made a decent living. I always wanted to eat out, both to experience other restaurants and because I spent all my waking hours sweating over a stove. But P said no: "You cook better than anyone, so why should we pay for dinner?" He was so cheap that when we did go out to some pub like the Quiet Man, we'd each get a beer and then split the hot dog basket. To this day, my Southie friends give me shit about that.

They couldn't stand him, and neither could my mother. She disapproved of his family and where he grew up—on McDonough Way, a low-class (in her view) section of the projects. She didn't like the fact that he was never around and probably didn't appreciate the way he treated me when he was. For a time I was semi-living with him and wound up painting the apartment while he didn't lift a finger. I kept wishing that he'd change his answering machine to say, "Barbara and I aren't here right now . . ."—any gesture to show that he considered us a real couple.

P wouldn't even give me a house key. At one point, a guy he'd met on the Ireland junket came to crash at his place for a couple of months. When I rang the buzzer, the guy would say, "Hello, identify yourself." "It's me," I'd say, pissed as hell, and he'd repeat, "Identify yourself." That killed me.

More damaging, P never took my career seriously, even when it began to skyrocket. He went so far as to say that I'd never amount to much; that my dreams for the future weren't realistic. "And yours are?" I'd ask. P was sure that he'd become a millionaire. On Sundays, when he made cold calls, I'd plug my ears because it was so painful to hear him wheedle customers, then get shot down and have to dial again to launch into a new sales pitch. But P seemed to love the word no; getting rejected fired him up. It seemed like a hellish job.

Why did I stay with P so long? One reason was that I was working so hard. My schedule was too brutal and my immersion in work too total for me to stop and consider what I wanted, never mind find and build a new relationship. P was handsome and more quirkily intelligent than most of the local guys I knew, and since he was from Southie, we had that cultural bond—he instinctively understood me. Besides, it wasn't like I'd seen a lot of examples of great partnerships. I grew up in a world of single mothers. Like many women, I'd caught a dose of the "eat shit" disease—the belief that, no matter who adored me and praised me, the one who ignored or belittled me had the only opinion that counted.

Today, though I'm still processing it, I suspect that the rape was a factor too. I was too walled off for real intimacy—which P wasn't offering—and, since deep inside, even beyond consciousness, I felt so damaged, maybe he seemed like the best I could hope for or deserve.

To my restaurant friends, P was a ghost boyfriend. Few of my coworkers had ever met him, and the ones who had didn't think much of him. Funnily, the one exception was Siobhan. A couple years after I left Pomodoro, when I called to invite her to my wedding, she said, "Really, Barbara? Are you sure you want to marry this guy? What about P?"

*   *   *

One night during the time I was working at Pomodoro, I had a dream. When Cat and I were at Rocco's, we'd sneak around the corner for an espresso at Galleria Italiana, a breakfast-and-lunch place run by two Italian women, Rita D'Angelo and Marisa Iocco. It was like a hidden treasure, known mostly to the faculty and students of Emerson College, who raved about their muffins. At lunchtime, they'd set up steam tables and Marisa would create an Italian buffet, to be eaten on paper plates in the back dining room. The food was good, based on the traditions of Abruzzo, where Rita and Marisa had grown up together, and a real bargain.

Cat and I often fantasized about setting up a dinner service at Galleria. In my dream, that fantasy came true.

The next morning I called Cat, who was as up for a new challenge as I was. So I popped the question to Rita and Marisa, who went for it. We would provide dinner service from Wednesday though Saturday, with Cat as sommelier and me as chef.

The Galleria women had once tried to offer dinners, with little success. Scoping out the space, we thought we understood why. As Cat put it, it had terrible feng shui, with a huge, empty front room where they put steam tables at lunch and hideous deli cases with fluorescent lights. From the street, you'd never be able to tell that a vibrant restaurant was in the back.

Cat came up with a brilliant idea—to set up the front room as a wine bar, with appetizers, to pull in dinner customers. To give it the cozy, romantic atmosphere we wanted, somehow we'd have to furnish it. Luckily Cat is the opposite of me. I like clean, spare, uncluttered spaces, while she's a girly-girl, with an apartment full of colorful rugs; silky, flowing fabrics; books; and lots of artsy accent pieces.

She brought in a mahogany console, oriental rugs to scatter on the floor, tablecloths and scarves to drape the ugly deli cases, and candles, potted roses, shaded lamps, and other knickknacks to add charm. She created a display in the front window, using her own wine books, and positioned cases of wine everywhere. The transformation was magical. Our decorating scheme probably violated a dozen provisions of the health code, but we converted that bare, empty lunchroom into a warm, inviting nightspot. At closing time, we'd roll up the rugs, tablecloths, and scarves to stash in the basement, along with the wine and other accents, and restore the room to its daytime identity.

As a joke, we called the new wine bar Miss Kitty's Salon, but the name stuck. The place was like our laboratory, where we could play with any food and wine ideas we wanted.

The food we served at Miss Kitty's was small-plate fare, which varied daily and included mix-and-match offerings like Ligurian potato salad—potatoes vinegared while warm, tossed with lemon aioli—still one of my favorite dishes; lamb skewers; garlic bread with mortadella; *porchetta* with apple cider chutney; crostini with tuna and fried capers, or with Gorgonzola and beet and leek salad; *sformatti*, which were tiny cheese and spinach soufflés with aged salami; and little pizzas with thinly sliced potato and rosemary or caramelized onions and anchovies, just to name a few. We kept the prices low so people could order a big array.

I also wanted the dinner menus to reflect the flavors of Abruzzo, a region just south of the calf of the Italian boot. I'd brainstorm with Marisa and Rita, then each night handwrite descriptions of seven to twelve small courses that Marisa and I would execute. I'm especially proud of antipasti like my Parmesan soufflé with porcini-chanterelle mushroom sauce; fresh mozzarella and eggplant *tartina*, like a pizza with black olive spread and prosciutto, touched with caramelized balsamic; tuna carpaccio with white bean crostini, served with black olive aioli; and grilled calamari and white bean puree with white truffles and fried leeks. I actually tried grilling the calamari over a wood fire, like the restaurant that inspired the dish, Paolo e Barbara in San Remo, Italy, but the smoke drove the neighbors crazy.

One of my big innovations was to have beautiful pastas and breads made in-house. Norma Cicolina from Abruzzo, who spoke no English, and Zoya Kogan, who spoke English and Russian, managed to collaborate beautifully on those. Two interesting pastas were a three-grain version topped with anchovies and turnip greens and *riccioli*, dough wrapped around knitting needles (my mother's) to create a tight curl, served with a sauce of artichokes, chicken stock, and touch of cream.

My favorite entrées included veal loin with sausage and fennel stuffing and a cherry glaze; seared rabbit loin and braised rabbit with wild mushroom ragù, served with creamy polenta in a copper pot; a slow-braised veal shank on minted risotto with veal ragù, which Mat Schaffer of *Boston* magazine called "centuries of Italian cooking on a plate"; and crispy duck, cured for four days in a dry rub then cooked in its own fat, served with a butternut squash risotto and cherry balsamic sauce.

The highlight of my time at Galleria was the Big Night party we threw to celebrate the restaurant's anniversary. We re-created the famous meal from the movie *Big Night*, starring Stanley Tucci, Tony Shalhoub, Minnie Driver, and Isabella Rossellini. It's the story of two immigrants from Abruzzo, running a failing restaurant in New Jersey, who are tricked into believing that Louis Prima is coming there to eat. They cook up a lavish meal that nearly bankrupts them (the real goal of the competitor who deceives them), centering on a *timpano*, or *timballo*, an impressive creation of layered and molded pasta.

Norma helped me make the pasta for the dish, gorgeous *garganelli*, which are little squares of dough rolled on a gnocchi board, around a pencil-size stick, to form horizontally scored tubes. The word *timpano* means "kettle drum," so we needed to bake the pasta in some kind of dome-shaped mold. A huge stainless steel mixing bowl did the job.

We lined the bowl/mold with *garganelli*, then layered it with tiny veal meatballs and my homemade mortadella, studded with pistachios and lots of fat. After binding the layers with béchamel and tomato sauce, we covered the bowl with a dish towel and steamed it. What a sight it was, unmolded, like a perfect half moon. A triumph! We served it to a fanfare of Louis Prima songs. As in the movie, we spread the rumor that a famous person—Isabella Rossellini, in our case—was coming by to eat. But if she had, we probably would have been too drunk and exuberant to notice.

Since Galleria was only open for dinner Wednesday through Saturday, I wasn't killing myself working every night, as I had at Pomodoro. Free to travel, I spent some three-day weekends in Florida, having a blast with my coworkers Christine Smith and Daniel Phillips. But, being a young chef, I was always itching to cook or to check out restaurants for inspiration. Soon, instead of partying in the sun, I'd head to New York, often with Cat, who was an opera lover.

So was my old boss David Petri, who was the owner of Port Terminals Company, the dry-goods warehouse where I'd worked until Kerri sprung me. I'd remained friends with him and with his wife, Judy. Cat and I would attend the Metropolitan Opera with them or with Ron Della Chiesa, the Boston host of shows on classical music and jazz. Like the Petris, we'd become good friends with Ron and his wife, Joyce, and I'd often house-sit to care for Rodemere, their cat. I loved that because they had a huge selection of movies and the first DVD player I'd ever seen. I'd curl up to binge-watch with Rodemere, a plate of pasta with Bolognese, and a big bottle of red wine.

For Cat and me, any trip to New York meant research—squeezing in all the stops we could at the top or up-and-coming restaurants. We had a hit list of places—Daniel, Jean-Georges, all the hot spots. So we rolled our eyes when Ron and Joyce insisted on eating at the Duomo, a faceless Italian joint where they said opera singers hung out. It was behind Lincoln Center, next door to a dry cleaners.

"Christ," we said to each other. "Who's the chef? There's no name listed. Is this place even rated?"

Once we sat down and looked at the wine list, which came in a red school binder, we got even snootier. The plasticized pages cataloged the wines—mostly grocery-store quality—with prices and no vintages. Though the waitstaff were incredibly nice and the smells coming from the kitchen were amazing, we grew more high and mighty by the minute. "We'll stay for appetizers," one of us said. "But then we need to hit some important places"—emphasis on *important,* meaning restaurants we'd read about in the *New York Times.*

Ron and Joyce ordered a mess of dishes for us to share. The first to arrive was a globe artichoke. It was glorious, perfectly steamed, with bread crumbs and oregano, diced olives, and delicious olive oil. The basic table wine was a perfect complement. Cat and I were stunned.

Everything coming out of the Duomo's kitchen was impressive—a delicately sauced spaghetti, an exquisitely grilled fish. We wound up spending the whole evening there, yakking with the regulars who drifted in. It was like a big, joyful dinner party with lively guests.

The pleasure of that meal confirmed the theory of Italian cooking I'd hatched on my first trip to Tuscany—that what made it great was its bold simplicity. The spirit of welcome that I felt that night, and the shared enjoyment of beautifully prepared food, seemed to me the definition of hospitality. That was the feeling I was determined to nurture in any restaurant I headed. I came to the Duomo thinking, *Shit, what can I learn in this dump?* and left with a powerful inspiration.

• • •

Our Galleria dinners, happily, pulled in a steady clientele right away. In the beginning, I begged reviewers to hold off until I fixed some dining room glitches, like ditching the Fiestaware and convincing the ladies not to fan out the napkins as if it were a Chinese joint (both were almost as bad, to me, as having glass-topped tables). When the reviews came in, they were raves, both for the food and for Cat's wine selections. *Boston* magazine called Cat—then barely in her thirties—one of the city's "most knowledgeable sommeliers." As for the food, the reviewer said, "Everyone's talking about Lynch's cooking," and that the restaurant was "not to be missed."

It must have been those reviews that attracted the notice of *Food & Wine* magazine. When I got the FedEx letter, I nearly threw it out, assuming that it was some bullshit scam. But I showed it to a friend, who said, "This is for real! *Food & Wine* has named you one of America's Ten Best New Chefs!"

Not only would I be featured in the magazine, I would be showcased at the annual *Food & Wine* Classic in Aspen, Colorado. That meant conceiving—and shipping premade—a special signature dish to serve to hundreds of food professionals.

I thought Rita and Marisa would be psyched by the attention but instead they seemed insulted because only I, not Marisa, had been honored. They refused to help. So I was on my own preparing and packing my creation to represent Galleria Italiana, foie gras ravioli, which I would serve with crispy duck and fig sauce.

I traveled alone to Aspen. When I got off the plane, drivers were waiting, holding up signs: Julia Child, Patricia Wells, and . . . Barbara Lynch! *Oh my fucking God*, I thought. *This is big time!*

My beautiful boxes of ravioli, so painstakingly assembled, were already at the hotel. But when I undid the packaging, I found that nearly all the ravioli had split open. *Fuck, fucking, fuck*—I was ready to burst into tears. All that hard work, preparing hundreds of perfect pasta pouches of foie gras, lovingly packing them, anxiously entrusting them to the shipper—I had no idea what I was doing—gone to waste. I felt so defeated I wanted to collapse.

Finally pulling myself together, I remade hundreds of ravioli with the kind help of another Best New Chef nominee, Maria Helm Sinskey of PlumpJack, in San Francisco.

For setup, I had reinforcements coming, my boyfriend, P, and a waitress pal from the restaurant, Christine Smith. Not the ideal team, but I needed help and they were free. Christine was never much of a waitress but she was one of the funniest women I knew. When customers checked coats at Galleria, we had to stash them in the kitchen. On the way Christine would model them—especially the furs—with fashion show commentary that would crack us up.

The next day, time blurred as I cooked feverishly and set up my food station. Mostly, out of shyness, I kept my head down, serving, as guests filed past to fill their plates. Through the fog of focus, I heard a kindly male voice, with a French accent, ask, "Oh, so what is this?"

"It's foie gras ravioli with crispy duck and fig sauce," I replied. Then I looked up. "My God, do I know you? You seem so familiar!"

"I'm Jacques Pépin," the guy said.

Jacques Pépin! "You're one of my heroes!" I told him, because I'd heard that, early in his career, he'd invented the fried clams at Howard Johnson's. "I didn't invent them," he corrected, but had developed a recipe that could be flash frozen, so every franchise would serve the same version. "We'd get in these giant clams," he said, "and then have to cut them up into pieces the same size."

"By hand?" I asked, imagining him hacking and sawing through chewy masses.

"No, Barbara, we figured out that we could run them through the bread slicer."

Genius! I told him my "canning" story, begging money for HoJo's instead of the fake school band, and we laughed.

That night, after service, a bunch of us went out to the Caribou Club, a private party place that had great music. Christine spotted me across the dance floor. "Get up here," she said. "I just asked Patty to dance." She meant Patricia Wells, the queen of food critics—the only American and only female restaurant reviewer for a major magazine in France. She taught cooking and, that year, won a James Beard Award for her cookbook *Patricia Wells at Home in Provence*.

"Goddamn it, don't call her Patty!"

"Why not? She likes it," Christine said.

I went to get a drink, and when I next saw Christine, she had Jacques Pépin up dancing, with his red bowtie wrapped around her head.

That's fucking Boston for you, I thought.

• • •

Christine and P had come with me to Aspen because Cat had left Galleria. She'd reunited with her childhood sweetheart and moved with him to Alaska. It was hard to imagine Cat living there with no opera, going trekking or fly-fishing or whatever in her Hermès scarf. I missed her so much, but as she said, she was sick of the Galleria lifestyle—problems that intensified when I returned from Aspen.

The place always had a makeshift vibe—from the salon that we had to pack up every night to the single cordless handset we used for reservations, which was lost half the time. With my award, the restaurant got so much buzz that the phone was ringing off the hook. I swear that Rita and Marisa spent hours lying on the office floor, having heart palpitations—they were that overwhelmed. Their little seedling, a charming lunch buffet, had shot up into a beanstalk, beyond recognition. Even if they liked the success—and I'm not sure they did—they couldn't handle the business.

I fantasized more than ever about opening my own restaurant, with proper, permanent fixtures, a kitchen I designed, nice tableware and linens, and trained line cooks and waitstaff—a professional backbone that would make me proud and leave me free to focus on the food. Even more, it would let me stretch and breathe, to escape the prison of other people's fears. How I'd reach that goal, I didn't know, but I began poking around town, looking at spaces that I could visualize making my own.

• • •

Moving from Figs to Rocco's to Galleria, I'd developed a little following. My regulars included my old boss David Petri and his wife, Judy. David would entertain customers at Rocco's, which was great for me, since it filled seats, and good for him, since he could brag that he knew the chef. Cat and I often went to the Petris' country place in New Hampshire, where I would cook, Cat would break out interesting wines, and Mike, a musician they knew, who played at the Bostonian Hotel, would entertain on the piano. I loved those visits and thought of David and Judy as dear friends.

So I was honored when David decided to hold his sixtieth birthday party at Galleria. I ordered a great cake, to make the night special, and retrieved my car, which P had borrowed the night before, just in time to pick it up. But when I was driving along, the car sputtered to a stop. I was out of gas. What the fuck?

"You piece of shit," I shouted. I meant P, not the car. How could he forget to fill it up? He knew how much David's birthday meant to me—that I wanted everything perfect. Was he trying to sabotage the party? Was he just too cheap to buy gas? Did he care so little about me that he never even gave it a thought?

At that point, the reason didn't matter. I was sick of P and his stinginess with emotion and affection, as well as with cash. I couldn't stand the way he shot down my ideas, as if my ambitions were stupid. I hated his indifference to my passionate curiosity—about food and wine and culture and the great big world beyond Southie. He didn't love me enough—or just wasn't willing—to share my life. I was done, once and for all.

* * *

I got to Galleria late but pulled off a proper birthday meal to honor David. While I was cooking, a tall man dropped by the kitchen, wearing big, serious glasses and a goofy seersucker suit. He was the emcee of the party, I knew. He introduced himself as David's brother, Charlie.

I was surprised that I'd never come across him in New Hampshire, where I'd met the rest of the Petri clan. Charlie was in his fifties, a year or two younger than David, and also in warehousing, with a seafood specialty. The father of three children, he'd lost his wife three years earlier to stomach cancer.

We shot the shit, and he was funny enough that I hung out in the dining room after the party to get to know him. He was an opera buff, so I claimed to be a serious fan. (Hey, I'd been to the Met a few times.) He was gracious enough not to call me on my bullshit.

In the weeks that followed, he'd pop by Galleria's back door with some delicacy from his warehouse, like a box of langoustines. Or he'd come for dinner, often bringing his thirteen-year-old son. The more we talked, the more I liked him. He was such a great listener that I started to confide my restaurant dreams.

"Of course you should open your own place," he said. "Why kill yourself and waste your creative energy so someone else gets rich?"

No one in my life had ever offered that kind of affirmation. I was a risk-taker, always motivated by a dare. But there wasn't a hint of "I bet you can't" in Charlie's words. He assumed I could, without convincing. He recognized my yearning for freedom and autonomy as perfectly natural, and thought, *Why not go for it?* He saw windows where other people saw walls.

"Do you have a plan?" he asked.

Well, no. I could definitely run a restaurant, having handled all the administrative chores—ordering, furnishing, controlling overhead and payroll, managing personnel, and all the rest—in several jobs. But to open a restaurant cost money, and I had no idea where money came from. What I could scrape together, after living with my mother to build savings, certainly wasn't enough.

"You get investors," Charlie explained. "You write up a business plan and, if it's persuasive, people back you. I can show you what to do when the time comes."

• • •

From the beginning my feelings for Charlie puzzled me. He was twenty-four years older—a gap big enough for him to be my father—but I never thought of him that way. He had business knowledge that could help me, but I didn't see him as a teacher. He made me laugh. He offered genuine praise and encouragement, which I sucked up like a dry sponge. I felt powerful around him, and womanly. Pretty soon, I had to admit that I was in the grip of a deep crush.

That insight struck me one night during a lull in the kitchen at Galleria. I couldn't keep it to myself, so I called my mother, who I knew would be home, cocooned in her recliner.

"I think I've found the guy I'm going to marry," I announced.

"Oh my God!" she said. "Tell me it's not P."

"No, it's not P," I assured her. "But this guy is older than the president of the United States right now."

Who happened to be Bill Clinton. That didn't faze my mother. "So, he's lived his life," she said. "That's good. He won't be cheating on you."

I took that as her blessing, but then she confused me by asking, "Does he like graham crackers?"

"What the hell?"

Graham crackers and orange juice were her favorite snack, an alternative to peanut butter cups, which were hell on her diabetes. Maybe, because of his age, my mother was identifying with Charlie—though, looking back, I wonder if this was an early hint of Alzheimer's, the disease that would claim her life.

Getting Charlie's blessing was harder because, at the time, we weren't really dating. He was definitely interested but very conscious of our age difference. "I'm too old for you," he insisted. "You'll be younger than I am now when I turn eighty."

"So what?" I said. "Why not try for ten or twenty good years? Isn't that what matters, not some arbitrary age number? Who says that you'll turn decrepit in your sixties or seventies or even later? None of us can see the future."

I won him over. Charlie and I began to see each other romantically. I'd dumped P right after David's birthday party, so I'd been single for only a couple of days. But when you're in love, you're in love. Three months later Charlie and I were engaged.

• • •

I left Galleria Italiana as abruptly as I'd left P, but this time, it wasn't by choice. In my discontent after leaving Aspen, I really began checking out real estate, trying to picture what my own restaurant would look like. Somehow word of my explorations got back to Rita and Marisa. They seemed to view it as a betrayal and freaked out.

I guess they figured that the three of us would expand into a new and bigger restaurant. But I was the one making money, winning awards, and getting press. I felt they were holding me back. In the end, they fired me for supposedly stealing a leg of lamb.

"Seriously?" I said. "I don't know if I should fucking punch your heads in right now, throw you in the oven, or just laugh."

It was so crazy. Not that I wanted to stay at Galleria—I was too restless. But I couldn't even say good-bye to my sous-chef, Baz (David Bazirgan, who'd come to me through Susan Logozzo), or my line cook, Suzanne Nasuti.

Rather than raise holy hell, I just walked out, shaking my head. When I got home, the ache of humiliation set in. I'd never been fired, so I didn't realize how much it could hurt to be kicked out, even from a place I wanted to leave.

I fell on the couch and just sobbed for an hour. "For God's sake," my mother said, from her recliner-throne. "You're throwing yourself a pity party. Quit feeling sorry for yourself. Get over it . . ."

I had to mourn, but I knew I'd shake it off. When one door closed another door opened was how I looked at it.

8

OTHER DOORS

Over the next few years, my early thirties, I kept busting through doors, never stopping to worry about what lay on the other side. *I'll figure it out* had always been my mantra, and I stuck by it, even while taking some hair-raising risks. Which is not to say I have regrets—or at least, I don't have many.

One big risk was rushing into marriage. Beforehand, I did test-drive Charlie with my family and friends. My mother loved him on sight and, to my relief, didn't mention graham crackers. After we hung out awhile with Mary, I asked, "What do you think? He's old, right?"

"Yeah," she said. "But you laugh a lot. You have a real connection."

When I told other Southie friends that I was madly in love, some were doubtful. They appreciated the way Charlie treated me—dropping me off at work and picking me up, opening doors for me, always springing for the check—but they didn't know what to make of it. That kind of old-school etiquette was unusual in our world, especially in guys our age. At first they thought that I was having a fling with Charlie because he was so exotic.

Or because he was a substitute father. That's what Kerri thought, being fatherless herself. At the time she was living in New York, waitressing at the then-new Gramercy Tavern. When I brought Charlie in to introduce him, the first words out of her mouth were, "Who's Captain Kangaroo?"

Now we can laugh, but that wasn't a good start. Charlie was already nervous, knowing that Kerri was so important to me, and that she was also my fiercest critic and protector. But he rolled with it. For a while even his cheeriness was a liability, as friends analyzed whether he was too nice or too crazy about me: Was he sincere? Eventually, even fear of the age gap faded as my friends fell for Charlie's big-heartedness and sense of humor. Today, even Kerri calls him a great guy and says that, in his seventies, he has "more energy than I'll ever have in my entire life."

We were spending a long weekend at Turtle Bay, in the Virgin Islands, when Charlie proposed. Most of my travels at that point were related to cooking, doing food research or chefs' showcases. So it felt luxurious to relax in the sun, just the two of us. One big drawback, however, was that ground was thick with land crabs, then at the peak of mating season. We rode around in golf carts, comically trying to dodge them. It was like playing Pac-Man. But when Charlie popped the question, it was a fairy-tale moment. "Yes," I said, with joy.

We didn't see the point of a long engagement. I wanted a big wedding with everyone I knew—about 350 guests, including a shitload of Lynches, Southie friends, restaurant friends, and Charlie's people—so the planning was intense. I decided to hold it in Westport, Massachusetts, a rural town near the Rhode Island border, which had a glorious state park, Horseneck Beach, right on the ocean. For a few years, Cat and I, along with a few other friends, had rented a summer place there and thrown many huge,

wild, and deliciously memorable dinners. The town was charming and close to Boston—about forty-five minutes away, or what
we called a two-beer drive (the number you could drink on the
road). A family-run vineyard there, Westport Rivers Winery, had
enough space and agreed to host the wedding.

Getting married seemed like such a cozy family ritual that I
asked my sister Beth to help pick out my dress. When we stopped
at a plant store along the way, she wound up smashing a huge
terra-cotta pot. She seemed a little glassy-eyed, making me wonder
how much of a second opinion she would offer. Still, I'd made the
sisterly effort. But as it turned out, at Yolanda's Bridal in Waltham,
the classic salon, the opinion that counted most was Yolanda's.

As we entered, Yolanda herself, dressed in her signature all-
white getup and cradling a little dog, swept down the spiral staircase. "Who's the bride? Who's the bride?" she called out.

When she heard it was me, she announced, "Oh, I see you
look like a cappuccino."

Did I?

"So I want to do beige and white and off-white."

Not knowing how to respond, I placed myself in her hands.
My faith was justified when Yolanda decked me out in a gorgeous
Vera Wang gown that I loved. I didn't even want to guess how
much it cost.

I also chose Vera Wang for the bridesmaids' dresses, in the
cream-latte shade that Yolanda recommended. The fittings were
insanely hilarious. Three of my bridesmaids—Beth, Kerri, and
my old roommate Annie Copps—were full-busted women,
which made them tough to fit. As Annie tried on her dress, I
could hear the little Russian seamstress bitching, "This dress is
not for you. It's for a skinny girl. Who ordered this dress?"

She wanted to stick a bow someplace for coverage. Annie kept
protesting, "No, stop it. No bows. Barbara hates bows . . ."

Then I heard, "What the hell?" The seamstress had come up

behind Annie and was kneading her boobs, trying to mash them into the dress. "You need modesty panel," she was saying. She was also alarmed by the grapes tattooed on Annie's back.

Meanwhile, behind the next curtain, Christine Smith from Galleria was all pinned up. But she starting laughing so hard that the pins kept sticking her—"Ow, ow!"—leaving droplets of blood all over her dress.

I, the bride, came close to ruining my perfect Vera Wang/Yolanda image with a couple of ugly injuries. Both times, I got hurt at Charlie's home in suburban Winchester, eight miles north of downtown Boston, where I spent a lot of time, even though I lived with my mother until my wedding day. We had gotten a golden retriever puppy, which we kept in Winchester, named Perrin. One day, I took Perrin out back to the woods for a run. I wasn't big on nature, being a project rat, so I didn't expect the ground to be booby-trapped with gnarled roots and rocks. When the puppy took off, I chased after him and tripped, sprawling flat on my face in pain. "Fuck!" I'd twisted my ankle and fractured it in several places.

After a few months on crutches, I hoped to stand on my own two feet at my wedding. But some weeks before, I was hobbling down the stairs at Charlie's when my crutch missed a step and I fell, smashing my forehead and splitting it open. "Leave me alone," I insisted, with blood streaming down my face. "It hardly hurts. I'm fine."

Charlie and Ryan, his son, said, "Oh, no," and whisked me to the emergency room, where I got dozens of stitches. Luckily, by the big day, my wound had healed enough that no one thought Charlie was the groom of Frankenstein.

After all that drama, the wedding was phenomenal. Everything from the food and wine to the music was a labor of love, created by people who were significant in our lives. Paul O'Connell, the sous-chef I'd worked with at Olives, had moved on to his own restaurant, Chez Henri, and did me the honor of cooking for the wedding. I kept the menu bold but simple—pasta served family style, pork, and quail.

Susan Logozzo, the high school teacher who'd nurtured me as a cook, was also an accomplished pastry chef. She made me a kick-ass wedding cake: four tall tiers with beautifully sculpted icing and a cascade of real roses spilling down them. Inside was a delicious surprise: half the cake was chocolate with raspberry filling, Charlie's favorite; the other half was white, filled with fresh fig jam, the flavors I loved. It was un-fucking-believably fabulous.

Though Cat couldn't attend—Alaska was too far away—three liquor purveyors she'd brought in to Galleria supplied our prosecco, champagne, wine, and beer. I had to laugh when, at the end of the night, the cleanup crew found cases of empty Budweiser bottles. Right away, I knew who to blame—my brother Kenny, who'd been bellyaching about drinking "that Italian shit." He'd smuggled in a stash of Buds to share with Southie friends who felt the same way.

Charlie's family had a farm, so that's where a lot of our flowers came from. We had two bands, the first one led by Mike, the piano player from the Bostonian Hotel, whom I'd met through David, Charlie's brother. They set the mood with suave, Ella Fitzgerald–era standards. Then, after dinner, the second band, featuring Toni Lynn Washington and Diane Blue, got everyone up and dancing with jazzy rhythm and blues.

We would have partied till dawn if the winery hadn't begun to worry that someone would call the cops. "Like who?" I said. "The cows?" I hated to see the wedding end.

I had only a few disappointments. First, I'd forgotten to confirm with the photographer, so we never got official wedding pictures. Then there were guest glitches that I still get shit for, like failing to mail an invitation to my dear friend Kevin Tyo. I did invite food critic Mat Schaffer, but he showed up on the wrong day. Finally, I'd hoped to be married by Father Quinn, the young priest I'd cooked for at Saint Monica's, who'd tried to enrich our teenage lives through the YES program. He was out of the country at the time, so a local Presbyterian minister married us. Then we retied the knot properly with Father Quinn in a Catholic ceremony on our first anniversary.

• • •

Even marriage madness couldn't distract me from the dream of opening my own restaurant. While Cat and I were still at Rocco's, I'd sketched out a plan for a sixty-seat place called Diva. I was so enthralled by the idea that I carefully blocked out menus for bar food (like grilled sardines with garlic and lemon aioli or barley and quinoa salad with roasted veggies, plated with marinated olives) and dining room food (with entrées like saddle of rabbit and sausage-stuffed quail), to be preceded by free appetizers (a selection of possibilities like creamy salt cod with crusty bread, grilled calamari and chickpea salad with warm pancetta vinaigrette, and semolina pudding with wild mushroom ragù), and first plates of interesting pastas, plus four special gnocchi (goat cheese with white truffles, potato with classic Bolognese, black olive and chèvre with roasted tomato sauce, and basil with yellow tomato sauce). I was so deep in my vision that I even wrote: *Please note: Gnocchi are served only on Thursdays.*

At the time, I had no clue how to realize that vision. I wound up using many of the food ideas from Galleria. But what Cat and I created there—remodeling on a shoestring to make the place a seductive nightspot, developing an award-winning menu—totally stoked my imagination. After *Food & Wine* named me one of its Ten Best New Chefs, Gordon Hamersley, who'd won the same honor earlier, told me, "You can play this two ways: either get overwhelmed by the press and fail, or take this award and ride it." I was definitely ready to ride.

Charlie, who'd run a business all his life, had offered to help me draw up a real plan—not just a food vision—to attract investors. We decided to work on it in Hawaii, where *Food & Wine* was holding a Mother's Day event and had invited me to be a featured chef. As usual, I accepted without asking questions, so I didn't realize that I'd be cooking for hundreds—maybe even a thousand people a day.

My first clue was the size of the hotel where the event was staged. The kitchen was so huge that we rode bicycles to fetch supplies from the pantry in its bowels. For my menu, I chose to feature fresh pasta, which I usually cranked through my little tabletop machine. But when I asked for one at the hotel, I was given a contraption that looked like it didn't belong in a kitchen but in a factory.

"What's that?" I said.

It was a dough sheeter. *Yeah, right,* I thought. *What the hell . . .* So I took a two-pound hunk of pasta dough and stuck it in the machine. I hit the button, as I'd been shown, and then—*whump!*— the fucking dough shot out of the sheeter and—*poof*—vanished into thin air. It's probably still stuck on the ceiling somewhere. I never did find it. The whole time, the hotel chef was sneering as if I'd unleashed a bad smell.

Maybe I wasn't quite as ready to launch a restaurant as I thought. But I came home with a business plan and an even stronger sense of resolve. The Hawaii event was a steam valve, releasing just one short blast of the creative pressure that I had building up inside.

•   •   •

When I was at Galleria but semi-looking for my own space, I'd identified an area to target. It was the stretch of Back Bay—along Commonwealth Avenue leading to the Public Garden and on the streets ringing the Boston Common—where the private clubs are clustered: St. Botolph, Algonquin, Harvard, Somerset, Union, and others. The Massachusetts State House is right nearby. Around there, I knew I'd find a core clientele to sustain the kind of restaurant that I envisioned, with white tablecloths, fine dinnerware, and elegant food and service.

It wouldn't be one of those intimidating places that try to make you feel, "Oh, I'm so lucky I get to eat here." I hate that mystique thing, which also puts a shitload of pressure on the chef. But beautiful china, glassware, and silver, as well as professional service (and interesting food), create a mood. The mood I wanted was warm hospitality.

Realtors had shown me lots of uninspiring places, but there was one that stuck in my mind. It was a former shoe store, right next door to the Union Club on Park Street, overlooking the Common. There were no windows and the façade was pink fake marble. "How big is this space?" I asked the broker.

"Three thousand square feet," he said.

"Great," I replied, as if that made sense. What a fucking square foot looked like, I had no clue, never mind how many I'd need for a kitchen and a roomful of tables and chairs. But I liked the bones of the space enough that I asked some Southie girlfriends, including Mary and Cheryl, to come see it and give me a second opinion.

"My God!" Cheryl said when we pulled up. "We know this building."

The ground floor was the shoe store, and upstairs was the place that sold the uniforms for South Boston Heights Academy. I'd attended it so briefly before getting bused to Roxbury that I didn't remember uniform shopping there. But for my friends whose families had sprung for the tuition—and who hadn't bailed on high school and were refitted there year after year—the building held strong memories.

The place also held a lot of shoes. The previous owner had

cleared out, leaving piles of stock behind. "Maybe we can sell them," I said, half-serious. I gathered an armful in my mother's size, seven and a half, to bring home. Later, when she was trying them on, she grabbed a shoe and smacked me in the head. "These aren't pairs," she said. "They're all left feet!"

Mary shuddered, thinking of the building's creaky elevator, vowing, "I'm not getting in that godforsaken thing again." So she climbed the rickety stairs as we rode up, sticking our hands out at each floor to try to grab her. We got a little boisterous, so a tenant on an upper floor, a lawyer, came out of his office to scold us for making noise. *Oh, yeah?* I thought. *If we seem noisy now, wait till we're neighbors.* That elevator, I learned later, is one of oldest in the whole city that's still running.

Back downstairs, we walked around the cavernous space as I tried to visualize a design. "The kitchen could be over here," I said. "Then, maybe a bar up front with some tables—that would be the more casual, fun place to eat. You'd walk through the bar to the dining room, which would be kind of formal but cozy and warm with banquettes . . ."

"I don't know how you can picture that," Cheryl said. "You'd have to tear everything out. I just don't see it."

Mary agreed. "This place is gross. How can it be a restaurant? And that elevator . . ."

Still, they had to admit I'd done plenty of things in the past that they didn't believe. Since I knew I'd have to gut whatever space I found, their doubts didn't discourage me. The immediate obstacle was that landlord wasn't keen on renting to a restaurant.

* * *

Then, of course, there was the money. You'd think it would be scary as hell to raise—and then have to repay—$3 million. But in a way, my Southie background paid off. The words *financial obli-*

gations didn't mean much in a culture where scamming and theft were reasonable, acceptable options for getting by.

So when I got a bill, I'd chuck it in a drawer, assuming that I'd hear when I was really in trouble. For years, I viewed paying taxes as optional, the way I saw getting licensed to drive. Since I couldn't both live on my income and pay the IRS, I chose life. Who wouldn't? There was no difference, in my mind, between $30,000 and $3 million. Both sums were unimaginably huge and out of reach.

What I *could* imagine was cooking good food—maybe even great food, judging by the reviews—to draw an even bigger, more loyal base of customers than I ever had at Rocco's, Figs, or Galleria Italiana. All I needed was professional space and the freedom to create, without limits. I was twitching with energy, flooded with ideas, aching to get back in the kitchen.

Amazingly, there were investors willing to gamble on my dream. I remember meeting the first one face-to-face. I was so anxious that I practically dissociated from my body, circling it like a soul in a near-death experience. Hard as I tried, I couldn't work up my usual *fuck it, I'll figure it out* attitude. This wasn't like bullshitting a cruise-ship captain to get a job. It was much more intimate, exposing my heart—my deepest, most private vision of my own future—to a judge who would decide if it was worthy.

The day was wet and snowy. The investor met us in a coffee shop, wearing a baseball cap and soggy rubber boots over his shoes. I tried not to stare as he took off the cap and shrugged off his trench coat, which wasn't fancy, like Louis Boston, but just normal and good-looking. He shook hands with Charlie, who stood beside me, and then with the management guy who'd helped us refine the business plan. Then, finally, he turned to me. "Miss Lynch," he said, in such a gentle, humble voice. "I'm very glad to meet you."

He took my hand with a grip so sincere and expressive that I almost cried. Even now, recalling that moment, I tear up. Instead of being what I expected—critical and arrogant—he was so kind and open that I wanted to blurt out everything: how I grew up in the projects, fucked up academically, started cooking in home ec class, dropped out of high school, and had zero formal culinary training—and yet, I was determined to open a restaurant on the hill, meaning Beacon Hill, the most aristocratic part of town, that would be elegant but welcoming, with informed, intuitive service and sophisticated food, not the big bowls of pasta I became known for at Galleria, but food created from my personal palette of Italian and French influences, the French accents coming not from any hands-on experience but from close study of my large collection of cookbooks by Alain Ducasse and other masters, some not translated, which I understood with the help of a dictionary and, mainly, the pictures; a restaurant that would be different from any in Boston . . .

I didn't spew out this whole torrent, but must have presented it convincingly, along with the business plan, because on Christmas Eve, 1997, my investor called with an amazing gift. "I'm in for six figures," he said. "People are gone for the holidays now, but I have a couple friends who might also be interested."

"Wow . . . wow," was all I could choke out. Then, "My God, thank you, thank you so much."

My whole life I'd had to fight—to teach myself, to achieve, to prove what I could do, to overcome a million doubts and fears, including my own. Now, someone had given my skills and accomplishments a definite value, in dollars. That degree of respect stunned me, touching me at level deeper than any glowing review or award. It granted me a professional stature that I had hardly dared to envision for myself.

I wanted to be that respected professional, both as a person and as a chef. I pledged right then—to myself and the universe—that I'd earn that esteem not only by racking up reviews, but also by committing to repay my investors. Restaurants are such notoriously high-risk investments that big institutions like banks usually won't underwrite them. Startup costs are high, profit margins are low, and success depends on variables like the weather, which is as fickle as the public's interest. A huge proportion—some say as high as 50 percent—of new restaurants fail in their first year. So I am proud that within three years of opening, I repaid my investors in full; and nearly twenty years later, my first restaurant is still going strong.

I am so grateful to the investors who've gambled on me, making my life as a chef-owner possible. I've benefitted not only from their generosity but also from their business acumen, moral support, and more. Some might be embarrassed if I named them, so I'll remain discreet while expressing my profound appreciation. Their faith in me has meant the world.

● ● ●

Now I had to earn that faith by getting up and running. I won over the landlord at the fake-pink-marble-shoe-store space and started in on the gut renovation. To save thousands of dollars, Charlie and I decided to do the interior demolition ourselves, with the help of our families and friends. Every night after work, a bunch of them would come by to help rip out the shelves and flooring and sledgehammer the walls down to the studs. What a hell of a lot of fun it can be to trash a place.

To create the atmosphere of warm hospitality I wanted, I turned to Jeffrey and Cheryl Katz, a power couple I'd met when they were customers at Michela's café, who've been close friends ever since. He's an architect and she does interiors, and they'd designed retail spaces, like the Domain home furnishings stores. I loved their home, which was a comfortable, restful space—the opposite of what you'd expect from such hot-shit designers. They had a great blue glass chandelier in their kitchen and other quirky

accents that offset the soothing, muted colors they used everywhere. The walls were lined with shelves of books and personal
treasures, but the house didn't feel at all cluttered. It was unpretentious, clean, and open, yet also cozy.

That's the feeling I was after. The Katzes had never designed
a restaurant, but they were intrigued by the challenge of doing
mine. I knew that they understood me, and that I could trust
them. They magnified my vision into a spectacular design that
isn't overly trendy or boringly classic, but timeless.

Siobhan stopped by while the build out was going on. After
checking out the construction and hearing my plans, she opened
the backpack she was carrying. It was full of money—which
looked like thousands of dollars. "To me, this is an investment,"
she said. I had to laugh. Cash on the barrelhead was always h
way. "Well, that's one way to get backing for your new place,"
told her. "Good luck, but that's not my path."

At the time she was opening Matt Murphy's Pub in Brod
line, run by and named for her husband. I'd been mulling o
what to call my place, the precious expression of my dre
"Lynch" doesn't make you think of elegant food with Fr
and Italian influences, and there was nothing in my pers
history to suggest the kind of restaurant it would be. I cou
exactly call it The Projects. The solution I finally reached wi
simplest, an easy-to-remember name highlighting the hi
neighborhood—No. 9 Park, the building's address.

• • •

Now I had to assemble my team, starting with Cat. I'd
sworn to her that I'd open my own restaurant, and that
did, she'd be wine director. So I called her in Alaska to s
happening! You have to move back."

"Where's the restaurant?" she asked. "Is it in one o
beautiful buildings we used to look at?" Cat would reci

tations in front of them, saying, "You will be mine, you will be mine . . ."

"This location is even better," I told her. "It's at the foot of the statehouse, right on the park. Tell your guy he has to get a transfer."

Cat did convince her boyfriend to transfer back east, not to Boston itself but to Connecticut, within commuting distance.

To staff the kitchen, I happily hired Baz from Galleria, giving him a lead role as my chef de cuisine, and Suzanne Nasuti, whom I promoted to sous-chef. Then, for assistant manager, I tapped Kerri, who was still in New York. When I visited, we'd sit up nights drinking and fantasizing about working together. But I thought she'd never come home. Kerri was done with Boston, having spread her wings to San Francisco and now New York. So I was surprised to get a letter from her explaining that her experience at Gramercy Tavern could help me. Was I interested? Hell, yes, I was. To open No. 9, Kerri came home to Boston—temporarily, she insisted—and wound up staying.

To find a general manager, I asked around. One of our liquor wholesalers recommended Garrett Harker, another Boston expatriate who wanted to move back from San Francisco. His résumé looked great. Lydia Shire and Todd English were both interviewing him, so I said, "Sure, I'm willing to meet him." A few years ago, Garrett recalled his job interview in the *Boston Globe*. "She's a woman of few words," Garrett said of me. "She told me, 'I want the best restaurant in Boston. Maybe you know how to do that.'" However I put it, that was definitely my goal. I hired him.

With my key staff in place, I started writing a kitchen manual, covering everything from sanitation (noting, "God knows we have enough hand sinks") to job descriptions and ideal hires. I knew the kind of employees I wanted:

All of our staff should possess a sense of style but no preten-
sion. We should also hire people with good intuition, so they
can sense how much attention a customer wants . . . Passion
is all-important. We should actually hire an inexperienced
person if he or she demonstrates genuine enthusiasm.

I listed guidelines for the waitstaff under the heading, "My
Feelings on How to Reach 4-Star Service in an Unpretentious
Manner"—I hated the fuck-you attitude of too many fancy
restaurants—and also for kitchen behavior:

Being a sous-chef is like coaching . . . You want to get the best
work out of your people but to motivate by example rather
than intimidation. I favor a calm supportive tone . . .

In those days, many, if not most, career workers in high-end
restaurants saw abuse on the job as a rite of passage. In a hot
kitchen, under intense pressure, executive chefs were expected
to freak out and get verbally and/or physically violent. I wanted
my restaurant to be more or less free of drama. I wrote, "If we
get slammed with a rush of orders, I'll add a little urgency . . ."
hoping it would be possible for all of us to stick to those words.

I also didn't want sharks on the waitstaff, knifing each other
for extra tables to score tips. I set up a tip-pooling system that
my first crop of servers, picked from the best in the city, naturally hated. They also didn't understand the style of service I
wanted; for example, I had them bring proper silverware with
each course, rather than make the guest sort through whatever
was lying beside the plate. They bitched so much to Garrett and
Kerri that I finally had to call a mandatory meeting, as I had at
Rocco's.

"I have a wait list of servers who want to work here," I announced. "If you're unhappy, you don't have to stay. I'm shutting

down the restaurant tonight, and if—only if—you want to work on my terms, show up tomorrow."

Most did. They grasped that I wanted to create a different kind of restaurant, staffed by professionals—not moonlighting actors or students or whatever, but lifers, to whom hospitality was a career. I wanted them to have predictable incomes, not crumpled wads of random dollars at the end of a shift, so they could raise families, buy houses, pay taxes, and lead regular adult lives. Like Mario Bonello, I wanted them to find dignity in their work and take pride in being part of a food and wine culture.

That's why my kitchen manual was so idealistic, upholding the vow that my restaurant would be educational. Cooking, to me, was a vocation, and I wanted to give my employees the chance to discover that in themselves and to learn the way I did— not in cooking school, but on the job. I wrote:

No. 9 will be one of the most challenging kitchens you will ever work in. Our staff has been chosen because we feel strongly that you, collectively can promote the kind of atmosphere we love . . . Teamwork is an assumption. Running an exceptional restaurant is our mission. We want to have fun, which includes listening to music during prep time or joking around on the line. However, we must still be focused . . .

Everyone in the kitchen should be learning constantly. The atmosphere should be one with an open exchange of knowledge . . . Take this opportunity to put hard work into the restaurant and food; it is an investment in your future. Read (and swap) cookbooks whenever you can; go out to eat as often as you can afford. Experience, live, and think about food. Your part in No. 9 is more than a kitchen job.

Other chef-owners I knew thought my educational scheme was airy-fairy. "Your staff won't give shit about learning," some said. "They want to do the job, get paid, and go home." Others insisted, "You'll be too busy—you hope. When the doors open at five, you better have more to do than hold class." But I was determined to try it.

I created handouts describing the food—ingredients and techniques—and, now and then, gave a pop quiz to be sure the staff was up to speed. When I introduced a dish, everyone would try it and discuss it. At first I wanted to hold a weekly wine class for the staff, but Cat and I soon settled on having a more efficient nightly tasting. That helped the knowledge stick, and as Cat said, "Why not have ten sommeliers on the floor instead of one?"—a staff that actually knew something about the recommended pairings. For further exploration, we set up a small library of food and wine resources.

I'm proud to say that my education model has paid off. Some employees have been with me nearly from the very beginning. In my footloose business, that kind of loyalty is rare. Some of those who've left—often heartbreaking but necessary—have gone on to major careers. No. 9 is the mother ship, defining the culture for all the restaurants in my group, and that kitchen manual, expanded with experience and input from the staff, is like our bible. There's a sense that we're all in it together, like members of a family, striving for excellence side by side.

• • •

Naturally, for me, the most creative and satisfying challenge at No. 9 was the menu. I'd built my reputation by riffing on traditional Italian food, but French cooking, with its crazy precision and focus on technique, is the most respected in the world. When people talk about "classical training" in things like ballet and cooking, they mean French. Never having gone to cooking school, I hadn't experienced the French kind of discipline, except for observing Mario Bonello at the St. Botolph Club.

So I remained intrigued but a little intimidated. Over the years, when I'd traveled to France I'd found my way into a few kitchens. Unlike Italians, who are generous, the French chefs I encountered tended to be snobbish. Often the male cooks I met on the line were mean; they smirked at the sight of a small woman straining to lift a stockpot weighing as much as she did. I'd always admired Julia Child, but those experiences elevated her to sainthood in my mind. Being the only woman in her class at Le Cordon Bleu in 1949, when even the idea of a female chef was radical, took some serious balls (or as the *Boston Globe* later said of me, *quenelles*). And when I think that she created her great work, *Mastering the Art of French Cooking,* with no modern conveniences like food processors or standing mixers, I genuflect in awe.

What empowered me to embrace French cuisine was *White Heat*, a book by Marco Pierre White, the bad boy of British cooking, who looked more like a rock star than an executive chef. The youngest chef ever to win three Michelin stars, Marco bragged that, at the time he won, he'd never even been to France. *White Heat* inspired a generation of chefs, like Mario Batali and Gordon Ramsay, both because of its brilliant recipes and its harsh truths about kitchen life. "The book gave us power. It all started here," Anthony Bourdain has written.

For me, Marco was a special hero because of what we have in common. He grew up working-class in Leeds and, like me, dropped out of high school. He learned to cook under fire in restaurant jobs, the way I did. He's even dyslexic, as I am. I loved his badass attitude and also his admission that his notorious drive and perfectionism came from "low self-esteem."

One of the highs of my life as a restaurant owner would come a few years later when Marco—in person!—dropped in to No. 9. It stunned me to see that he was skinny and huge, well over six feet tall. I instantly called Lydia Shire, whose restaurant, Biba, was right across the street. "You won't believe who's here!" I said.

Excited as I was, she ran right over. When she asked him to sign the back of her chef's jacket, Marco kindly did, or so she thought. Above his signature, he drew a giant cock and labeled it *THE GREAT WHITE SHARK.*

Long before he made me laugh, Marco motivated me. I'd taught myself to cook Italian food by plowing through *The Food of Italy* and, thrilled by *White Heat,* puzzled my way through enough cookbooks—including Waverly Root's *Foods of France,* Julia Child's *Mastering the Art of French Cooking,* and even a substantial chunk of Alain Ducasse's eleven-pound masterpiece, *Grand Livre de Cuisine*—to grasp the foods of France. By the time I opened No. 9, even if I wasn't 100 percent fluent, French cuisine was part of my vocabulary as a chef.

One of the best expressions of the dual French and Italian influences in the No. 9 menu is prune-stuffed gnocchi, my signature dish. In Northern Italy, gnocchi with marinated prune filling are served as dessert, but the flavors I wanted were savory. I started with a bow to Italy, marinating prunes in vin santo, the dried-grape wine I'd first tasted with Mita in Tuscany, and making gnocchi dough with the traditional riced potatoes. After sticking a prune in each pillow of dough, I reduced the vin santo marinade to add to a sauce made of two ingredients that are quintessentially French: butter and foie gras.

The finished dish, with the gnocchi cooked, sauced, and served with more sautéed foie gras, is surprisingly light. The marinated prunes counterbalance its richness. Yet the taste and texture are so luxurious that *Food & Wine,* praising the dish, called it "over the top." In the *New York Times,* Mark Bittman did a four-part feature on me in "The Chef," his 2002 interview-and-recipe series. My prune-stuffed gnocchi, which he hailed as "a no-holds-barred spectacle," got an entire segment.

Of course, the whole menu couldn't rest on my adventures in mixing traditions. I was lucky enough to have a loyal following from the days of Figs, Rocco's, and Galleria, and they expected to see at least a few of their favorite dishes. One of the biggest hits was crispy duck, inspired by Todd's, with changes to make it my own. It's a killer dish, literally and figuratively—half a duck slow-cooked in duck fat, then crisped up in more duck fat before serving. Everyone loved it.

That is, everyone except for one guy, early on. Kerri, who oversaw the dining room, came into the kitchen all blotchy, which is how her skin got if she was nervous or angry. "This guest," she said, steaming. "He says that we served him veal instead of duck."

"Was there a mix-up?" I asked.

"No, it's a boneless breast and leg, right there on the plate."

"What does he want, the fucking feathers?" I said. "Tell him it's duck and to shut the fuck up."

A few minutes, Kerri was back. "He won't listen," she told me. "He says you're lying."

I grabbed a whole duck with one hand, and with the other, a boned half. Then I stormed into the dining room. "This is what you're eating," I said, holding up the ducks in my hands to compare them with the food on his plate.

He couldn't see the resemblance. "I don't believe you," he insisted.

"You don't believe me?" I said. "Then don't eat here, now or ever again."

He looked surprised. So I clarified: "Just drop your fork and get the fuck out."

* * *

One guest down. No loss. Happily, though we opened without a lot of hoopla or a big party, we were jammed. During those first few weeks, it seemed that every food professional in town came in to check us out. They liked to congregate in the bar, which has twenty-five seats and a casual, limited menu, and then demand to try everything. I had to lay down the law, with humor: "So make a reservation in the dining room! No special treatment just because you're a chef!"

The bar was Charlie's headquarters. Though a little shy, he was an enthusiastic host, who loved meeting and greeting diners. That drove Kerri a little crazy at first because it was her job to wrangle guests, ensuring a smooth flow of orders. Eventually, though, they settled into a rhythm. Today she says, "All of us together made such a great team. It was very satisfying to work there."

I was glad to see Charlie happy, since he was the one who pushed me and showed me how to achieve my dream. He was so different from me, enjoying the social whirl while I hid out in the kitchen. His nature was so generous that I sometimes worried that he was buying drinks for the whole city. By the end of the night, when I was dead on my feet and dying to go home, he'd always have new friends for me to meet. "Let me introduce you to so-and-so . . ." That made me want to sneak out the back. But I appreciated how much the staff and guests loved him. He was my bedrock, my biggest fan.

My girlfriends who'd seen the place in its "before" state came to marvel at the changes. Funnily, they mostly came for drinks because the food seemed too complicated. As I recall, Tina and Cheryl—maybe a few others—braved a meal, but not Mary, who was a plain-food gal, strictly steak-and-potatoes. Once, during the holidays, another group of Southie friends dropped in wearing loud Christmas sweaters with blinking lights. One of them asked for a glass of wine. "What would you like?" I said. "Chardonnay?"

"Yeah," was the answer. "If it's the white kind."

Seven minutes and a world away . . . That thought so often crossed my mind when I thought of Southie or saw old friends while building a clientele of Boston Brahmins. I knew people from the projects were proud of me, and I was grateful. I wanted them to feel welcome at No. 9. Without a North Star, I'd managed to steer myself into thrilling but unknown waters, and it felt good to keep a foot planted on the solid ground of where I came from.

●   ●   ●

One of our early guests at No. 9 was Boston's greatest food personality, Julia Child. When I heard she was there, I was excited but kept working, too self-conscious (and scared of fucking up the food) to make a fuss. At the end of her meal, I came out to greet her and thank her for coming. "That was delicious!" she told me, then asked, "But why do you have to make so much pasta?"

"Uhhh . . . " I was flummoxed. Though I was known for pasta, I wasn't serving heaping bowls of it at No. 9. I almost joked, "Why do you only like French food?" but squeaked out the answer, "Well, it's an Italian restaurant."

Some time later I was invited to Julia Child's home in Cambridge. Not personally but for a party, and not really to the house but to the garden. Sheryl Julian, food editor of the *Boston Globe*, who was one of Michela's best friends, put me on the guest list for the bridal shower of Jane Levine, food writer and coeditor of the *Zagat* restaurant guide to Boston. That was kind of Sheryl, but the invitation freaked me out. I'm uncomfortable around strangers—and to make matters worse, these strangers would probably be critics who could make or break my restaurant. I wanted to decline, but Charlie put his foot down. Blowing off the invitation would be insulting, he said, and besides, if I wanted to run a business, I had to network.

The first thing I saw when I arrived was a buffet line, which I couldn't handle. The food might have been great, but I'd be too nervous standing there, forced to chitchat while trying to dish

gether. On Christmas Eve, we always had Chinese food, to lay the groundwork for the delicious roast my mother made on Christmas Day. The house was festive, with her plastic Santa Claus tablecloth anchored by a bowl of walnuts, complete with matching silver nutcracker and pick. Pots of geraniums, brought in from the yard for the winter, would be lined up on the radiator.

For Saint Patrick's Day (shamrock tablecloth), she'd set out a deli platter, along with her famous meatballs made with saltines soaked in milk: "You have to broil them!" She was fanatical about that. If serving them with spaghetti, she'd dump the broiled meatballs, along with the fat from the broiler pan, right into the sauce. Extra virgin olive oil couldn't compare to the delicious grease of ground meat fresh out of supermarket Styrofoam and plastic.

She'd make an excellent coffee cake by adding apples, cinnamon, and sour cream to a Duncan Hines vanilla cake mix.

For holiday drinks—a celebratory break from the usual Budweiser and Schlitz (or for Steve, Taylor's Port)—she liked highballs, like the classic Seven and Seven, made with Seagram's Seven Crown whiskey and 7 Up or her preferred ginger ale, or else Irish coffee, hot Sanka with a glug of booze and the powdered coffee whitener, Cremora.

On New Year's Eve, she'd invite friends like Peggy Mahoney and Peggy Harrigan over to watch the Times Square ball drop on TV, while enjoying appetizers like a shrimp cocktail platter, crackers with cream cheese and pepper jelly, or chips with her favorite dip made with sour cream and a package of Lipton onion soup mix. When I got older and learned a little about food, that dip struck me as boring. "Ma," I said, "you need to jazz it up. Like, try adding two packages of Lipton Soup mix."

"Barbara, don't screw up my recipe!" she scolded.

The kind of memories that flooded me then are still dribbling in. I can see that "closure" isn't a quick good-bye, with a door slam, but a process of letting go that continues, on and on. Just recently, I was driving and had to pull over to the side of the road, suddenly, because my mother came so strongly to mind.

She never had the time and energy or even much use for me, with my big ideas and ambitions, apart from the care she demanded when I lived at home. She didn't nurture, coddle, or protect me. It often seemed that all her affection had dried up by the time that I, the last of the Lynches, came along (even if she managed to pump out another trickle when my brother John was born). What I'd accomplished seemed to confuse or intimidate her, rather than make her proud.

Yet, as I laid my forehead on the steering wheel, I was overwhelmed with grief for the harshness of her life—her two drunken husbands, the challenge of seven children, the burden of relentless work—and then, when I could finally afford to offer her a few luxuries, the cruel disease that made even a bubble bath too frightening to enjoy.

I forgive you, I thought, silencing the litany of grievances scrolling through my mind. Letting go of them seemed to unknot the angry tangles in my brain that blocked the flow of energy. It eased my sadness to formulate *thank-yous,* even if they were mixed ones:

Thank you for sharing your personal style of cooking, for showing me that food mattered.

Thank you for your certainty, even misguided, teaching me to ignore other people's judgments.

Thank you for your fuck-you pride, checking my insecurity over my Southie address, accent, and lack of education.

Thank you for exposing me to threats—playgrounds with piercing sharps and choking bars, boiler rooms with the stench of piss—leaving me with little to fear.

Thank you for who I am today—someone I wouldn't be if you, or our lives, had been any different . . .

• • •

In the meantime B&G was going strong. The *Boston Globe* reported that, on opening night, we had 116 diners—incredible for a thirty-seven-seat restaurant—all attracted by word of mouth. The article noted the age of the staff, which, as I told the reporter, was part of my mission: to give "young, driven kids working room to test their wings." That's how I got my culinary education, and karmically, I was repaying the favor.

The ten to twelve kinds of oysters we offered were a draw, and so was our kick-ass New England chowder. But right away, two entrées on B&G's simple menu grabbed the spotlight. The first was our fried calamari. Fried calamari appears on so many menus, and 95 percent of the time it's bullshit. It's been frozen and thawed, then battered, heavily or tempura-style, before being dunked in boiling fat and emerging a soggy, tasteless, too-mushy or too-chewy mess.

At B&G, we use only fresh squid, right from the docks. We marinate it briefly in buttermilk to enhance the texture, then coat it in a special mixture of cornmeal and semolina, to give it bite. There's even an art to frying it. When the temperature's just right and you drop the basket of calamari into the fryer, it bubbles right up. Then, all of a sudden, the bubbles will slow down—that's the instant the squid is done, so it's crispy and light instead of greasy.

Our other super-popular dish was our lobster roll, also common on menus and rarely done well. There's nothing I hate more than biting into a lobster roll and hitting a big, stringy chunk of celery hidden in a glop of mayo dipped from an industrial-size jar. That's a sacrilege.

So for our lobster roll, we peel and then *brunoise* the celery— chop it into eighth-inch dice—before mixing it with the cooked lobster and freshly whipped mayonnaise. The bun is the top-split Pepperidge Farm classic, but the coleslaw and pickles that come with it are house made. The french fries we serve on the side are hand cut and dusted with fines herbes. The *Boston Globe* listed our lobster roll among its "54 Divine Dishes" of 2004.

Both the calamari and the lobster roll are expressions of B&G's philosophy: casual, clam-shack food at its finest, prepared with fine-dining-style love and care. When we first opened, guests seemed almost shocked by the real china and stemware, expecting to find cardboard boats and plastic cups. But now I think most would agree that thoughtful preparation, a pleasing table setting, and a real glass or two of interesting wine are what good seafood deserves.

At first, the Butcher Shop was a little harder for people to grasp—a meat market that was also a little wine bar. A piece by Sheryl Julian in the *Boston Globe,* which ran six weeks after the doors opened, began:

> I was describing the Butcher Shop recently to some people who had never been there and I realized that halfway through my story—no matter how detailed I got—they wouldn't be able to picture this place . . . Yes, it is really a butcher shop in the back, with the finest naturally raised organic meats money can buy. The shop also serves the same little meaty meals it offers at dinner during lunch. At night, when the foot traffic starts along Tremont Street, the 800-square-foot [dining] space turns into a neighborhood party . . .

But it too was successful, as the article noted: "On a busy night, 100 people can come through the place, some stopping to have a glass of wine after putting their name on the list at B&G Oysters Ltd., across the street."

Even more than B&G, the Butcher Shop focused on education. Chef Jason Bond and butcher Fred Donovan had a staff of five artisanal-butcher trainees, who would make the sausages and pâtés served in my restaurants. Cat, who was wine director for all three restaurants, expanded our teaching mission with an open-to-the-public Tuesday-night series. For a modest fee, each class offered a discussion and tasting of the wines and assorted appetizers of a particular region of Italy or France. We announced the series simply by pinning up a notice, and instantly forty-five people signed up. It quickly became a hot ticket.

* * *

Of course, the launch wasn't all bliss. Garrett and I clashed when he wanted to hire Gwen Butler as the opening manager. Four years earlier, Butler, a glamorous six-foot-plus, red-haired model-type, had been tending bar at the Federalist in the XV Beacon Hotel, when she got the ultimate tip. A grateful customer, who happened to be a Swiss tycoon, gave her nearly $3 million to open her own restaurant.

Gwen's story made headlines all over the world. She was on the *Today* show and CNN. As she told interviewers, the restaurant, which would have a church-like décor, would be called Zita, after the patron saint of waiters and waitresses. The waitstaff would dress in modified Catholic school uniforms. Everything was under way, right down to the monogrammed silverware and matchbooks. A launch date was announced. But for unknown reasons, the place never opened and Gwen's backer pulled the plug.

I wanted to steer clear of the whole mess, but Garrett seemed determined to give Gwen a second chance. At a certain point, I let him have his way.

One long weekend, to get away, Charlie, baby Marchesa, and I, along with my friend Annie Copps, headed to Montreal. I'd started menstruating again, which I knew happened when you eased off breast-feeding, but the bleeding never stopped. All weekend, Annie kept telling me, "Something's wrong," but I kept blowing it off until I could no longer deny that I was hemorrhaging.

Back in Boston, I went into the hospital for a D&C. During the procedure, the doctor nicked my uterine wall. I had to have emergency repair work to save my life, and then also some kind of gastrointestinal patch-up. I was too out of it even to grasp what was happening. All I remember is Charlie saying, over and over, "You're going to be okay," and feeling a little scared by the blankness on his face—a weird expression for a guy who was usually so cheery.

Luckily, I escaped winding up with a colostomy bag, but I did get septic. As Annie tells it, she brought chicken soup to the hospital but I couldn't eat. I was the color of pea soup, hooked up to bags and tubes, literally on my deathbed.

I was hospitalized for fourteen days. Once discharged, I was supposed to stay flat on my back at home for five weeks, with a nurse coming in daily for wound care. Even as sick as I was, I hated being stuck in bed, and worse, I had a little baby who needed me. Thank God for Sarah Gulati, our Winchester neighbor and an old friend of Charlie's late wife, who had embraced me—even encouraging Charlie to remarry—and came to help. She lovingly babysat Marchesa for what was supposed to be a couple of nights but turned into weeks.

Before I had a chance to recover, there was a mutiny at the new restaurants. Key staff members were quitting and I had to try to sort out the mess.

Charlie urged me to stay calm. I felt so patronized—as if Charlie were saying that I was overreacting and, worse, that a dumb girl like me from the projects couldn't possibly manage the business. "Stick to the kitchen," is the message I heard.

It took a while before I realized that Charlie was only trying to spare me out of concern for my health. I'd nearly died, and I was supposed to take it slow. I had an infant to care for, and I was responsible for three restaurants. Charlie worried that I was headed for collapse. But at the time, I felt disrespected in my own business, abandoned by the man I thought I could count on, and outraged.

In the end I bought out Garrett's share of the restaurant, but kept the name B&G.

Then there was Gwen. One night she came waltzing into B&G with two guys and plopped down at the bar to eat dinner. I had a strong sense that she was mocking me—as if she'd had gotten away with something and was flaunting it. So I went up to her and said, "Gwen, it's over for us. Now please get out."

She didn't protest. She just went down to the kitchen office to clear out her stuff. Gwen came back up the spiral staircase carrying a laptop—equipment I'd bought for the office, containing my contacts and other proprietary information. "That computer belongs to me," I said, from the top of the stairs. "So drop it."

But she kept coming. I raised my leg to kick her back down the stairs, and she retreated. After a minute, though, she made another run for it, clutching the computer. Angrier now, I lashed out with my foot again, but my waiters yanked me back. "Chef, don't do it," they said. "You'll go to jail. She's not worth it."

"I ought to chop you up and fucking fry you," I said to Gwen.

She left, finally, without the laptop.

• • •

In the meantime, I had to get on with the hard job of retaking control and rebuilding a staff that I could trust. I started by literally cleaning house, shutting down B&G for a day. You know how you burn sage to get rid of bad energy? Well, I went in with buckets of a compound containing sage, along with other evil-eye busters, and washed down the walls in the upstairs and kitchen offices. I totally redid the menu. I did everything I could do to drive out the bad juju.

Only then did I feel that I had really turned the tables and could make a totally fresh, clean start.

10

THE SOUTH END

When Garrett was handling the business side, I'd been immersed in the creative work of running my restaurants, as well as starting a family. Now I had some catching up to do, checking the profits and losses and future projections that would let us keep the doors open and the lights on. I had a reasonable grasp of the numbers, having twenty years' experience as executive chef and chef-owner, but of course, I had no business education. *What the hell*, I told myself. *I had no fucking training for anything I've ever done.* As always, *I'll figure it out* was my mantra.

The bookkeeping shit took some puzzling to understand. At times my head ached from the effort to grasp it all, and I kept wondering, *Am I too dumb for this?* But I felt so leery of outsiders that I was determined to work out every calculation. Never again, I vowed, would I just place my faith in someone else's "professional" knowledge. (That promise proved hard to keep.) It was my business, born of my creative vision and built with my blood, sweat, and tears. I had to get a grip on the math.

It was a hell of an education, but I'm proud to say that, within the next couple years, I not only boosted my bottom line, but actually doubled the company's profits.

• • •

At a certain point, I could afford to expand. Catering seemed like a logical way to go since we'd been doing a steady stream of private events like, say, a home birthday dinner for ten. I called the catering division Niche Catour (*nichée* being French for "nest" and *catour* an old-fashioned word for "catering"), which led to goofy mispronunciations. We were constantly getting calls for Nicki or Nee-che Cator-ey, so I had to wonder if people were skipping us for easier names. I soon changed Niche Catour to Nine at Home.

The greater challenge was cracking catering itself. To be effective, I had to hire a sales team to drum up bookings. That's when I started hitting walls. Many of the best event spaces and annual bashes had established affiliations with certain caterers. Being new to the business, we hadn't stockpiled china and silver and had to rent them, making our bids less competitive. The biggest sticking point of all was staffing. We weren't serving rubber chicken, but high-end cuisine, which had to be executed by great line cooks and a talented chef. Around the holidays, when catering gigs tend to cluster, my senior staff would be stretched to the limit juggling bookings and restaurant traffic. Of course, hiring a dedicated catering staff wouldn't make sense until the business grew enough to ensure them steady employment.

Though we did some fabulous parties, I came to see that branching into full-scale catering was a misstep. We could keep doing private functions on an individual basis, without building a new sideline that might or might not turn a profit and that would distract me from my mission: creating elegantly simple, Italian- and French-inspired food.

I'd been thinking of myself the wrong way—as a chef seeking exposure—when, in fact, I already had a public identity. My reputation was my brand. Why wasn't I selling that? By linking my three restaurants under one umbrella, with my name, I could leverage that reputation. That's how my company, Barbara Lynch Gruppo, began.

During this time, a tiny storefront—just a couple hundred square feet—opened up next to the Butcher Shop. *I might as well be my own neighbor,* I thought. So I leased it as a complement to the Butcher Shop, a place to sell produce that was as exquisite as our meat. Along with more down-to-earth products, I brought in hard-to-find vegetables, like wild asparagus and morels in season, and designed beautiful displays. Plum Produce was like an art gallery for fruits and vegetables—the cutest little greengrocer you've ever seen.

I loved hanging out there, spritzing the lettuces and creating fruit-and-vegetable tableaus. The displays were so gorgeous that shoppers would sometimes pause before ruining the design. Whatever I couldn't sell, I had to preserve in some way, so I came up with the idea of dehydrating vegetables and fruits and selling them in mason jars. Customers quickly grasped how handy it is to have, say, some dehydrated carrots, mushrooms, or greens on hand to round out a dish. I also discovered that some fruits and vegetables take on new dimensions when they're dried. Watermelon, for example—when dehydrated, it's delicious but tastes more like the squash it is.

The dehydration process got me interested in powders, made from either fresh herbs or vegetables like asparagus or beets, to add a jolt of nutrition and flavor to other foods. Those too became popular. My experiments in that itty-bitty storefront laid the groundwork for a business I launched a decade later, B. Lynch Made, which I first imagined benefiting urban "food deserts"—Boston has its share—and may have the potential to help fight world hunger.

Of course, I also preserved fruits the traditional way, by creating interesting jams. In fact, peach jam was the very first thing Marchesa ever helped me make. She was still in diapers, so by "helped," I mean she bit into every peach in the bushel. But she loved watching me cook. I have an adorable picture of her standing on the kitchen counter, which was her observation post, smeared with peach juice.

My third new venture, which proved a major success, was born out of need. Since all my restaurants are open for lunch and dinner, their kitchens are constantly bustling. At my home in Winchester, I could experiment with recipe ideas, but I couldn't really mentor my staff there. So I rented a new space for a test kitchen, combined with a cookbook store. I called it Stir.

Lots of people adore cookbooks as much as I do, but I soon realized that those sales wouldn't pay the rent. So I circled back to my strong commitment to education. TV cooking shows had multiplied like crazy. Surely the public would find it more satisfying to see a chef create a meal up close, in a small group, and actually get to enjoy the food, with expert wine pairings. The minute I posted a sign about cooking demonstrations, we were swamped. We started to offer them three nights a week, and for the first couple years I personally conducted nearly every one.

Now and then, I'd give a hands-on tutorial on, say, knife skills or sauce making, but the most popular format—and the most fun to demonstrate—was a four- or five-course meal. Cat and I would work up a special theme for each night. Like we'd do "Champagne and Butter"—all kinds of luxurious elements like French lobster with butter, different kinds of caviar, and rich brioches, paired with dry champagnes, and foie gras, served with sweeter versions. Or "The Chef's Night Out," featuring foods we'd love to order in a fine restaurant (my favorites were sweetbreads, squab, rib eye steaks with béarnaise sauce, or sometimes just spectacular pastas).

We'd choose a cookbook and prepare a meal from it, with flights of wines. One of the favorites was *Mastering the Art of French Cooking* by Julia Child (which, of course, got an extra boost from *Julie and Julia*, the book and film). We made everything by hand, just as Julia had, without benefit of electric blenders, food processors, or other modern devices. The featured entrée, a cassoulet with handmade garlic sausage and duck confit, was a labor-intensive challenge but always a hit. So was the dessert, baked Alaska; my arm aches from the memory of whisking all those egg whites for the meringue. Watching us sweat it definitely deepened the class's respect for and awe of Julia, our local hero. I loved describing my encounters with her over the years—how humble she was, and what a ham.

Some of our other very popular classes were armchair travelogues, with Cat and me telling stories about our visits to different regions of Italy or France. People loved hearing our tales of Tuscan boar butchers, smoky fire pits, and artisanal vineyards as much as they enjoyed the delicious dishes and wines that we brought back. We'd describe how we put together menus, sometimes reading from the notebooks of wine flavors and meal scenarios that we'd compiled (I've saved most of them):

Wine: Muscadet from Loire
Food: Oysters, almost needs smoke in a mignonette

Wine: Provence rosé, Château Viranel, Saint-Chinian; they drink
  it with a really garlicky aioli
Food: Red mullet with toasted garlic rouille, crostini with charred
  bread

Wine: Bourgogne, Claude Maréchal, tastes of earth and fruit and
  ocean

Food: Grilled salmon or snapper or potatoes with poached oysters,
    needs butter to soften; charred octopus with potato cake and
    green olives

Wine: Macon La Roche, Château de la Greffière, soft, not a lot of
    malic acid
Food: Scallops, lentils, langoustine tart, shallot sauce; a sharp
    wine that definitely needs cream and leeks; cassoulet of
    escargot, blue cheese, and bread crumbs, farro, or barley

* * *

A decade after its launch, Stir is still going strong. It's completely
sold out months in advance. Thanks to the energy and enthusiasm of Abby Gregory (who started out as a server and worked
her way into management), it's become the Little Engine That
Could—a two-hundred-square-foot profit center.

Stir has expanded its range from French and Italian specialties
to more global cuisine. For example, a class recently put together
by Gruppo executive chef Michele Carter was called "Some Like
It Hot." It featured five courses of foods with different sources
of heat: stuffed jalapenos and *shishito* peppers to start, followed
by mulligatawny soup with curry and cayenne; then, for entrées,
Korean fried chicken served with Korean chili paste plus haba-
nero and poblano sauces and sole en papillotte layered with bok
choi and sauced with Thai chilies, ginger, mirin, and lime; and
for dessert, spicy gingerbread zinged with ginger, cloves, and nutmeg. Armchair travel sessions, in any given month, might center
on such far-flung places as Israel, Mexico, Spain, Latin America,
and Japan.

Stir has helped me in ways beyond profitability. Though I can
be badass when it comes to jumping off roofs (or into romances
and restaurants), I've always found public speaking, and even
conversations with strangers, to be tough. I don't know how to

stand or what to do with my hands. I squirm. I can't find the right words. Distracted by feeling awkward, I blurt things out and get pissed off. I need to be moving instead of sitting or standing still. Cooking is how I communicate best, even in my own home.

Today, though, a chef can't stay holed up in the kitchen. You have to greet guests, talk to the press, and at least sometimes appear on TV. Of course, many chefs host television shows. To be successful, I had to boost my performance skills, and I did it by teaching night after night, year after year, at Stir. I had to explain clearly, without mumbling or rambling. I had to project confidence and charm. It was like total-immersion media training, or being shoved out onto a Broadway stage. It taught me to master my nerves—more or less.

I also found those classes very rewarding. I loved seeing ten people, most of them strangers, enjoy the great food and wine, and then start to bond. A surprising number of people have told me that they made new friends for life at a session at Stir. It is also gratifying that so many attendees gain the courage to cook creatively from observing a chef. I often hear, "I made the tomato tart for Easter"—or whatever occasion—"and it's now it's my signature dish. Sometimes I add such-and-such as a variation . . ." They'd watch and learn the techniques and get empowered.

At Stir I could cook one-on-one with members of my staff. Daily life in a restaurant is usually frenetic, focused on the demands of the moment—prepping, cooking, and literally or figuratively putting out fires. But at Stir, while executing a single meal, a cook and I could interact closely. That led me to fascinating discoveries; for example, of the remarkable strengths of Kristen Kish. Born in Seoul, South Korea, Kristen was adopted and raised by a Michigan family. She probably could have done whatever she wanted but found her way to culinary school in Chicago, then came to Boston, where after a couple of entry-level cooking jobs, she started with me.

Cat and I had developed a class called "Birds and Burgundy," pairing the complex and lively wines of the renowned region of France (including wines like Chablis, Côte de Beaune, Chassagne-Montrachet, and Pouilly-Fuissé) with different preparations of poultry like quail, squab, and roast chicken. Kristen was fairly new, but one night, when I was totally slammed, I asked her to execute all the dishes for me. Wow—I was blown away. Kristen is such an incredibly precise, clean, and elegant chef. Her food was gorgeous. So I told her, "From now on, you own this class. Instead of assisting, I want you to teach it."

I love that, seeing young chefs really shine. Sometimes, they've been learning and then there's a sudden breakthrough moment, when they crush it. In others, like Kristen, there's a certain magic or inborn skill, which they just need a chance to express. Either way, these are the times when it's thrilling to be a mentor.

Kristen would go on to become my chef de cuisine at Stir and then at my fine-dining venture, Menton. Along the way, we had some hilarious adventures, like the one we called the "Bruiser incident." We get our delicious butter from Animal Farm in Orwell, Vermont, which is run by Diane St. Clair. One day she called to ask, "Could the Butcher Shop use some veal?" Though primarily a dairy farm dedicated to "cow-comfort"—you can taste the difference in the milk—now and then there would be a humanely raised, grass-fed animal ready for slaughter.

"Of course!" I said. The condition was that I'd have to arrange its transportation. "Hell, I'll come and pick it up," I told Diane.

Kristin came along to keep me company on the four-hour drive. When we reached Orwell, Vermont, we packed the bed of my SUV with ice, then loaded in plastic-wrapped sections of a calf so huge that we named him Bruiser. By the time we got back to Boston, it was around 9:00 p.m., and the dinner rush at both B&G and the Butcher Shop was in full swing.

How do you move large animal hunks into a shop past scads

of diners? There's no graceful way to do it. I'm short in stature and Kristen, though somewhat taller, is thin and looks more delicate than she is. So I pulled the car up on the sidewalk, as close as I could to the building, and the two of us small women wrestled the plastic-encased body parts out onto the ground— legs nearly as big as we were; giant, meaty haunches; and of course, the huge, forbidding head. We felt like a couple of mob assassins dumping bodies in Savin Hill (aka Stab and Kill Hill.) Even through the windows, I could feel people's stares of horror and see them mouth the words, "Oh my God." *This is where meat comes from*, I wanted to say, half-laughing, but I was huffing and puffing too hard.

Owner, executive chef, teacher, and catering supervisor; produce-display artist, spritzer, and dessicator; butcher (self-taught, with the help of *The River Cottage Meat Book,* by Hugh Fearnley-Whittingstall), shopkeeper, and now meat hauler—I was doing it all. It could be utterly overwhelming, but now I had the satisfaction, after all the conflict and betrayal, of feeling completely in command of my world.

• • •

With so much going on, I decided to get a pied-à-terre, a loft in Southie, minutes from the restaurants, where I could collapse at the end of my fifteen-hour days, rather than commute to Winchester. Of course, that meant not seeing Marchesa as much, but I was hardly around during her waking hours anyway. I'd found a great nanny, Meg, who was one of seven kids, as I am, had a young daughter of her own, and studied child psychology. She got to be a member of the family.

Another constant presence, from the time Marchesa was about one, was her godmother, my Southie friend, Dyan LaRosa. She spoiled Marchesa like crazy, but I was grateful for her help, because of the demands of my business and because she seemed so good with kids. With my meager experience of parenting, I didn't quite know how to cope with a toddler—maybe nobody does, I realize now. Maybe people ultimately learn to manage kids through constant exposure, which I never had, since I was working so hard. But at the time, feeling incompetent compared with Dyan shook my confidence as a mother.

Still, I adored Marchesa and marveled at her every move. Once she grasped that there was a big world around her, she rarely cried. If I put her down on, say, a counter, she was content to look around, always observing, instead of crawling off. She seemed so curious, so intuitive.

Also, from a very young age, she had a sense of precision. For example, one Thanksgiving, I was making pumpkin fritters from a recipe developed by my close friend Ana Sortun, a great chef whose restaurants, all in the Boston area, include Oleana, Sofra, and Sarma. Marchesa, who was no more than two or three, wanted to help, so I had her lay out the fritters on a sheet tray. Even today, unless I look at the photo I snapped, I can hardly believe how she arranged them—all in perfectly straight lines. What kid that age has such a good eye, as well as that kind of coordination? It was amazing.

One of my parenting ambitions was to give Marchesa a more expansive upbringing than mine. I never wanted her to feel culturally limited. My own sense of how the world worked and of my place in it had come with travel, which gave me a perspective that my mother, who never left Southie, couldn't offer. So when I had the chance to go abroad, if I wasn't on some crazy business junket, I liked to take Marchesa along.

She made her first trip to Europe in the womb, when I was invited to join an international club of women in food called Les Nouvelles Mères Cuisinières or New Mothers in the Kitchen. It was founded by Hélène Darroze, a three-Michelin-star chef with restaurants in Paris, London, and Moscow, along with Ariane

Daguin of D'Artagnan, the major gourmet food purveyor in New York. Members included the three-Michelin-star Anne-Sophie Pic of Maison Pic in the South of France; Elena Arzak of Arsak in San Sebastian, Spain; Christine Ferber, the famed pastry chef and maker of artisanal jams in Niedermorschwihr, France; Caroline Rostang of L'Absinthe in Paris; Judith Baumann of La Pinte des Mossettes in Switzerland; and Léa Linster, chef of three restaurants in Luxembourg; among others. I'm mentioning only the Michelin stars, but all the women were winners of major awards. It was humbling to be included in such a prestigious and accomplished group.

The club was founded to highlight the too-often-ignored achievements of women chefs in Europe. The idea was for a bunch of us to get together and cook, then invite the press to cover the event. The first meeting I attended was held in Alsace, which is like the French mother ship for salamis and sausages. Unfortunately, being pregnant, I couldn't enjoy either one or try the world-famous wines like gewürztraminer and dry Rieslings.

The dish I planned to make, representing Boston, was butter-poached lobster, with baby vegetables on the side, in a *vin jaune* sauce. *Vin jaune*, or "yellow wine," from the Jura region of France, is matured under a film of yeast (the *voile*) for six years and three months. In that time, it evaporates so only 62 percent of the original volume remains, which is yellow in color, with a unique, nutty aroma and flavor resembling that of dry Fino sherry.

I wasn't feeling well, so I had the young chef I'd brought along handle the prep, including Cryovac'ing our beautifully turned tiny carrots and brussels spouts. After being introduced at the opening press conference, I didn't bother to check up on him. As it turned out, I should have.

I didn't see what had gone wrong until cooking was under way. I was already off balance because they asked that I use an Alsatian wine in my sauce. That was fair enough, and I loved the

Trimbach Rieslings they had on hand, but they tasted very different from *vin jaune*. While I was coping with that difference, my sous-chef was assembling the lobsters and vegetables—somehow oblivious to the fact the brussels sprouts and carrots in the vacuum packs were gray. I mean *gray*, the color of cement. All I could say was, "What the goddamn hell!"

"Don't worry," he said. "They taste fine. The dish will be great."

"No fucking way!" I had to insist. Since he'd already combined the lobsters with the gray roughage, I had to shitcan the whole mess. In my very best sketchy French, I had to beg for more lobsters and baby veggies from the hosts of the event.

Meanwhile, I could feel the stares of the French *nouvelles mères*. Not only were they more meticulous and elegant than I was, most of them headed restaurants with illustrious histories, some stretching back generations. The family restaurant of Anne-Sophie Pic, for example, had won three Michelin stars back in 1934 under her grandfather André, lost one after the death of her father Jacques, his successor, and then Anne-Sophie won it back. Hélène Darroze is a fourth-generation chef; Elena Arzak is second generation; and so is Christine Ferber, who inherited her father's business, along with her siblings, then brought it to international renown. Even Ariane Daguin, who founded her own business, D'Artagnan, is the daughter of a celebrated chef.

I heard all these distinguished pedigrees when we were introduced to the press. And what could they say about me? "This is Barbara Lynch from the projects?" Maybe pregnancy hormones were clouding my brain, but I thought I sensed some animosity—as if they resented the fact that, unlike them, I didn't have to uphold a legacy; that I could follow my own whims and be accountable only to myself. My lack of culinary breeding was all too evident.

Seeing the wreckage of my meal, one of the chefs asked—

snottily, it seemed—"So, do you sous vide often?" Sous vide is the name of the method for slow-cooking food in vacuum-sealed bags. "Well, obviously not," I answered, as politely as I could, while thinking, *Go fuck yourself.*

What a shit show.

So I was surprised to be invited back, the following year, to the meeting of Les Nouvelles Mères Cuisinières. This time I took along my pastry chef, Kristen Daniel Murray (whose place in Portland, Oregon, Maurice Luncheonette, named for her pet rabbit, recently made *Bon Appétit's* Top Ten), Charlie, my niece Stacy, and Marchesa, who was six months old. We flew into Paris, where Marchesa had her first taste of grown-up food, *pommes Robuchon,* which are fingerling potatoes boiled with bay leaf, riced for fluffiness, folded with equal parts butter and cream, then pressed through a *chinois,* a china cap, to create a silky, rich puree. She loved them.

We met up with the other chefs to board the train from Paris to Courchevel, a ritzy ski resort in the French Alps. Everyone at the station oohed and cooed over Marchesa. I spotted Hélène Darroze from the back in a beautifully cut Marni coat, which I'd seen in a magazine and could never afford but coveted. The press swarmed around us, looking as stylish as the chefs, the *Madame Figaro* editor puffing the most elegant, slim cigarette. It was like being in a photo shoot for French *Vogue.*

The platform was groaning under stacked-up crates of Lynch-Bages, incredible Bordeaux with echoes of ripe cassis, truffles, and tobacco; and Veuve Clicquot Grande Dame, the good stuff, a top-of-the-line champagne. Each of us was supposed to make a regional treat for the trip. My very American offering was a chef's version of s'mores, made with homemade graham crackers, fine chocolate sprinkled with *fleur de sel,* and stabilized crème fraîche instead of marshmallows.

Pinch me, I thought, caught up in the party atmosphere, feeling more of a sense of belonging than in Alsace. *This is definitely* la belle vie, *"the good life."*

It was *la belle vie* big-time in Courchevel, a playground for the superrich and famous. Site of some of the world's top ski slopes, it's full of luxury hotels and fine restaurants, including seven with Michelin stars. There, for the first time, I tasted real fondue and also raclette, a traditional Swiss dish of cheese melted next to a fire, scraped off the block onto a plate, and served with potatoes, air-dried meat, and garnishes like gherkins and pickled onions. It is earthy and deeply satisfying.

Our home base was Le Chabichou, a two-Michelin-star restaurant in a five-star hotel. The theme of our event, to which we all contributed dishes, was "French picnic." I cooked along-side and got to know Elena Arzak, one of the chefs who'd seemed so off-putting my first time around. And this time my dish, black truffle tomato tartines, came out beautifully and proved a big hit. *Whew!* To boost the festive picnic mood, Ariane had booked an alphorn band, playing traditional horns so long that they stretched from their mouths to the ground, with a sound more *oompah* than R & B. So French!

What an adventure. It was the most glamorous scene I'd ever experienced. I was glad to give Stacy a real taste of the world in her teens, an age when my idea of travel was flying to Bermuda on stolen credit cards to booze on the beach.

When we got back to Paris, I encouraged her to join Kristen Daniel Murray on a trip to see the *Mona Lisa* at the Louvre. "Okay, I'll go," she told me. But it wasn't long before the phone rang in my hotel room. It was Stacy, bored to death. "Auntie Bub," she said. "I don't care if Mona fucking Lisa is crying. You've gotta get me out of here."

She was tired of being around grown-ups, sick of acting like an adult, lonely for her friends, and wanted to go home. I didn't blame her one bit.

• • •

Because my life got so busy—expanding into B&G, the Butcher Shop, Plum Produce, Niche Catour, and Stir; and then, almost immediately plunging into the even more ambitious Fort Point development—I didn't reconnect with Les Nouvelles Mères over the next few years. Then one day, when I was in New York, Ariane Daguin and I met for lunch at Prune, the tiny East Village gem owned by my dear friend Chef Gabrielle Hamilton. "You know, Elena Arzak will be in New York pretty soon," Ariane told me, "and Hélène Darroze adopted two daughters."

"Wow," I said. "Why don't we get all our kids together and have lunch? Maybe we could do a potluck . . ."

The next thing I knew, we were staging a huge event. Geoffrey Zakarian, the New York restaurateur and chef famous for appearances on such shows as *Chopped*, *Iron Chef*, and *The Kitchen*, among others, offered his restaurant Country as the setting. All kinds of stars were invited to lunch, ranging from chefs like Jean-Georges Vongerichten and Drew Nieporent to food celebrities like Ruth Reichl and Martha Stewart.

I took Ana Sortun with me from Boston, along with her daughter Siena. Since Siena is a year younger than Marchesa, they've played together forever. I thought they'd be good company for each other in the mix of kids, and though Ana wasn't cooking, that she'd enjoy the other chefs (and be moral support for me).

While Ana took the girls to the zoo, Gabrielle Hamilton and I joined the visiting French *mères* in the kitchen. Gabrielle is like me—a self-taught, intuitive, freewheeling chef. The French chefs, of course, were the opposite: expertly trained, confident, and precise, even perfectionist in their technique. They took the luncheon very seriously.

I was dropping spoons, fumbling ingredients out of containers, sticking my fingers into pots to taste the food—you name it—and all the while, feeling painfully self-conscious.

Gabrielle asked, "Why do you let these women intimidate you? I bet they don't even plate their own food."

"Okay, okay," I said. She was right that I shouldn't feel intimidated, but something about them—their superior air, the fact that none of them was rumpled or sweaty or food-splattered—unnerved me. Of course, once I got to know them well, I found them charming and fun-loving, but back then, around Frenchwomen, I could still revert to insecurity.

● ● ●

But the French gang can be a lot of fun. After James Beard Award ceremonies, I often hit the parties with Ariane, whom I call the French mayor of New York. I like to tease her by whining, "Can't we go to an Italian party? Why do we have to go to Daniel again?" Daniel is Daniel Boulud's incredible Upper East Side restaurant, one of the few in Manhattan with two Michelin stars.

When Ariane hosts a gathering, you never know what to expect. Once she held a Duck-a-Thon in New York, in honor of the gourmet food that launched her business, American-sourced foie gras. It was a scavenger hunt for D'Artagnan products hidden all over Chelsea. At the last minute she told me, "You have to come in costume." So I shipped our chefs' coats ahead to my cousin Brian in New York, who is a wizard—then staging events at the Botanical Garden—to be covered with duck feathers.

Besides the scavenger hunt, there were wild competitions, like a relay race that everyone ran wearing flippers. Watching an elegant Frenchwoman run in flippers is hilarious—almost as funny as trying to do it yourself. I peed my pants so many times that I lost track. Ariane drives around town in a little Mini Cooper, beeping a horn that goes, *Quack, quack.* She's a great partner in crime.

● ● ●

One of my other favorite partners in crime is Annie Copps, who's joined me on a few of the promotional missions that chefs often embark on to extend their brands (usually to support some worthy cause). Some of these junkets are wonderfully memorable, like the one that took me (alone) to Ireland for the first time. Having been so deeply steeped in Irish-American culture, it was almost mystical to experience the motherland—the country had spawned all the sayings, traditions, and even personality traits that were part of the fabric of life in Southie. Ireland is beautiful, green, and rocky, with magnificent castles; I felt like I'd been transported to the world of *Downton Abbey*. I couldn't believe that Boston was just five hours away.

I was there for the Kerrygold Ballymaloe Litfest of Food and Wine in Cork, following in the huge footsteps of such chefs as Alice Waters and René Redzepi. It's a long weekend of music, dancing, storytelling, and of course, sharing ideas about Irish food and drink. Irish food isn't one of the world's most celebrated cuisines, but I have to say that the ingredients are amazing: the lamb, the trout, and especially the butter and cream—oh my God. And real Guinness is so different from what we drink in the States. For one thing, it isn't served cold but is pulled from the spigot warm and creamy and aromatic. It's delicious.

One of the highlights of Ballymaloe is its Cookery School run by Darina Allen, situated on her family's hundred-acre organic farm. Along with outdoor plantings, it has acre-wide greenhouses blooming with every imaginable fruit and vegetable. There are also magical gardens, including one with herbs contained by sculpted hedges, one with fanciful topiaries, and a wildflower meadow with a Celtic maze of yew trees. In one of the gardens there's a little house with a pointed slate roof and an interior—

floor, walls, and ceiling—completely encrusted in a mosaic of scallop and mussel shells.

While I was at dinner with Darina Allen and her family, someone asked, "Where do you come from? You're a Lynch. Are you from Cork?"

I've heard that my family has roots in Cork, where the name is common. At first I improvised, "Yeah, sure. I'm from Cork." But who the hell knows? So I backtracked, "Where do you want me to come from?" Since I'd been welcomed so warmly and since everyone at the table was older than me—some the age of my grandparents (had I ever known them)—it didn't feel right to bullshit.

I never made it to Dublin on that trip. I met some interesting young chefs, but didn't get to hang out with as many as I'd hoped of the up-and-coming ones, who are redefining Irish cuisine. So I'll have to go back.

• • •

Annie was with me on a wilder trip, a Mediterranean cruise sponsored by the marketing arm of *Food & Wine* magazine. Normally, Sarah Hearn, my right hand, would have come along, but she was pregnant and suggested, "Take somebody fun."

When Annie got my text, *Free trip to Europe?* she was lying on the beach in Nantucket. *Free?* she shot back. *Sure!* We flew into Rome and made our way to Civitavecchia, the departure port for the cruise. It's an ancient walled city but what struck me was its very modern frozen food industry. An interesting store there is like the Italian answer to Picard, the amazing supermarket chain in France that sells only frozen foods. Picard stores sell everything from what they call "cooking essentials," like frozen minced shallots and beurre blanc, to prepared dishes like mini boudins blanc with morels, *dorade* with truffles, and *saumon en croute*.

You'd think countries like Italy and France, with food-centered identities, would turn up their collective noses at frozen products. But convenience counts too, and the quality of these offerings is high enough—even if not as good as homemade—to satisfy fairly sophisticated tastes. These stores make me think that the frozen food business in the United States is just beginning to fulfill its possibilities.

On the ship, I was scheduled to do two cooking demonstrations in the onboard restaurants, each time prepping food to show the guests, having the meals executed by the regular chefs, then presiding over the service. When I met with the kitchen crew to describe my meals, I was assured that they had all the ingredients I needed, including, for the prune gnocchi that is my signature dish, plenty of foie gras.

When the ship docked at Livorno, Annie and I decided to get off and poke around. On the shuttle into town, we chatted with a woman from New Zealand, who introduced herself as Jax. "I'm going to Lucca," she told us. "It's just an hour away by bus and train."

"Let's all go!" we said. There wouldn't be that much open to interest us in Livorno on a Sunday.

In Lucca, a lovely medieval Tuscan city, I had one of those meals that makes me marvel at the simple genius of Italian cooking. Melon at the utter peak of ripeness—another hour might have tipped it over the edge—with delicately cured prosciutto, just sliced and warm, and a crackling of black pepper; followed by perfectly cooked octopus and potatoes with parsley and aromatic olive oil. It was most satisfying version of the dish I've ever had.

After lunch Annie and I hit a flea market, then met Jax to head back to Livorno. After about forty minutes on the train, we realized that we were going the wrong way—inland, instead of toward the coast. Jumping off at the next stop, we had to tear through an underpass to catch the train to Livorno, which was just pulling in. Jax, a big girl, was huffing and puffing behind us as we ran. We didn't make it.

We got the next train, which put us into Livorno more than an hour after our ship was supposed to sail. Jax had a cell phone but couldn't figure out how to use it, so there was no way for us to communicate. "Well, if the boat's gone, it's gone," I said. In Livorno, we grabbed a cab to take us to the dock. On the way, we heard the radio buzzing with alerts using the word *americani*. None of us spoke Italian, but Annie said, "Holy shit, I bet they're talking about us."

They were. The cruise line held the boat and had been calling the cops and the hospitals. The cabbie radioed ahead to tell them we'd been found. The minute we boarded—we were in the elevator, rising to the deck—the ship hauled anchor and started moving. For the entire rest of the cruise, we were branded by the incident. I heard, "Oh, Ms. Lynch, you were one of the late girls," as often as I was told, "Oh, we loved your food."

The cooking demonstrations were a passive-aggressive battleground. I can see why people who cook anonymously on ships, probably enduring plenty of bullshit from the passengers and staff, might resent a "celebrity" who comes aboard, demonstrates a recipe or two, and then reaps glory from the ungrateful guests. But a "name" chef is what attracts passengers to these cruises and keeps everyone employed. So there was obviously something more, like sexism, motivating the all-male kitchen crew to stoop to the dopey stunts they pulled.

The first day, they refused to give me parchment paper, which must have been a hot commodity—why, I can't imagine. When they finally coughed up a used piece, I thought, *Fuck it,* and made do. Why even bother to fight such pettiness?

But the hits kept on coming. They had me prep on a folding table at the pass of the restaurant, presumably because the kitchen, then in the middle of service, was too cramped. I had to keep ducking as trays of food were lofted over my head. I had an ingredients list, but rather than let me stock up at the provisions center, a guy made me wait as he brought out the items I needed one at a time. "You don't have to do that," I kept saying, meaning, *Knock it the fuck off.* "Just show me where to go." But for some reason, I was barred from the inner sanctum and reduced to asking, "Would you bring me a big bowl so I can mix this stuff?"

When I finally had my supplies and was nearly done, someone evidently decreed that I was underfoot—no fucking kidding!—and had to move. After the interruption, I was installed in a large auxiliary kitchen that had been standing empty the whole time I'd been dodging trays. I could have finished my work, efficiently and comfortably, in less than an hour instead of the four it took me. It was crazy.

I wish I could say this was a one-time clusterfuck of errors but when it came time for my next demonstration, making the prune gnocchi, I was told that all the foie gras was gone. Someone needed it, so they'd sold it in Monaco. Seriously? It was a preposterous scenario, even as sabotage.

* * *

While all this was going on, Annie and I kept telling each other, "This is a free trip to Europe." It became our mantra. So we made the best of it, enjoying a magnificent lunch at Le Grill, the Alain Ducasse restaurant in Monte-Carlo on top of the Hotel de Paris, with its retractable skylight roof and breathtaking view of the Riviera; and in Barcelona, stopping in at Quimet y Quimet, a quirky wine and beer bar that's world-famous for its *montaditos*, improvised little sandwiches, with up to a hundred different variations offered daily. We tried so many that the staff there marveled, "God, these girls can eat," as they kept giving us wines to taste. We stumbled out of there blissful and hazy.

We got back to the ship at happy hour and settled on the pool deck for a smoke. By that point on the trip, we'd developed a role-reversal routine that always cracked us up. I, who could normally party all night, considered the cruise a chance to relax. So when we got a little toasted, I'd say, "Okay, tonight's a TV night. I'm turning in early." Annie, usually the restrained one, would tease, "Yeah, go catch up on *Masterpiece Theater*," while she planned to hang out and possibly find romance.

We were kicking this joke around—and I really did intend to hit the sack—when a guy came sidling up and asked, "What are you girls drinking?" He introduced himself—I'll call him Dave. As we started talking, he ordered a round. We were laughing about something when, all of a sudden, Dave dived into Annie's lap. "God," she said. "What's wrong?"

"My sister's here," he whispered. "We both just got out of rehab. Don't let her see me drinking."

So the night was getting interesting. No way could I go to bed. We wound up changing, putting on makeup, and meeting Dave to dance on the deck. At one point while dancing, I was whipping the end of my long Dries Van Noten scarf, when someone grabbed it and pulled it taut. "Limbo!" I called out. The band launched into the song.

Though a lot of the passengers on deck were elderly—some on walkers or with oxygen tanks—many got into the limbo line. "Lower, lower," people were chanting.

"Barbara, some of these people can't even bend over to tie their shoes! How can they limbo?" Annie asked.

But they did. Even a guy in wheelchair scooted under the limbo scarf. I was laughing so hard I had a mini tsunami in my pants.

"Okay, we're leaving," Annie said. "You're sopping wet, and with the vodka I've been drinking, nothing good is going to happen . . ."

As we tried to slip out, cackling hysterically, the band kept begging, "Don't leave! It's still early." We were the life of the party.

The next morning was brutal, but we recovered enough to explore when the boat docked in Tunisia. At the bottom of the gangplank were huge woolly creatures. "Oh, my God!" I said, smacking Annie's arm. "Camels!" I'd never seen one before. Back on the ship that night, and on nights to follow, we hung out with Dave. He was our Scheherazade, with One Thousand and One tales to tell.

He was traveling with his whole family—his newly widowed father, in his nineties, who was paying for the trip; his father's girlfriend; and his sister and brother-in-law. The plan was that they'd all have dinner together at night and spend the rest of the time on their own—each of them, it seemed, consumed by deep, dark secrets.

There was a pedophile in the family—someone's father, who'd left people traumatized. That was heavy. When the talk shifted to our limbo experience, Dave mentioned my Dries Van Noten scarf, musing, "I wonder if that's something my brother-in-law would like."

"What?" I said. Dave surmised that one reason for his sister's substance abuse was her suspicion that her husband was cross-dressing.

"I know he's doing it, but she still isn't sure," he explained. "It's a new thing. It's only since he got out of jail that he's been a tranny . . ."

"Jail!"

And so it went. The only thing Dave ever told us that we might have guessed was, "Oh, by the way, I'm gay . . ."

But there was more: "I met this new guy. I don't even know his name. Or maybe I just don't remember . . . Anyway, the first time we were together, we recognized that we both had a lot of excess fat hanging off us. That's because we'd both had gastric bypass surgery. Imagine, what a coincidence . . ."

What a life. Every conversation with Dave led deeper down the rabbit hole of stranger-than-fiction human experience.

But his amazing openness sparked dialogues deeper than ever before between Annie and me. We'd known each other forever and been roommates, so I knew I could tell her anything. But since we hadn't spent time alone together in a while, I hadn't filled her in on some discoveries I'd been making. I'd barely admitted them to myself. So now I confided, "I think I might be gay too, but I'm not sure yet."

"Really?" Annie said. She wasn't at all shocked, but she was curious: What made me think I was gay? Was I only attracted to women? Was I in love or did I just have some great experience? What was it like? How did it happen? All the normal questions . . .

"You should try it," I told her.

"Uh, I don't think so," Annie said. "When I was in college, we all experimented, but it never flew for me. So, I'm just not into it. But thank you . . ."

"Not with me! That wasn't a come-on. I meant, in general—for romance, for fun—because I'm getting laid more than a carpet!"

Okay, that was an exaggeration, but it gave us a laugh.

It was also funny how many people claimed that they knew I was gay before I had an inkling. My old friend Cheryl recalls once telling me, "You're a lesbian." I don't remember that. Todd English had said cryptically that I plated "like a dyke." Then there were some South End lesbians who came to the Butcher Shop but weren't just drooling over the rib eye. I heard through the grapevine that they were rolling their eyes and asking, "When is she going to realize she's gay?" At one point, in an interview, I mentioned having a girlfriend and the word went out: "Finally!"

But how could they know? Was I emitting some vibe? And

even if I were, did it mean that I'd crossed a line and suddenly morphed into a new human genre? Like in the childhood rhyme, "Step on a crack, break your mother's back . . . ?" I've been among gay people all my adult life, and I've never considered "gay" to be some separate category of human being. More than changing, I felt I was expanding.

Annie had some thoughts on my possible gayness. One was that, growing up, I never experienced much love. That is true. Even as an adult, going from one long-term boyfriend straight to a husband, I didn't really have a chance to practice or experiment with relationships. So now, I'm like a plant growing toward the sun, leaning in whichever direction the rays feel strongest. Sometimes that analogy seems accurate.

Of course, I can't pretend to speak for anyone else's grasp of sexual identity—whether people, including me, are born gay or bisexual or whatever. I'm still working it out for myself.

Annie also said, "It's extraordinary how open-minded you are, how you can just go, 'I'll try that.'"

I wouldn't call it open-minded as much as curious—just being so conscious of what I don't know about the world. Curiosity was the force that drove me into the pages of Waverley Root, to travel to Italy alone, even to pipe pudding mix into pastry swan boats for Susan Logozzo's class. Sure, some of my risk-taking springs from that jump-off-the-roof, take-a-dare mentality, but often it's sparked by a spirit of discovery. My default position when encountering the unfamiliar is usually, "Until I understand it, I can't judge it." I think my sexual experimentation started with that desire to understand.

"A lot of people wouldn't be that curious," Annie said. "They'd be too scared to step outside their comfort zone."

But I was someone who never quite fit, not even in my own body. My life as a child was chaotic and crowded, with no sense of security at home. I felt like a perpetual outsider: in school, because my brain was racing; in Southie, because of my ambition; in Cambridge, Back Bay, and Beacon Hill, because of my background and accent. Even in the culinary world, when I got successful, I felt like a novelty, a pull-yourself-up-by-your-bootstraps story.

As a wife and mother, I was hardly the norm, with my crazy work hours, city apartment, need for personal space, and the sense that I was making up marriage and parenthood as I went along.

Then there was the challenge of staying creative, of keeping my business vital and fresh. Though deeply rewarding, that was like a tap dance on a treadmill in itself.

So, a comfort zone? I don't think I ever had one or even recognized the concept.

11

FORT POINT CHANNEL

Expanding was the theme of my early forties—on all fronts, professional and personal. It happened just as I thought I was settling down, getting a little bit of a life. I'd retaken control of my five restaurants, which were thriving, and I had a routine going at home. Marchesa was in preschool, and I tried to offer her extra enrichment activities that I'd never even conceived of as child. One was French for Kids, a reflection of my own regret at not being exposed early on to a different language and culture. Also, I thought it would be cool if she could help translate my French cookbooks.

The first year was fine. The main drawback was the monthly potluck, when groups of mothers took turns bringing dishes for the class lunch. And we were all mothers, not fathers—French expatriates, for the most part, trying to ensure that their kids grew up bilingual. I wanted Marchesa to feel that she belonged, so although I was one of the few working mothers in the group, I did my part.

My first contribution was a crowd pleaser: yogurt *panna cotta* with homemade blueberry jam, served in lovely vintage jars with decorative spoons and little cakes on the side. Perfect for four- and five-year-olds, yet also elegant. Next I made a selection of beautiful quiches, which everyone loved. Why the hell was I trying so hard?

Obviously, being a professional chef, I had a reputation to uphold, but an even bigger reason was that all the other mothers were French. I mean, French with a capital F, with an air of superiority over Americans when it came to food. Les Nouvelles Mères Cuisinières were less daunting than the suburban mothers at French for Kids. So no way was I slapping a couple slices of bologna or, God forbid, tuna salad with pickles, onto Sunbeam bread and calling it lunch. Every dish I was asked to bring, I sweated.

Then, one morning during the second term, Marchesa announced, "I don't want to go to French anymore. I don't want to say, 'Bonjour.'"

"Really?" I said. Late for a meeting, I was racing to brush Marchesa's hair and smooth it into a ponytail. "I'm sorry, but you have to go."

She whined and sulked, dragging ass about putting on her shoes. "Come on," I said, "Let's go. Bon-fucking-jour."

I must have told a friend because the next thing I knew, some T-shirts turned up with *BON-FUCKING-JOUR* on the front, along with a child-size version for Marchesa reading BON-F-ING-JOUR. I had to laugh, thinking, *Thank God the kids can't read well enough to understand.*

I was losing patience with the potlucks just as Marchesa was losing the will to learn French. (To be fair, she'd been on her own since Charlie and I, not speaking French, were never much help with her homework.) The last straw came the day that I was assigned to bring the class snack. I made individual servings of

delicious Tomme cheese with sprigs of Muscat grapes, still on the vine. "You can't serve grapes like that," scolded one of the mothers. "You must cut them in half."

But the kids seemed too old to choke on grapes. I took the rebuke as a sign that I was destined to translate my own French cookbooks. As Marchesa and I made our final au revoirs, I was muttering, "Bon-fuck-you" under my breath.

Around the same time, I enrolled Marchesa in classes at Boston's Museum of Fine Arts. They had a wonderful program for four- and five-year-old kids. The children would make masks and zoos full of animals, paint with watercolors, or sometimes just walk through the museum to sketch the paintings. I loved that. I was very interested in painting and could wander the galleries for hours. It reminded me of the times when Kerri and I, growing up, would hang out in the Venetian garden at the Isabella Stewart Gardner Museum, pretending to be Italian ladies. It was a magical escape into imagination.

Marchesa complained about going because none of her friends were taking art classes. I felt mean for insisting, but I knew she'd value the experience someday. Sure enough, a few years later, on a school trip to the museum, she was amazed to find how much she remembered. She was like a junior tour guide, pointing out highlights to the class. Not long afterward, she even dragged me there to show me her favorites, like the huge John Singer Sargent painting of Achilles riding the centaur, half man, half horse.

Later, when I started to paint, I got obsessed with that mural and with Sargent's genius. There's a special white light in some of his works that I kept working to re-create, studying books on his techniques. I learned that he started with thinned paint then loaded a thick layer on the brush to use in places where he wanted the colors to pop.

Marchesa continued to shadow me in the kitchen and enjoyed

cooking on her own. One of the dishes she mastered was Scrambled Eggs a L'Escoffier, which is a forty-five minute process. You melt butter in a pan over low heat, then just perfume it with a clove of garlic speared on the tines of a fork. After whisking the eggs lightly in a bowl, you very gently pour them into the pan and let them set. Every ten or fifteen minutes, you walk by and give them a tiny nudge with a rubber spatula until they're done, more heavenly and creamy than any scrambled eggs you've ever eaten. Marchesa would start her eggs, then go watch *SpongeBob*, warning, "Nobody touch them," and return to give them a little riffle at the commercials. She had her technique and timing down.

Once, Charlie made us breakfast, and I'm sorry to say that we both turned up our noses at his scrambled eggs, saying, "What's that?" like a couple of food snobs. Today I'm getting payback because Marchesa makes fun of my microwave skills. She actually stuck a note on the microwave with a big arrow pointing to the button that says "Popcorn."

Because I was working so many hours, I would have Charlie bring Marchesa into the restaurant I was managing for lunch or dinner. "Why do we always have to eat out?" Marchesa would protest. "I'm sick of it!"

"Because I need to see you," I'd tell her. "I miss you!"

And I did—and do—and love her more than life itself. I hoped that she'd understand—and maybe even appreciate—that I'd never fit into the mold of a suburban mom. With five businesses to oversee, I was wildly busy in a way I like to be—fully engaged, keeping restlessness in check. I was content.

• • •

Then, one day over lunch, Young Park, head of the development firm Berkeley Investments, described his seven miles of vacant warehouse space in Fort Point Channel. Just hearing him talk, I felt a familiar prickling, an urge to stretch that I barely knew I had. Fort Point was a ghost town of shuttered warehouses with a few colonies of settlers, but to me, it was home ground. "It can't hurt to look," I told him, thinking, *I'll be fucked if we see that building I love* . . .

Circling the blocks, we passed the old button factory and there, right across from it, stood my favorite, 348 Congress Street, with its strips of scrollwork dividing the rows of bricks and radiating from the doorway, like sunbeams. I suddenly got a powerful flash of the building's past life as a textile plant: sheep, bleating, crossing its walkway bridge to the shearing room; women gathering wool by the armful, separating the thick and thinner stands, pinching out the burrs and nits; the wool boiling, with dirty steam rising, then being forked into vats of dye, to emerge in the vibrant colors of the rainbow . . . *Boy, was I screwed* . . .

I wound up leasing a whole city block in no-man's-land. I had to wonder, *This time, have I finally gone too far?*

But some ideas that had floated in my mind for a while now came into sharper focus. If I could develop a few of them at once—creating different dining options under the same roof—my building could draw a broad clientele to an area never known for its nightlife. It could also offer Fort Point residents, who had almost nowhere to eat nearby, a choice of places to enjoy. Making the building the destination, rather than a single restaurant, could multiply my chances of success. Looking it at that way, leasing fifteen thousand square feet of space didn't seem as nuts.

Having so much space gave me the freedom to create a dream layout, including elements like a grocery receiving dock, where deliveries could be weighed, washed (produce), butchered (meat), or filleted (fish), and refrigerated in special sections, that all the dining establishments could share. Instead of focusing on the décor of the dining rooms and squeezing the kitchens into the basement, I dedicated almost half the space to well-designed cooking areas. The *Boston Globe*'s business section covered the construction, publishing the floor plans, describing all the state-of-the-art culinary equipment I was installing, and marveling at my plans for a huge prep space plus multiple finishing kitchens. What really impressed the writer, Thomas C. Palmer, was the Molteni cooking suite, with a flat high-temperature range, refrigerator drawers, and cooktops with griddles, where the staff could take a "holistic approach" to assembling plates and learning from each other. Richard Griffin, a vice president at Berkeley Investments, told the paper, "She's building the *Starship Enterprise*."

• • •

One of the businesses I definitely wanted to establish was a bar. I love dives and have done my time in them, playing the jukebox and enjoying the honest pours and old-school camaraderie. But that's not something you can create; the beauty of a dive is its authenticity. I didn't want to open a pub, either. Places like the Quiet Man embodied the best of that tradition, and there was no reason to improve on it. I certainly had no interest in developing some overdecorated, fashion-conscious spot for scene makers, with an attitude and a wine list.

So I decided to concentrate on cocktails, which didn't yet have the cachet they do today, and to serve them in a place, which I named Drink, which reimagined the bar experience.

In bars, I always got confused by the rows of bottles along the wall and never understood how someone who ordered, say, gin and tonics, could sample enough spirits to vastly prefer one brand over another. Too many of those bottles sit there moldering while the widely advertised brands get served. So, instead of having a slew of commercial gins, vodkas, and so on, I focused on finding spirits that were unique: artisanal, sourced from small distilleries, that might never make it into national distribution.

I discovered a Boston-made brand, Bully Boy Vodka, distilled from potatoes grown on the local family farm. I brought in Monkey Gin, which was almost unknown back then, from London. While you don't normally associate gin with Italy, a lot of juniper grows there, and I've begun to investigate that budding industry. Drink was one of the first bars to serve mezcal, sourced from families in Mexico who cultivate maguey, a kind of agave, which is then roasted underground for three days before fermenting. The long roasting time gives it a smokier taste than its cousin, tequila, which is made from a certain species, blue agave.

Besides serving unusual spirits, at Drink I've eliminated the back bar, with its rows of dusty bottles. The bartender never turns his or her back on you to mix a drink. Instead, there are nine little *mise en place* pans, with mint for muddling, diced lemons and limes, and other flavorings laid out in a row in front of the bartender, above refrigerators keeping the fresh-squeezed juices chilled. Also right at hand are our house-made simple syrups, bitters, and tonic water. The bartender is like a chef, creating a drink right before your eyes.

At first, some bartenders were skeptical, asking, "How the hell do you work like this?" But for John Gertsen, who developed the cocktail program at No. 9, the layout gave him the stage he deserved. He was that awesome. Now his understudy, Ezra Star, has assumed the lead role. She comes from an interesting academic background—biochemistry—which seems to dovetail perfectly with mixology.

My old friends Cheryl and Jeffrey Katz designed the bar in three horseshoe-shaped sections to make it easy for customers to see each other and, if they wanted, to connect. As Michele Carter puts it, "The Drink experience, with highly curated cocktails and a small water glass on the side—so the bartender pays way more attention to you, constantly checking in, filling your shot glass of water—and great appetizers, plus a lot of interaction, is like the best cocktail party you've ever been to."

The appetizers started out simple—fried mortadella sand-wiches, pepper jelly and crackers—and have gotten a bit more sophisticated, like steak tartare on brioche with truffle aioli, or little duck pot pies. But I've always limited the menu to finger food, served on wooden boards or in fun bowls, to keep Drink true to its identity as a bar.

Harvard and MIT have food-science programs, and my restaurants welcome students who come to explore the physics and chemistry of cooking. For example, I once participated in a contest to create better gluten-free pasta. Some doctoral students came in with little silver weights to measure the noodles' elastic-ity. The whole staff got a big kick out of that.

But we got an even bigger thrill when two sons of Harold McGee came to Drink to study our cocktails. Harold McGee is a *New York Times* columnist and visiting scholar at Harvard, whose famous book, *On Food and Cooking: The Science and Lore of the Kitchen*, launched the field of food science and is still its bible. His sons were fascinated, in particular, by our milk punch. Traditional milk punch, which dates back centuries, is a mixture of bourbon, brandy, or rum with milk or half and half. When the ingredients are blended cold, they yield a sweet, fizzy, frappe-like drink that's a famous hangover cure in New Orleans. But if the milk is heated first, it curdles, leaving milk solids to be removed by repeated filtering, which takes hours. What's left is a perfectly clear liquid that has to rest for a day or so before serving. When you taste it, you can't quite tell what it is, but it's mellow and complex, with an incredible silky smoothness.

I don't know all the scientific insights the McGees gained from their observations, but it was an honor to host them. Drink has racked up its share of formal honors as well. I was so proud when, at the 2013 Spirited Awards, presented by the international beverage group, Tales of the Cocktail, Drink was named the World's Best Cocktail Bar.

• • •

The Katzes had even more fun with my next venture, Sportello, which was inspired by Brigham's, a soda fountain on Broadway in Southie that seemed magical when I was a kid. Brigham's ice cream chain, a Massachusetts firm dating back to 1914, still sells ice cream by the quart throughout New England. Today, some of its flavors have regional meanings, like the Big Dig (vanilla, caramel, brownie bits, and chocolate chips) and Curse Reversed (vanilla with swirled fudge and chocolate-covered peanuts and caramel nibs; a name changed from Reverse the Curse after the Red Sox beat the Yankees in the 2004 World Series). But when I was young, the options were the more typical chocolate, strawberry, coffee, maple walnut, and my all-time favorite, vanilla, which was seriously good. Once, in an interview, I mentioned my love for Brigham's vanilla, and an executive took notice. The company sent me a batch of coupons in the mail—enough to keep me in ice cream for years. You can believe I used them, with joy.

One of Brigham's other claims to fame was that, in the 1940s, it introduced chocolate sprinkles or "jimmies" to Boston. For as long as there were Brigham's soda fountains, you could get jimmies free of charge on any cone or dish of ice cream.

I loved going to Brigham's with my mother, and actually worked at the branch on Park Street for a while when I was in high school. It was the kind of comfortable lunch counter you rarely see anymore, where you could park on a stool and have an excellent grilled cheese with an ice cream sundae or tuna-fish sandwich with a black-and-white frappe. When a customer came in, I'd pull the paper place mat and silverware out from under the counter, slap them down, and handwrite the order in my book of paper checks.

To one side of the counter was the ice cream freezer, with its drums of different flavors, and behind me was the flattop where a cook flipped burgers and did the grilling. Half the time either he or the manager didn't show up or vanished for hours. When they weren't there, I did it all—taking orders, cooking, dishing out ice cream, or (the worst) hand-packing ice cream into containers. That took brute strength. At those times, or whenever else I could get away with it, any cash plunked on the counter to pay a check found its way into my pocket.

By the door at Brigham's, there was a wall of gorgeous candy: saltwater taffy and gumdrops in a rainbow of colors, nonpareils (those dark chocolate disks studded with white dots)—you name it. I loved them all and could never resist stealing some. One holiday, in Susan Logozzo's home ec class, we made gingerbread houses. I shaped mine like a South End brownstone, decorated with colorful candies nabbed from Brigham's.

Down the street, there was a competing ice cream parlor, Bailey's, with a different atmosphere—marble tables, terrazzo floor, more upscale charm than the dime-store lunch-counter look of Brigham's. To me, Bailey's seemed colder, if more elegant, and Brigham's felt homey.

Brigham's was the image in my mind when I sat down with the Katzes to talk about Sportello, a name that means "counter service." I wanted the place to feel like a diner—with that promise of welcome for breakfast, lunch, and dinner—but offer the food of a trattoria (the Italian equivalent of a diner). They came up with an interpretation of a lunch counter that is sleekly modern, without corny nostalgia—two parallel U-shaped bays, so guests can see each other, fronting an open kitchen, so they can watch the food being made. As at Drink, the dining experience is interactive. The press got the concept right away. In a January 2009 dining roundup called "The Best of the New," the *Boston Globe* Sunday magazine said Sportello "looks like a gleaming white mod diner but tastes like modern Italy."

I'd envisioned Sportello partly as a hangout for the Fort Point community. The artists who'd settled there worried that my building the *"Starship Enterprise"* meant gentrification, driving them out of their homes. So I made a point of offering food service they could use: takeout coffee, espresso, yogurt, hard-boiled eggs, and homemade pastries (including *bomboloni*, or Italian doughnuts) in the morning; sandwiches and other items like chicken salad at lunch; and fresh-baked bread, cakes, pies, cookies, and other goodies all day long. To announce our launch, Sarah Hearn and Abby Gregory braved subzero cold to run a makeshift stand on the street serving free hot chocolate. It was heroic guerrilla marketing.

Sportello also had a small retail section, selling house-made chocolate bars and exquisite jams from Christine Ferber, my fellow Nouvelle Mère Cuisinière. There was an Italian section with offerings like incredible Ligurian olive oil, bronze-die-cut pasta in beautiful packaging, and fine jarred tomato sauce and *pepperoncini*. Since there was nothing else around—never mind such delicacies—the neighborhood was appreciative and very supportive.

Once we officially opened, we served full sit-down lunches and dinners with wines, the *Boston Globe* noted, "put together by wise Cat Silirie," featuring "unusual Italian grapes, all great with the food." The *Globe* praised our pasta specialties: little twisted *strozzapreti* (aka "priest stranglers") with rabbit and olive sauce; *gnudi*, poached ricotta pillows with brown butter and walnuts; and pappardelle with Bolognese and fried basil. The *Improper Bostonian* went for the *bigoli*, hearty noodles with littleneck clams, sea urchins, and flecks of salty bottarga. Even the *New York Times* weighed in, recommending the gnocchi with peas and porcini and the *baccalà*, pureed salt cod with fennel, crispy potatoes, and olives. But what pleased me most was that the *Times* reviewer caught the Brigham's connection, saying that Sportello reminded her of "an old-fashioned ice cream parlor with stemless wine-glasses instead of ice cream dishes."

When other food sources moved into the neighborhood—grocery stores, casual breakfast and lunch spots—our retail, take-out, and bakery operations stopped making sense. Since the locals didn't need those services anymore, I decided to refocus and concentrate on the restaurant's true mission: serving bright, modern Italian food. But though I could close the bakery, there is one wildly popular holdover that I just can't seem to stop serving: our sky-high coconut cake.

Yes, it was delicious, full of fresh coconut and cream, and beautiful—towering layers of snowy cake swathed in pure-white frosting. But on Sportello's menu, it was a fish out of water. It wasn't Italian. It wasn't a dessert you'd crave after eating pasta or gnocchi or gnudi. Making it was an effort that tied up a staffer for hours. But every time I tried to take it off the menu, there was an outcry. So, for long while, that coconut cake was grandfathered.

Eventually, when it came time to refresh Sportello's menu, I refocused the desserts on lighter, more authentic choices, like house-made gelati and sorbetti, that complement the entrees. Change is always tricky and can be painful, even when necessary. But serious-sweet-toothed guests seem to be finding consolation in our cannoli, crisp, delicate pastry shells with a creamy filling that changes daily.

If ever I threaten to take it off the menu, there's an outcry. So what can I do? Like it or not (and of course, I do love the taste), that coconut cake is grandfathered.

• • •

Charlie had told the *Globe* that both Drink and Sportello started off "at the pointy end of a spear," meaning that it was scary to launch restaurants in an area with a sparse population and little foot traffic. Luckily, it wasn't long before that gamble paid off. But the jewel in the crown of my Fort Point Channel development—a glamorous but unpretentious restaurant serving my interpretation of contemporary haute cuisine—was the riskiest of all.

I envisioned an elegant sixty-seat restaurant offering two options: a four-course prix-fixe meal for $95 and a seven-course chef's tasting menu for $145. But it was 2008, a depressing stretch of a seemingly never-ending recession. No one believed that diners were in the mood for a formal, expensive night out.

One of my investors noted if any pricey restaurant could weather the downturn, it was Aujourd'hui at the Four Seasons Hotel, which served travelers on top of its local clientele. But Aujourd'hui was struggling like everyplace else and would close in the summer of 2009. That just stoked my determination. It meant that there was a vacuum at the top. Still, I decided to postpone my opening for a while to give the economy a chance to rebound.

A few years before, Rux Martin, an editor at Houghton Mifflin Harcourt, had signed me to write a cookbook that would be, in her words, the story and recipes of a "raw outsider who was consumed and driven by a love of food." That pretty much sums me up. The deal was surprising because I wasn't a celebrity with a "platform," like a television show. I've never liked that kind of attention, and get my greatest satisfaction from hands-on creative work, not from talking about what I do. I don't have a restaurant in New York, which can attract the national media. Boston is my turf—where I come from—and I don't feel the need to try to "make it" anywhere else.

Still, Rux took a chance on me. Because I love (and owe) cookbooks so much, I envisioned writing the kind of cookbook I buy. When I'm in New York, I love to visit Kitchen Arts & Letters, a shop dedicated to cookbooks, founded by Nach Waxman. Nach or his partner, Matt Sartwell, greet me: "Oh, here comes the hurricane!" Then they start pulling out new, oversize, lavish food-porn books from all over the world, with gorgeous art photography.

But Rux said, "No, we want a book of recipes that you make at home."

"When am I ever home? I have five restaurants. Why would I cook?"

Distracted by expansion and motherhood, I put the project on hold. When I finally caught my breath, I thought about my vow—that my restaurants would be about education. So would my cookbook, I decided. Instead of creating some glamorous collectible, I would feel proud doing a book that anyone could use, even a beginning cook. I named it for my teaching kitchen, *Stir*.

Stir: Mixing It Up in the Italian Tradition is like a collection of greatest hits from all my restaurants. Its recipes run the gamut from appetizers like Butcher Shop beef tartare and B&G oysters with sparkling mignonette; through homemade pasta with (Butcher Shop) meat or spicy lobster Bolognese, ricotta *gnudi*, and prune gnocchi with foie gras sauce; main dishes like lobster roll with lemon aioli, spice-rubbed roast goose, and rack of lamb with fresh mint gremolata; side dishes like braised Tuscan kale, and homemade pickles and potato chips; and on to desserts like yogurt *panna cotta* and homemade apple-butter tart (sorry, no coconut cake).

I dedicated the book to Marchesa, "the best carrot peeler/sous-chef ever," which thrilled her. She sat beside me for the book launch at Stir and added her name, along with eyebrows and a smiley face, to each book I signed. At the end of the acknowledgments, I thanked Charlie "for everything"—shorthand for "more than I can say."

• • •

Meanwhile, I continued to refine the concept for the new restaurant, to be called Menton. It's named for a small French town on the Mediterranean Sea, right at the Italian border, next to Ventimiglia, Liguria. Its official symbol is the lemon because citrus trees flourish there, bearing huge, sweet lemons, oranges, and tangerines. William Butler Yeats, the great Irish poet, died there; and Jean Cocteau, the French artist and playwright, decorated some of its public spaces. Because of its charm, it's known as the Pearl of France.

The Katzes proposed a silver and gray palette for Menton's décor, which I love. White Murano glass chandeliers, hanging from the high ceilings, add a note of simple elegance. I personally chose the German porcelain dinnerware, the Austrian glassware, and the French table linens and silver. I wanted to experience the feel of a bread knife in a diner's hand and the sensual roundness of a wineglass. Everything on the table had to please the eye and be pleasurable to touch.

As the name Menton suggests, the menu echoes my two culinary inspirations, the cuisines of Italy and France. But my interpretations are more imaginative than literal. If Menton has a signature dish, it might be butter soup, which is very refined, creamy and tangy, with a velvet texture. It's made from the exquisite butter I get from Diane St. Clair's Animal Farm in Vermont. I start by boiling a little water to make a *beurre monté*, that is, whisk in chunks of butter so the mixture emulsifies. To this soup, which is not at all greasy, I add lightly poached shellfish of all kinds—clams, mussels, scallops, crabmeat, and delicate bits of lobster tail. I top it with a foamed honey emulsion and a dollop of black caviar. People go crazy for it. When I made it one year for the James Beard Awards, Audrey Meyer, the wife of Danny, the renowned restaurateur, took home a few gallons. It's one of my all-time favorites.

With the Menton concept taking shape, I had to think about personnel. The Gruppo had grown so much with the Fort Point development that it was more than I could handle. I had a great team, including a terrific operations manager, Eli Feldman, who started out as a server at No. 9. He was brilliant at hospitality. Where I needed help was on the business side. I was scared to lose control, but I had to be realistic. A company the size that mine had become needed professional management.

So Jefferson Macklin came along at just the right time. I met him through my friend (his then wife) Shannon Reed, who'd left a mass-market fashion career to start her own line of cool chef's wear, Utility Chic. After graduating from West Point, Jefferson fought in Desert Storm, then got his MBA at Darden. From there he went into the music business and wound up managing bands, including Wilco. Though he didn't have restaurant experience, his background appealed to me: a combination of military discipline and dedication, and a passion for music and fun.

He made a big presentation with a convincing pitch, to the effect that I was a small speedboat on my way to becoming a luxury liner, with his help. I was all for that. I handed over the files and said, "You're hired."

Jefferson started out strong by telling the press, "Barbara is known as a girl who grew up in Southie . . . But her business instincts continue to amaze me. I think there's something to be said about street savviness."

Colin Lynch (no relation), executive chef of the Gruppo, would oversee Menton. A decade before, he came on board as a cooking school intern at No. 9, then worked his way up from garde-manger through sous-chef all the way to the top. In a business notorious for constant job-hopping, I was proud to have lifers on my staff. Nothing made me happier than developing talented people like Eli and Colin (among many others) and giving them the opportunity to shine.

* * *

As 2009 wore on, I was getting anxious to open Menton. "It's too soon," people kept telling me. But I'd noticed that Boston, like every other city in the country, is full of steakhouses, where it costs as much to eat hunks of meat from huge commercial feedlots, plain old baked potatoes, and iceberg lettuce, while drinking ordinary booze and wine at sky-high markups, as it might cost

to dine at Menton. Of course, some steakhouses are special, but often you pay top dollar for a meal you could easily make at home on the backyard grill. Compare that typical steakhouse meal with a fine-dining experience, with food that awakens your palate, paired with expertly chosen wines, delivered through flawless service. Which is more worth the price?

During the recession, the steakhouses didn't go broke, because people always need a place where they can celebrate with food. They might be too intimidated to choose a high-end restaurant, fearing a stuffy atmosphere, snooty service, or food that's too fancy or weird. I understand that, which is why we need warm, unpretentious places where people can discover and delight in the new. I wanted Menton to be one of those places, a welcoming setting with stimulating food.

I also felt a sense of responsibility to Boston. A world-class city has restaurants where innovation is going on. They're an essential part of the cultural landscape. It was a sin that we'd lost so many. And young chefs need kitchens where they can observe and start to experiment with flavors while stretching their techniques beyond bistro food.

When I announced the launch in December, the *Boston Globe* wondered if I was doomed. In a piece called "The Gambler in the Kitchen," Bella English ticked off some reasons why: I was "launching an ultra-lavish restaurant in a weak economy that has shuttered other upscale establishments; in the middle of winter, normally an off time in the industry; and in the Fort Point Channel neighborhood, an area . . . that has yet to truly take off commercially."

The upshot: "This time she's defying convention as never before."

But I went ahead and pulled the trigger. Menton opened in spring 2010. In April, the *Globe* gave us a housewarming gift that still gives me a shiver of joy: a two-page rave in its Sunday magazine.

Devra First, the reviewer, praised the

> "ravioli stuffed with fava leaf . . . truffles flung about . . .
> like rose petals at a wedding"; "foie gras terrine . . . richness
> punctuated by sweet wine gelée . . . squiggles of rhubarb gel
> cavort exuberantly on the plate"; "a pea velouté the color of
> Kermit . . . pools around candy colors . . . tiny pink radishes,
> bright carrots, asparagus tips, elfin mushrooms . . . spiced
> with wisps of curry yogurt"; "fat langoustines with blunt
> pink tails wrapped in shredded phyllo dough"

—it was downright poetic. A pull quote read, "A Menu Offering
Maximum Pleasure"—that was my goal, exactly what I wanted
to achieve.

One paragraph that grabbed me discussed the controversy
about the opening: whether it was arrogant to open an expensive,
high-end restaurant in tough times. Devra First didn't think so
and credited the nerve it took. "Chef Barbara Lynch," she wrote,
"has quenelles of steel."

Quenelles of steel! Men have balls of steel, but how do you say
that a woman is bold? For a chef, what expression could be better?
I'd like *She Had Quenelles of Steel* to be my epitaph.

Menton would be listed in best-restaurant roundups in *Bon
Appétit* and *Esquire* and be nominated for Best New Restaurant at
the 2011 James Beard Awards.

Then, amazingly, the restaurant was inducted into Relais &
Châteaux, the prestigious international consortium of gourmet
restaurants and boutique hotels. Sophisticated travelers pay a
substantial fee to join in order to ensure that, wherever they are,
they can enjoy the finest quality accommodations and meals.
Restaurants are admitted because of their innovative cuisine and
outstanding service, confirmed by surprise visits. Of the 520
chefs scattered over five continents, only thirty-five are in the

United States. I was the only one in Boston and one of only six female Grand Chefs in the world.

All I could say was, *"Holy shit! I really fucking did it!"*

Then I went out and got the heaviest, most beautiful gold plaque I could find to hang out front, with the Relais & Châteaux designation in bold lettering. I could just hear my mother saying, "Barbara, you better make sure no one steals that. And what in God's name does it mean?"

What if I told her it meant that I'd opened a world-renowned restaurant? "Jesus Christ, Barbara, what a story," she'd say. "Some kind of château? Just where the hell do you come from?"

* * *

If professionally I was "defying convention as never before," in my personal life, I'd jumped off an even higher roof. I had fallen in love with a woman. I'll call her J.

I met her through Cheryl Katz, whom she'd consulted on an interior design project. Then, for an event, J needed a couple chefs to cook, and Cheryl recommended me. Though J was married, like me, and has two sons, we felt a visceral, electric connection. Nothing happened, but I was shaken—or awakened.

First with P, then much more so with Charlie, with no gap in between, I'd been in love, as I understood it. But my greatest passion was my work. Struggling to process the attraction I had to J, I let a few months pass before meeting her for coffee. The rush of feeling was just as powerful, irresistible. We made love then; and over the next year, stole away whenever we could for risky, secret encounters that were exhilarating.

J is a successful mixed-media sculptor whose pieces are shown and sold in art galleries. I wouldn't call myself a painter, exactly, but I thrill to the idea of pigments coming out of the earth, being mixed with egg yolk and water to make tempera, or with turpentine or linseed oil to create amazing, vibrant colors. Clay is another medium I love to work with. I take classes whenever I can and have set up a studio at home where I can lose myself in the smell and physical pleasure of daubing canvases with vivid paints. So I was fascinated by J's artistic world.

She is eccentric, which put me at ease. I've always felt a little socially off-kilter, on my home turf, certainly in suburban Winchester, and even in the food world among the celebrity chefs. It was freeing to be with an artist who saw the world differently too. J and I were always laughing our asses off and could tease each other about anything, including our own awkward, married-to-other-people romance. When I'd stay at her huge summer house in Vermont, she'd go out to garden in a weird hat, shorts, and sandals, wearing a tool belt. "Wow, now you look like a dyke," I'd say. "Am I really mixed up with you?"

J's primary home was an enormous place in the Boston suburbs. She came from a wealthy, warm Italian family, with an elderly grandmother, mother, sister, and aunts who, though all very elegant, were always shouting at each other and cooking together. One New Year's Eve, they invited me to join them in preparing the holiday meal. I'd taught J's son to make pasta, but her grandmother kept criticizing the formula, telling him, "Wait! You're adding too much flour." I'd have to counter with, "No! Just keep on the way I told you." All the back and forth was fun.

Then we all gathered around the table to make *cappelletti,* or "little hats," small filled pockets of pasta. It was an assembly line, with one person scooping up filling with a melon baller and passing it to the next, who would drop it onto a square of dough and fold to enclose it, then pass that on to be shaped by the next person, and so on. After an hour or two of this, I had to say, "You know, if you made *cappelletti* at this speed in a restaurant, you would be so fired."

"Why? How many do you think we made?" her mother asked. "Maybe ninety?"

"More like thirty," I had to tell her. We all laughed. But, after all, the company and the conversation around the table were as much the point as the number of *cappelletti*. I loved J's family, and they paid me the compliment of insisting that I was definitely Italian, not Irish.

At that point, they didn't know that I was romantically involved with J, and neither did Charlie and Marchesa. Marchesa enjoyed visiting J's suburban home because it had great play equipment, like a rock-climbing wall. I had no fucking idea what I was doing, but being with J felt good. It made me happy. The future was a blur.

Deborah Jones, who did my cookbook photography, lives in San Francisco with her lover and their daughter. She'd picked up some vibe and kept telling me, "You don't belong in that marriage. You're gay." I still wondered. At one point, I flew out to see her to get a sense of what it was like for two women to live together as a couple and raise a kid. Being the child of a single mother whose only spouse I ever knew was an irritable drunk, I didn't have much of a blueprint for any kind of partnership, straight or gay. I wanted to try putting myself in Deb's shoes.

I could see that there were differences in a female household. The two were more equal than people in most straight partnerships I'd ever seen. In straight marriages, men were usually helpless around the house (or did a little and expected praise), relying on women to run their lives. At dinner parties, the guests would segregate by sex and spend the time complaining or gossiping about things like schools and shopping, rather than all hang together and talk about ideas. These are gross, unfair generalizations, of course, but I was gathering information and puzzling over its meaning.

I returned from San Francisco without answers but leaning toward preferring the same-sex model. I wanted to feel challenged in a relationship, growing and changing, rather than settling into a routine. Somehow that seemed more possible with a woman. Since there was no cultural template for a gay relationship, with an expected role for each partner, I imagined that same-sex partners would be in a dynamic state of constant reinvention.

As I had with Annie, I sent up a trial balloon with Kerri, who knew me better than anyone, to see how my loving a woman fit into her sense of me. Irish-Catholic Southie, while we were growing up, was certainly not tolerant of difference. But to Kerri, it was no big deal. Her attitude was, "Whatever makes you happy." When Kerri told her mother, Diane, she shrugged it off too, saying, "Barbara is living her life."

• • •

When J and I had been together about a year, I knew I had to tell Charlie. I'd put it off partly because he was stressing over work. The warehouse industry had changed when the Walmarts and big-box stores got into the food business, with their own trucks and up-to-date storage facilities. Charlie's place, built in the 1930s, was like an eight-story refrigerator filled with ammonia. It seemed that every other month there'd be some crisis, like a leak or a broken elevator with a hefty price tag for repairs. Poor Charlie could never raise his rates because the competition was super stiff, so he was often skating on the financial edge.

"Why don't you shut it down?" I asked him. "We can certainly get by."

But warehousing was his family's business. He'd inherited the frozen-food warehouse, while his brother David got the dry-goods terminal where I'd worked way back when. To shut it down would feel like throwing away his legacy.

Even more important to Charlie, his employees were his second family. Most of them had worked for him for decades. Kerri had thought I worked with Q-tips at the dry-goods terminal, but by now Charlie's employees, of the same vintage, were past the Q-tip stage, some well into their seventies. Few of them would ever get another job.

That thought broke Charlie's heart. He felt responsible for his workers' welfare. That decency, loyalty, and sense of commitment are part of the reason I love him. But the problem was tearing him up inside.

The last thing I wanted was to cause Charlie any more pain.

But J wanted to tell her kids. I think her husband suspected that something was going on, and she didn't want him to break the news. So I had no more time to stall.

We were all at Ana Sortun's annual Memorial Day cookout. Ana and her husband, Chris Kurth, have a sixty-acre organic farm in Sudbury, Massachusetts, where Chris grew up, about twenty-five miles from Boston. The farm supplies beautiful, fresh-picked produce to her restaurants and a few others, including mine. For the party, the greenhouses became festive dining rooms, with long farmhouse tables.

I was making dozens of lobster rolls for the guests, mostly food-industry friends. But once J told her kids, word might leak to Charlie, so I had to pull him aside. "There's something you need to know," I began.

At first, he said only, "Hmmm . . . okay . . ." It was a lot to process.

Later, as we talked it through, he asked, "Is this a phase? The change of life? Something you needed to get out of your system?"

I didn't think so, but I honestly had no clue. On some level, Charlie was relieved that I'd fallen for another woman instead of a guy. And if it had to be a woman, at least he knew and liked J and her two boys.

"Are we getting a divorce?" he asked.

Weirdly, I hadn't considered it. Charlie and I were intertwined, to some extent professionally in that he'd helped me build the business and had remained my truest ally, but even more because we shared a daughter. We'd be in each other's lives forever. But we didn't live together full-time, so my romance with J wasn't destroying a household rhythm. Couldn't we keep the same pattern of space and connection without putting Marchesa through the pain and upheaval of divorce?

"We're great parents, and we can still be," I told Charlie. "You're a fantastic father."

It was true. He'd risen to the challenge of caring for three kids alone after his wife's death. When Marchesa came along, she united us as a family; and Charlie, as our friend Sarah Gulati puts it, having reached a life stage when he was no longer "rushing," experienced a "rebirth." We'd visit the Gulatis at their summer place in Gloucester, where Charlie would help Marchesa, as a toddler, climb over the rocks to the water's edge. There, he let Marchesa explore, turning over stones, peering into the water to spot the little fish, just "enjoying her inquiring mind . . . He was so patient," Sarah said.

Now Charlie was patient with me too. A more straitlaced husband would have hauled me into court in a heartbeat. But Charlie had already enjoyed a traditional marriage and recognized that ours would be different (though even I didn't expect that it would be *this* different). He "got me"—accepting my restlessness, my impulsiveness, my relentless work drive, my need for solitude. He knows who he is and was secure enough in himself to give me what some might consider a lot of breathing room.

Over the coming months, we functioned as a unit that must have looked strange from the outside. We all spent that Christmas Eve with J's family, the women with whom I'd made *cappelletti*—J and I as a couple, J's sons, and Charlie and Marchesa as my guests. It was awkward, but, with the truth known, I felt unchained. Charlie's family, unshockable, was more accepting.

Then, I threw a benefit party for the charity I worked to organize, the Barbara Lynch Foundation, at the Boston Children's Museum. My old Southie crew was there, including Tina, Cheryl, Mary, and Kerri, all sitting together with Charlie and various members of my family. At the end of the night, when I took the mike to thank the guests, I came out publicly, acknowledging J as my lover.

Mary laughed in sympathy. Kerri had known the announcement was coming. Cheryl said, "What's funniest is that no one even blinked an eye."

The definition of convention—and what it took to defy it—was expanding.

12

QUENELLES OF STEEL

One day in 2012, a Bravo TV scout called me to ask, "Are there women in your company who'd like to compete on *Top Chef*?" The popular reality show, which pits up-and-coming chefs against each other in cookoffs, has raised the profile of restaurant cooks in general and boosted the careers of its winners. So I was delighted to recommend two, sous-chefs Kristen Kish and Stephanie Cmar from Stir. They were friends as well as colleagues, with matching spoon tattoos.

Kristen didn't want to do it, but I pushed her. "You have to," I said. "You're a fantastic cook, and you're perfect for TV"—not just beautiful, willowy, and tall, which of course were assets, but also tough and assertive, a real leader. I wanted her to compete on behalf of women in professional kitchens, who even in the twenty-first century, according to Bloomberg News, hold only 6.3 percent of the head-chef jobs in prestigious restaurant groups. I was positive that Kristen could win.

I had tremendous faith in Stephanie, too, though she was less experienced. Letting both of them go compete really gutted Stir, but they deserved a shot.

The whole Gruppo cheered them on. Kristen and Stephanie couldn't breathe a word about the shows until they aired, so every Wednesday night, I'd throw a *Top Chef* party at my place in Southie for anyone who wanted to watch. My parties had food themes, like Marrow Night, when we roasted and scooped out something like fifty bones. Stephanie, who was eliminated in the first round, was invited to return in a later season, but for the first ten episodes, Kristen was going strong.

There was a cliffhanger in episode 11, when Kristen got kicked off because of her team's problems in developing a pop-up restaurant. "Noooo!" We all booed. But Kristen slugged her way back into the race by defeating all the other kicked-off chefs in "Last Chance Kitchen." In the finale, she went head-to-head with Brooke Williamson, the chef and co-owner of two Los Angeles restaurants. All the while, Kristen said, she kept an inspirational note from me in her pocket, as a good-luck charm. I guess it worked. We all howled and clapped and stomped when Kristen won. She was only the second woman named Top Chef in the show's first ten seasons.

I was so proud of both of them. I promoted Stephanie to sous-chef at No. 9, then let her take over the Butcher Shop in the morning for three weekends in a row to try out Stacked Donuts, her pop-up venture. It was a massive hit, selling out its entire first batch of 230 donuts—a choice of citrus-glazed with candied blood-orange peel, or Boston cream pie—within the first twenty minutes of opening. The next day, 500 donuts were gone within less than an hour. Clearly, Stephanie was onto something—*Zagat* called it "donut hysteria"—that was worth pursuing. She left the Gruppo with my blessing and congratulations.

Kristen was headed more in the fine-dining direction. Though she was locked into Bravo appearances for the year ahead, I promoted her to chef de cuisine at Menton in order to give her that high-level experience, as well as a chance to learn the Relais & Châteaux dining protocols. Like the traditional Escoffier service guidelines, the rules were strict: no computers in the dining room, fresh flowers as an amenity, and a waitstaff team, headed by a captain, for each table, just to give a few examples. With her elegance, technical precision, and attunement to detail, Kristen seemed like a good candidate to join me one day as a Grand Chef.

I took her with me to London to do a Relais & Châteaux dinner. Of course, we were the only women among the four or five teams of chefs, each responsible for one course of the lavish meal for a hundred guests. The place was a sea of men in bobbing white toques.

The chef ahead of us was constructing one of those food-tableau dishes, positioning elements with tweezers. There were so many steps that it was taking forever, so Kristin and I offered to help. Being a European guy, he blew us off, intent on demonstrating his technique, but also because he couldn't believe that Kristen was a chef. She was too attractive, he thought. Though he kept hitting on her, he wasn't impressed enough by her beauty to clean up his mess. We practically had to power-wash the station before we could start our own prep.

Meanwhile, though Kristen was reluctant to tell me, she'd been facing some tough challenges at Menton. Because of her Bravo commitments (and occasional travels with me), she wasn't working in the kitchen as much as other staffers. There seemed to be some animosity about that, or maybe jealousy—both over her *Top Chef* win and over our working relationship. I'm not always the most congenial person, as a colleague or as a boss. I'm introverted and can seem prickly and withdrawn. Some perhaps resented what they considered the special attention and privileges I was giving Kristen.

As for Kristen's new visibility, I've always encouraged my chefs to get airtime. Any television appearance, especially on a national broadcast, is fantastic publicity for my restaurants. When I'd push Colin Lynch to go on shows like *Top Chef*, he'd say, "I'm not that person. I'm not that competitive." I respected that, especially since I feel the same way. I'm slightly phobic about TV and can seem "a bit scowly," as *Grub Street* once said. But I think it's critical for female chefs to get television exposure, to counter the pervasive stereotype of the male "god of food," as a November 2013 *Time* magazine story dubbed the chefs on its "most influential" list, which totally omitted women. So I like to think I'm getting better at it.

When Kristen was deluged with job offers and wanted to leave, I wasn't surprised. "Go for it!" I told her. "If you don't feel respected and supported in your work, it's just too exhausting. Besides, you're riding a wave now that won't last forever. This is the chance of a lifetime."

●   ●   ●

During this time, my day-to-day involvement with the Gruppo had begun to shrink, almost without my knowing it. Part of the reason was the expectation that I'd earn enough in fees to cover the salary of my assistant, Sarah Hearn. The bigger aim, which I embraced, was raising the restaurants' profile in and beyond Boston. But maintaining an "onstage" persona night after night both exhausted and unnerved me—showmanship is not my strength—and I felt alienated from the world I'd created. I was traveling so much that I barely even got a chance to try out the Molteni cooking suite.

But there was one invitation I was thrilled to accept. Caroline Kennedy was appointed US ambassador to Japan, and she asked me to cook for her Fourth of July party at the embassy.

The preparations were nerve-racking. For one thing, there was no budget for me to take a team, so I had to go alone, to

work with the embassy chef and kitchen staff. I hadn't traveled by myself since my first trips to Italy, where, through a combination of naïveté and ADD, I got so confused that I still felt a bit traumatized. How would I function in Japan, which had a different alphabet, a language of which I couldn't guess a word, and a culture that was a complete mystery? I didn't even understand the cuisine, beyond sushi and the fusion cooking described in books by my hero, Gualtiero Marchesi.

But the Kennedys I knew—not personally, but as Boston's (and America's) First Family. Whenever Caroline had eaten in my restaurants, I felt deeply honored. So I planned a classic New England meal, the kind that I knew she had to be missing: seafood chowder, lobster rolls, and apple tarts for dessert. An all-American spread for Independence Day.

When I arrived in Japan, I was completely bewildered by the airport. The driver waiting for me looked at my tote bag and asked, "Is that all you have?" Somehow I'd left the secure area without collecting my luggage, since—bleary from the long flight and thrown off by the noise and signs—I hadn't spotted the baggage claim.

But I loved the Hotel Okura where they put me, a five-minute walk from the embassy. It felt like midcentury America, right down to the US Army frequency on the old in-room radios. The embassy attaché who welcomed me was new on the job, and it showed. When he went to shake my hand, a mess of condom packets fell from his pocket. For a minute everyone froze. To break the ice, I said, "Look at that. Multiple sizes?" The attaché blushed, the translator laughed, and all the polite Japanese women standing off to the side went, "Hee hee hee." The incident became the talk of my visit.

Caroline Kennedy doesn't do a lot of television, so she stunned her staff by agreeing to do a food show with me. The Japanese film crew sent over a hair and makeup team. It wasn't until I saw the footage that I realized the stylist trained my hair into a little flip, just like Caroline Kennedy's. Were they trying to make me look like a member of her family?

The diplomatic protocols were a pain. With the film crew standing by, Mr. Multiple Sizes put me through a two-hour tutorial on using chopsticks, napkins, and other tableware. "Couldn't we have done this beforehand, so we didn't keep people waiting?" I asked. "I'm so embarrassed—and I don't need a lesson."

"You have to use everything properly," he insisted. To me it seemed much ruder to hold up a film shoot than to risk some gesture that was culturally off base. The fact that Mr. Multiple Sizes disagreed, expecting perfection, sent my performance anxiety through the roof.

At last I was sufficiently schooled. Then he called in my hostess, Caroline Kennedy. After exchanging greetings, I couldn't help but blurt out, "A fucking two-hour chopsticks class? Seriously?"

She looked at me with just the sliver of a smile and said, "Mm-hmmm."

Now I was really mortified. "Uh—what did I just say?" I wondered, out loud. "Who the hell am I talking to?"

At that, Caroline Kennedy laughed. She never seemed high-and-mighty but always very human—shy and nervous. At the end of the show, she said, "Will you wrap up this food for me and stick it in the fridge? Later on, I want to finish it."

Hell, yes, I thought. I found that so endearing. *Girl, I've got you covered.*

Then I finally felt that I could breathe—that I'd satisfied my hostess and I'd earned the right to relax. I spent a couple of weeks touring the country, seeing places like the Mitsubishi factory, full of hundreds of men in uniforms—khaki coveralls or white shirts and black pants. "Where are the women?" I asked.

Mostly, they were at home. They are completely bound up in child care or elder care, more so than in the United States. I had a flash image of day-care centers designed for both groups, with a raised floor on the children's side, so the elders and youngsters could connect at eye level. Wouldn't that be something?

I also had a chance to meet with women who were would-be entrepreneurs at a culinary school. In Japan, they have even more limited opportunities than we do, which means almost no support. Some of them stood in line for as long as four hours to talk to me about how I founded a business. I'd love to go back and encourage them, if only by example.

I'd also like to spend some real time in Japan—like a month or two—absorbing more of their rich culture. There's such a reverence for beauty, even in everyday objects. One of their ancient arts I'd love to study is working with lacquer.

• • •

Back in Boston, there were problems at Menton. To me it was the special child, the one that would always need extra nurturing. Rather than count on a clientele—even with stunning reviews and Relais & Châteaux—we'd have to develop and earn that customer base. Restaurants perceived as expensive have to build a reputation, to become known as the best place in town for a special occasion or just a magical night. From the time we opened the doors in 2010, I'd figured that it would take Menton a decade to get that entrenched and really hit its stride.

So a few years in, we weren't seeing much of a profit, which I half-expected. To me that meant it was time to tweak, not panic or trash the original vision. I believe that the other daunting factor, beyond price, in fine dining is time. People don't always want to commit to investing a few hours in working their way through a tasting menu's scads of courses. So I thought we should consider an à la carte option, to give diners more control. We could add some salads and sides, plus a couple desserts, along with entrée-size dishes instead of the smaller tasting plates. That's the formula I've had at No. 9 Park—two separate menus, one tasting and one à la carte—and for going on twenty years, it's worked very well.

But I felt that no one listened. Never mind that I was the one who conceived and built the entire restaurant group, the one with decades of experience in the food world. Not only was my perspective dismissed, but it was suggested that I change my title from chef-owner to CEO/founder. That had a has-been ring to it, which should have been a sign. It was as if I were becoming a figurehead or a logo—the company's face for marketing and promotion but no longer its guiding force.

• • •

On the personal front, life was equally complicated. J's husband had initiated divorce proceedings. Though J was miserable in her marriage and wanted the split, it put a huge strain on our relationship. Since a lot of money was tied up in the marriage, it proved difficult to unravel. Inevitably, I got dragged in and was expected to meet with mediators, lawyers, and therapists—to share in the whole nightmare.

All the while, I was struggling to gauge what was happening in my business, fearing that, again, I'd lost control. Amid my travel and publicity commitments, I had to squeeze in time for Marchesa and Charlie. So I was pulled in too many directions, physically and psychologically, to offer much emotional support to J, who was growing increasingly needy and feeling unmoored.

• • •

At the Gruppo, when I asked for financial information, I often felt that I was being stonewalled. *Would a male superior be dismissed that way?* I wondered. I was like an intruder, unwelcome in my own restaurants.

The truth was undeniable—I had founded a mini-empire, employing hundreds of people, based on my personal, creative vision of food. But there was a disconnect: somehow I was sidelined, not at the center, as if my involvement had been incidental. Year after year, I'd show up on lists like *Boston* magazine's "50 Most Powerful" people or women in the city. Yet within my own company, I'd become the "brand" instead of the boss. Even people I trusted seemed to accept my marginalization. It was like being gaslighted.

Estranged from the world I had built out of thin air, for God's sake, I was lost. Cooking had been at the core of my identity since my teens. I'd worked like a demon—and for what? The planet had shifted on its axis, tipping me off it.

I'd been in perpetual motion all my life, and now, suddenly, I was stuck in a crazy, painful restlessness I couldn't exhaust through hard, physical work. I was hyper, angry, and hopeless—consumed by what I now know was clinical depression. That disease didn't exist in Southie when I was young, but I'd definitely caught it.

•　•　•

One fall day in 2014, Cat, Jefferson, and Sarah Hearn showed up at my door. They were on a mission. "We're concerned about you," they said. "We want you to go away for a while."

By "go away," they meant check into rehab for a few months—that, as the saying goes, I'd become powerless over alcohol. In the work-hard, play-hard restaurant world, with brutal hours and killer stress, lots of people have substance issues. Fewer kitchens are coke-stoked than in the past, but with fine wines and spirits always on hand, drinking is an occupational hazard. Certainly, alcohol lubricated every Gruppo promotion I'd hosted—champagne meet and greets, appetizers with drink pairings, demonstration dinners with flights of wines. I own what's been called the best cocktail bar in the world, for Christ's sake, though I myself can't metabolize liquor. That's ironic.

Of course, it wasn't just restaurant work that predisposed me to excessive drinking. It was also where I come from, and when. What today we'd consider alcohol abuse was standard operating procedure back then, in the larger culture, and more so in Southie. We drank and did drugs every weekend in our early teens, to the point that Tina wound up in AA (which didn't take then, but she has now been sober for decades, earned advanced degrees, and is regional director of a major social service agency).

But Tina's family was the exception. Most were much slower to acknowledge the dangers of drinking, even though four trashed kids collided with a bus and died; even as fathers (usually) got kicked out of the house for boozing—including my own, who died of alcoholism. Two of my brothers were headed down that path but got sober—one for thirty years—and my sister was hooked on drugs. That was our world. Intoxication was the Irish flu, the Irish scourge.

I wasn't immune to it. That wasn't exactly news. On plenty of mornings, I'd been told, "Boy, you sure had fun last night," usually by a hungover partner in crime. "Yeah," I'd say, racking my brain, trying to remember. As my mood spiraled downward, I had more of those nights and mornings, which deepened my depression. I hated the whole fucking cycle.

So I didn't deny what my visitors were saying. I blew off a little steam, but I didn't put up a fight about treatment. But I wasn't going to check in someplace. "Whatever help I need I can right here in Boston," I said. Nor did I express a shred of remorse. I might have risked my own health (maybe, once or twice, my life), but I'd never done anything to harm the business. That's what I cared about most.

* * *

I was forty-nine years old. I'd started working in my midteens. So, whatever challenges I was having with alcohol, another deep addiction I had to master was thirty-plus years of workaholism. My cure for whatever ailed me was action, part of which was probably an expression of my ADD. That drive was a great engine when I was teaching myself to cook, exploring the world, training in restaurants, and then starting my own But I'd been pushing so hard that I didn't know how to find my own dimmer switch or "pause" button.

A lover once joked that when I was asked, "How do you feel?" I'd say, "What's a feeling?" Truthfully, I didn't quite know. I had insecurities, worries, and bursts of emotion—joy, enthusiasm, anger, excruciating boredom, impatience, irresistible impulses, and so on. It was hard to imagine being in the eye, rather than in the full fury of the storm—to be in a resting state, of just being myself, without distraction.

The cusp of fifty seemed the perfect time to assess and, maybe, change my life. So I put myself in the hands of two terrific therapists, who got me properly medicated for the first time, while helping me recognize that, besides hitting the bottle too hard, I had more long-standing problems to handle. For one thing, it had been about a year since the news from Whitey Bulger's trial unleashed a flood of impressionistic memories of the rape. Those scary, stomach-churning images had been kicking around my psyche, unprocessed. Then, of course, there were the classic issues—absent, alcoholic father; impossible-to-please, unaffectionate mother; difficult environment growing up—on down through sexual identity. Luckily, I also had strengths to build on: creativity, curiosity, and long and loving friendships, to name a few.

So I hunkered down and got to work on myself. I went to therapy. I ate healthy food. I boxed for exercise. I painted constantly. I stopped drinking.

Weeks passed, and I wrote: *December 9, 2014. 70 Days Sober. And loving it! Well, not all of it. I do love the healthy me, the less tired me, the less stressed me. But I must be honest and say I do miss wine, like a great glass of Burgundy with cassoulet on a snowy, blizzardy New England day; crisp Chablis with oysters and lobster; and a great Saison beer with a hanger steak, Bernadine sauce, and fries . . .*

I hung out with Marchesa. With my relentless promotional schedule, being gone all the time, I'd missed her. I found Charlie to be a trustworthy listener and a great, helpful sounding board, offering an honest, clear-eyed appraisal of everything that had gone on.

I spent time developing the project that had long fascinated me, B. Lynch Made. It's a line of dehydrated vegetables, with each 2.5-ounce box containing a one-pound mixture of different varieties that you reconstitute by adding boiling water. The mixture can be a stew or soup on its own, or with added proteins, a full meal. I'd begun working on the idea back at Plum Produce, but now I could look at drying ovens and other equipment, as well as plan the product rollout. I got talked out of the name I really wanted to use, F'ing Easy, which I found catchy and funny, but which I have to admit it may be too edgy.

All told, I dedicated about eight months to cultivating my own well-being. How many of us ever get to do that in a lifetime? It should be mandatory, especially for women, who are so programmed to put the needs of others first. What started out seeming like punishment—being banished for my sins—turned out to be a luxury I never would have allowed myself: the chance, as I was turning fifty, for a full tune-up.

●　●　●

During that time, inevitably, I also examined my relationship with J. By then we'd been together about three years. Her divorce had come through, leaving her with a comfortable lifestyle. To her credit, she'd made it as an artist, but she'd never had to make a living, having grown up with money and advantages. The concept of work being your identity, of your creation being as much a part of you as an organ or a limb, was foreign to her. So as the conflict at the Gruppo escalated, I don't think she understood, at a gut level, what was at stake for me, a person who'd come from nothing.

She also wasn't temperamentally wired for independence. Maybe she was grieving her divorce, but she seemed to crave much more time and attention than I had to give. Not only was I stretched to the breaking point between my business and my own family, but to keep my equilibrium, I've always needed psychic space. In my twenties, I wasn't kidding when I said I wanted to marry an astronaut, who'd leave me in peace for long stretches. That was even less of a joke in my late forties. J wanted fusion; I wanted boundaries.

Now that I was in therapy, grappling with my relationship with my mother, I could see that I was playing out some of those tough old patterns with J. As with my mother, I felt judged, like I was always coming up short. I kept striving to please her—resenting the effort I was making—only to feel that it was never enough. I loved J, and I adored her children—the thought of no longer seeing them broke my heart—but I knew that I couldn't make her happy.

I also recognized that I wasn't going to jump into a marriage again. The partnership I have with Charlie, raising Marchesa and sharing in his now-adult children's lives, is a sustaining bond I'll never abandon. My work will always be a consuming force in my life. So I broke it off with J, convinced it was for the best. Neither of us could benefit by beating her head against the other's stone walls.

● ● ●

The other stone wall I'd been beating my head against was the Gruppo, with my sense of being invisible and unheard.

I'd been reading *No Ordinary Time* by Doris Kearns Goodwin, a biography of Franklin and Eleanor Roosevelt. I was struck by the way Eleanor, pushed out of her role as First Lady, found purpose in visiting wounded troops, helping to resettle European war refugees, and working for civil rights in the United States. At first I identified with her marginalization and felt inspired by her example—until I realized that I wasn't supposed to be the First Lady but the president!

But I tried hard not to dwell on the negative. I had to stay focused on the future of the company and the role I wanted to play in it. I might not have excelled in management or marketing, but I had vision and creativity. I could spot talent and help employees grow, earning their loyalty. As my track record showed, I knew how to make money. Until I got straight what I wanted, I planned to keep my eyes open and my ears to the ground.

Another area I wanted to focus on was the Barbara Lynch Foundation. It's a nonprofit I set up in 2012 to sponsor nutrition education and other food-related programs for inner-city kids. Our very first project, called "Meet the Worms," focused on gardening and farming, as well as cooking, in a South End school; and the following year, in partnership with the Cookbook Project and City Year, we helped train fifty-five food-literacy educators for third- through fifth-graders. I loved the program and wanted to see it expand throughout the city.

In April 2015, the foundation hosted two benefits on the same weekend: one an exclusive Relais & Châteaux dinner with a high price tag, and the other called Toques and Tonic, which was open to the public, with cheaper tickets, held at the Boston Children's Museum. As in the past, Toques and Tonic was totally sold out; it had become the city's top culinary fundraising event. But I was disappointed in the marketing for the Relais & Châteaux dinner, which I thought should have drawn more patrons.

At that point, I'd been on semihiatus for about six months.

When I got to the museum, all my chef pals were setting up their stations, but for some reason I was ushered to a room on the second floor. When the guests arrived, someone else—not me—played designated host, greeting them. My name was plastered all over the room, the chefs were all there at my personal invitation, and yet I felt shunted aside in the same way that I'd been at the Gruppo.

To add insult to injury, the upstairs room where they had me sequestered as the festivities got under way was evidently the repair shop. There was a sign over the door reading, *BROKEN, CAN BE FIXED*.

But a turning point came for me at that party when E. B. Maul, my head of human resources, who'd started out as a server at No. 9, came up to me and said, "Chef, I want you to know that I work for *you*."

•   •   •

That vote of confidence meant a lot. So did the support of my investors.

I had been demoralized enough—almost—to consider retreating into a new role, like developing B. Lynch Made. But now, with my strength and self-possession restored, I knew what I had to do. I spent the rest of the day calling the senior staff—all my general managers and executive chefs—to say, "Jefferson's no longer with us." They all thanked me for telling them personally. I let the dust settle for a few days, then for the first time in eight months, I chaired the staff meeting.

At first a couple investors were leery, asking, "Well, who's going to run the company now?"

"I am," I said. "Remember I'm the one with the track record. So hang on . . ."

I knew I had to rebuild a lot of trust. But I had the quenelles to do it.

13

GLOUCESTER

Now that I'd recovered my fighting spirit, I could finally appreciate that the past year or two, when I'd been lost in despair, had not been all doom and gloom. In fact, I'd had some shining moments.

One was an invitation to speak at the MAD3 Symposium in Copenhagen, an annual conference sponsored by René Redzepi. Redzepi, founder of the celebrated two-Michelin-star restaurant Noma, is a pioneer of New Nordic Cuisine, developed with the native, seasonal flora and fauna of Scandinavia. The ingredients are often unfamiliar and fascinating—lichens, mosses, seaweeds, and herbs like beach mustard and woodruff—and the methods of preparation traditional to regions with long hard winters, like fermenting, smoking, and salting. Redzepi launched a culinary movement by foraging for his ingredients in the wild. He is extraordinary, a true original.

Mad means food in Danish, and the yearly conferences focus on exploring the idea that (as its mission statement says): "Good cooking and healthy environment should go hand in hand, and the quest for a better meal can leave the world a better place . . . MAD is committed to . . . taking promising ideas from theory to practice."

I was invited to speak by MAD's guest curator David Chang, the badass chef-founder of the Momofuku empire, offering elevated-casual, Korean-accented dining. Chang supposedly chose the name Momofuku both to honor the inventor of instant ramen noodles and because it sounds like "motherfucker." I love that.

I'd just met David in June 2013, a couple months before the symposium, at the Aspen *Food & Wine* Classic. We were both staying at the Hotel Jerome, where he was hanging out with Wiley Dufresne of wd~50, the godfather of American molecular gastronomy, and some other modernist chefs I usually admired from afar. They were the hip guys with exotic influences and kitchens tricked out like chemistry labs, who turned everyday ingredients into new food forms, while I was a more traditional Mediterranean-influenced chef, interested in sensuality instead of science.

"Have a beer with us," David said. I joined them, feeling not 100 percent cool enough for school.

But I had a blast. David and I kept talking as people came and went from our group, mostly about how grateful we were to have discovered our true vocations. Then we got hungry, but the hotel kitchen had closed. "I'll go get a couple of pizzas," David said. "And we need some wine and beer."

"Great, I'll see what I can find."

The only place open was a gas station, where I loaded up on beer, peanut M&Ms, Pringles (sour cream and onion, since I didn't have caviar and crème fraîche to serve with them), and Marlboro Lights. We smoked the same brand. So we were all set.

We stayed up laughing and shooting the shit till dawn. David told me about the symposium, hosting some six hundred food professionals, from rebels to aristocrats, from all over the world. The theme that year was "Guts." "Your story would fit right in," David said. He convinced me to come and give a talk.

Guts can mean different things, including the intestines pulled warm out of a pig's carcass by the first speaker, Tuscan butcher Dario Cecchini, addressing the need for carnivores to be compassionate and responsible. He was followed by Vandana Shiva, the Indian community-seed-bank and sustainable-agriculture activist; Roy Choi, the Los Angeles chef and food truck king, who half-spoke, half-rapped on combating food poverty; and others, twenty-six in all, including me. What amazing, inspiring company. When I concluded my story of growing up in Southie, there was wild clapping when I said that the key to success was being honest and fearless and having "quenelles of steel."

Of course, in Copenhagen, I ate at Noma, where I bumped into one of my all-time heroes, Alain Ducasse. As I passed his table, I said, "Ça va?" in attempted French, meaning, "How's it going?" and he said it back to me. I didn't sit down, but we had a brief, fun conversation about our meal, which featured elements like pickled ferns, dehydrated deer moss, and kelp.

"Surprising, eh?" I said. The food was fucking delicious, especially paired with some dynamite biodynamic wines.

"And you can't beat the food costs," I added, since the ingredients were obviously foraged. Chef humor.

On the way back to Boston, I stopped in Iceland, where they bury rye bread dough in the ground for twelve hours to bake by geothermal energy. Amazing!

• • •

Then in May 2014, I became only the second woman to win the James Beard Award for Outstanding Restaurateur, given for setting "the highest national standards in restaurant operation and ownership." It was an umbrella award for all the restaurants in the Gruppo, with No. 9 Park, Menton, and B&G specifically mentioned. That was huge, and humbling.

• • •

In September, Daniel Boulud opened his version of a semicasual restaurant in Boston. His flagship restaurant, Daniel, one of the few restaurants in Manhattan to earn multiple Michelin stars, is more formal and serves the finest contemporary French cuisine. I love Daniel, who's a generous mentor and also a great believer in giving back to the community, especially through his favorite charity, Citymeals on Wheels, which he's supported for decades.

In 2008, the legendary Paul Bocuse, who thirty years ago set up the Bocuse D'Or—popularly known as the Olympics of food, in which teams from twenty-four countries compete—tapped Daniel to set up a screening process for the US team. Today, he, Thomas Keller, and Jérôme Bocuse run the screening, inviting chefs from around the country to judge the contestants in a range of food categories. I had been a judge in 2012 and helped pick the finalists for the 2013 Bocuse D'Or. The competition is held every other year in Lyon, France.

Daniel had invited me to come to Lyon in 2015, not to compete but as a member of "Les Ameriques sera place sous la direction de Daniel Boulud"—the elite team he was assembling to prepare a gala dinner at the Hotel de Ville for some 250 award-winning chefs. But it was not until the opening party for Bar Boulud, Daniel's new Boston place, that he told me what I was supposed to cook. "You are on fish," he said. I was thinking lobster until he added, "No shellfish—someone else is doing that." Then he delivered the final blow: "And it has to be served at room temperature."

Shit! What kinds of fish would be available in January and taste good at room temperature?

I recruited Colin Lynch to join me on the team, and together we came up with an interesting solution: cod poached in whey, which gave it a smooth texture. We served it with lots of truffle slices and truffle vinaigrette, over celeriac puree with just a hint of ginger. It was like a deconstructed French-ish interpretation of New England fish chowder.

A lot of the trip played out like a Lucille Ball routine. Colin and I took the red-eye and so arrived at our respective hotels hungry and badly in need of a nap and a shower. Though my room wasn't ready, I didn't worry because our itinerary said we had the day to relax. So it was a surprise to get a call from Daniel asking me to meet him in half an hour to check the setup. I begged for a little more time, got picked up by his guy, and spent the afternoon rearranging equipment. Then, just as I was about to escape, Daniel asked me to talk to the press. "How many chefs were coming?" the reporters asked. "How many women were among them?" I had no fucking idea. Day one blown . . .

The next morning I couldn't explain to the concierge that I had to leave—"Right now! This minute!"—dressed in the chef's wear I'd sent down for pressing the night before but hadn't received. Not even with my handy Pictionary. Finally the clothes showed up, and the hotel put me in a car to go meet Daniel. The ride took forever. When we arrived, I didn't recognize the place at all. Then I spotted a toque with Thomas Keller under it. *Holy shit!* I was at the Bocuse d'Or competition site, not the Hotel de Ville.

I called Daniel, who was furious. But by pushing the driver to go NASCAR, I managed to get there somewhat but not disastrously late.

What a Who's Who that dinner was. Every master chef in France seemed to be there—Frédy Girardet, Marc Veyrat, Alain Ducasse, Alain Passard, and Alain Senderens, to name a few. My head was spinning. It struck me that if the earth cracked open and they all fell in, we'd lose the culinary brain trust of just about the whole past century.

The next day, I had one of the greatest lunches of my life at Bocuse's own restaurant in Lyon, a brightly painted building with his name in huge, lighted letters rising out of the roof. Inside, the ceilings are beamed, the walls patterned or wainscoted and covered with photos and larger-than-life murals, and the initials PB stamped on the silverware. It's a glorious if fussy celebration of a long, illustrious life.

But all the decorations can't compete with the splendor of the food: the renowned truffle soup with a puff-pastry crown, invented in 1975 for President Giscard d'Estaing; the foie gras with pistachios; and the Bresse chicken, a special French breed, cooked in a pig's bladder, which arrives at the table like a full, round moon. (That inspired me to give Lydia Shire a pig bladder for Christmas. Imagine finding that under the tree—she loved it.) Any one of those dishes was worth enduring dozens of travel mishaps.

I think Daniel forgave those mishaps because I've been commissioned to design and paint the promotional poster for the next Bocuse d'Or. What an honor! But scary, because at the easel, as opposed to the stove, I am just a passionate amateur. Not that lack of training has ever stopped me before . . .

● ● ●

In 2015, my two great loves, cooking and painting, came together in an even more surprising invitation. I became the artist-in-residence for a month at the Isabella Stewart Gardner Museum. They'd never had a chef-in-residence before, so my role was wide open. I got to stay in a cool apartment in the new Renzo Piano wing of the museum, and after dark, I had the run of the place, by flashlight.

When we were kids, Kerri and I used to visit the Gardner more for the building than for the artworks. The museum was modeled on a Venetian palazzo and furnished with European antiques. We loved to act like grand dames waltzing through the airy, high-ceilinged rooms with tall cathedral windows and candelabra on the walls. Our favorite place was the interior courtyard, with its garden blooming year-round under a magnificent, peaked glass roof. Looking up from its mosaic floor, you were ringed by archways with balustrades trailing flowering vines, from which you could imagine lords and ladies in lavish gowns looking down at you. It was like traveling back in time.

But there was one painting that always grabbed me: a portrait of Isabella Stewart Gardner in Venice, throwing open French doors to see the fireworks flashing over the Grand Canal. Isabella seemed so alive, in motion, not stodgy and posed, like people in most old paintings. I could almost hear the fireworks exploding and feel Isabella urging her friends to come and see. I also loved her pearl necklace, dangling halfway to her knees, which seemed very modern and cool.

So that Isabella painting, by Anders Zorn, was one of the first things I visited during my residency. Then I went on a vision quest, studying other pieces in the museum to see what they evoked in me. I wanted to create dishes capturing the spirit of the artworks, without representing them literally. With the eyes of a chef attuned to presentation, I carefully studied the compositions and spatial relations of the works' elements, trying to imagine how I'd "plate" them.

I also thrilled to the colors. Years ago, when I took my first painting class, my technique was shit and I didn't even know the difference between oils and acrylics. Still, everyone said, "Wow, you have an amazing palette," meaning a sense of color developed through working with food. The teacher actually called it a "farmer's palette."

Working with the staff botanist, I harvested vivid red eugenia berries from the museum gardens and covered gardenias in sugar, letting them crystallize. Fascinating stuff. Then, inspired by artworks, I came up with four special dishes to serve donors in the museum's Café G.

I'd fallen in love with stained glass. So for the appetizer, I did an impression of a thirteenth-century stained-glass window, with red eugenia berries placed in a pink-tinged consommé along with almost-sheer rounds of pickled carrots, turnips, and beets. Then, I turned to my favorite, the Anders Zorn portrait of Isabella in Venice. In it, she's wearing a delicate white gown that I evoked with a mousse of celery hearts, cooked in butter and whipped with crème fraîche and a hint of citron. I used slices of black truffles to represent the dark waters of the canal. To echo Isabella's long rope of pearls, I assembled a cluster of tiny, translucent bay scallops. Over the top, I sprinkled daisy petals, which were like a flutter of fireworks.

For the entrée, I replicated a sixteenth-century tapestry's woven texture and earthy reds and browns with a lamb shank strewn with pomegranate seeds. And for dessert, as a tribute to Japanese art scholar Okakura Kakuzo, a big influence on Isabella Stewart Gardner, I positioned green rectangles of *matcha panna cotta* on a swipe of red-bean lacquer, with accents of white vanilla rice crisp.

The donors loved the meal and gave me a standing ovation. That was gratifying. But for me the experience itself—translating instinctive processes into conscious thoughts—was like a sensory adventure. It taught me to see differently.

• • •

Meanwhile, I'd been remaking the Gruppo a little more in my own image. Colin Lynch left to start his own restaurant with Jefferson. Since he'd grown up with me, I could understand his wish to move. I replaced him with Michele Carter, making her executive chef of the Gruppo, and named Scott L. Jones the chef de cuisine at Menton. Funnily, both of them were at Harvard, Michele as a biologist in the School of Public Health and Scott as a PhD candidate in biochemistry, before abandoning academia for food. They'd come up through the ranks of the Gruppo, working in various capacities at different restaurants. I've loved cooking with them, getting back into the kitchen, even if at fifty I'm a little slower on the line.

Abby Gregory, who'd built Stir so brilliantly, has become my right hand. Her MBA will come in handy on the finance side. As operations manager, I've installed Ben Kaplan, the general manager of the Butcher Shop. When he left New York, where he worked for Scott Conant (of Scarpetta and now a Food Network star), everyone mourned the loss. So I feel lucky. But the biggest news is that Kerri Foley, my lifelong friend, whose own restaurant Pigalle closed after twelve good years, is rejoining me as director of hospitality. She was assistant general manager years ago, when I opened No. 9 Park, so I know what a fucking ninja she can be. Just as importantly, I know I can trust her with my life, because I have. In her bones, she understands the hospitality culture I believe in. After all, we come from the same place, geographically and psychically.

Cat, a real pillar of my professional life, has helped define that restaurant culture as much as anyone. We're a duo: food and drink.

With the cast of characters shaping up, I've been concentrating on Menton, to heighten that elusive quality of elegant simplicity without stuffiness. The à la carte menu has helped a lot. We're offering some fun items, like a bucket of quail with aioli that you can eat at the bar, accompanied by a great burgundy. We fire up tiny croissants, just one or two bites, to serve with butter and honey. They're irresistible, at least to me.

These days, new businesses are popping up in Fort Port Channel, so I've opened Menton for lunch, with a bargain prix fixe. Cat has come up with a house champagne, sold by the glass, to add sparkle.

I'm changing the whole energy of the place—tearing out the carpet, which creates friction under your feet as you walk, while a polished floor will let you glide, lifting your spirits. I'm already feeling a new, joyful spring in my own step.

• • •

At midlife, what I find I care about most is community. I found it at MAD3—the gods of French cuisine like Alain Ducasse rubbing shoulders with upstarts like David Chang and culinary radicals like René Redzepi, as well as serious game-changers like Vandana Shiva—everyone coming together to think about our world and one of its essential forces: food. I even found it in Lyon, as a member of younger, looser generation cooking for the serious Old (mostly) Masters. Someone from my background can find a place in that world—and stand in the front row for the group photograph of that crew, the *étoiles réunies* (the returning stars)— because we've all dripped sweat onto a hot stove, gotten burns up and down our arms, and screamed *fuck, fucking, fuck,* in whatever language when a dish went wrong. Whether or not you're some kind of celebrity, there's kinship of shared experience and purpose that, to me at least, is as meaningful as praise from my peers (or betters).

From the start, I've tried to create community, a family feeling, in my business—building education into the job, all of us uplifting one another by sharing knowledge; stressing collaboration instead of competition; and promoting from within as staffers grow. I love working with people I've known for years, with whom I have an unspoken understanding.

I've always wanted Marchesa to feel like part of a community. When I was growing up, the projects were a buzzing hive, where everyone knew your background and all your business—whose father was a brute, whose brother was mobbed up, whose mother kept delicious snacks in the house, who hung out at Billy's Pizza and who preferred Papa Gino's, and so on. That small-town quality could be claustrophobic, everyone living in each other's pockets, but you definitely knew you were a thread in the social fabric.

So, every summer from the time Marchesa was four, we've shared a summer place in Truro with Ana Sortun, her husband, Chris Kurth, and their daughter Siena, who's a year younger. Chris brings up huge flats of produce from the farm, giving us all the fabulous tomatoes and watermelon we could ever want.

Unlike my mother and her cronies, who'd sit yakking and cracking beers, Ana and I (and whatever friends we have visiting from the city) share activities with the kids. I have some hilarious photos from when the girls were very young at the annual Provincetown Carnival, which is held in August. There's a Mardi Gras–like parade of drag queens, with the marchers tossing beads and lollipops into the crowd. The kids look absolutely dazzled by the costumes, as well as by the treats.

One summer when Marchesa was six or seven, Cat and Annie Copps came to visit and we went clamming. A big local guy, Isan, took us out in a boat stocked with coolers full of beer and wine. At the clamming beach, we all waded into the shallows, wearing goggles so we could peer underwater and look for breathing holes. Under the holes were clams, which we harvested by hand or with a rake.

We must have gotten about fifty pounds. Marchesa helped clean them, and I hand-made some pasta to serve with them. I also broke down a whole salmon and let Marchesa fillet it, tracing the bones carefully with a knife. She was so into it.

I laugh when I see what a mini-me she is. Like when she eats a lobster, she sucks out all meat and arranges the empty pieces of shell around the edge of her plate in a perfect design. I also do that unconsciously.

A recent summer was super fun because chef and author Yotam Ottolenghi and his new baby spent the day with us. Ottolenghi draws on the Jewish and Arab traditions of his hometown, Jerusalem, in his cookbooks, two of which are vegetarian. But he eats meat now and then, so I whipped up some rib eyes for lunch. I served them with five kinds of pasta, including *corzetti*, hailing from Liguria, which are thin disks of dough stamped with a wooden die to give them a sunburst design. They're very special. But I was laughing while I was cooking, because we could hear Marchesa outside, with a water balloon, showing Siena how men pee.

Of course, we don't make the kids stick with us all the time. I set them up with arts-and-crafts projects, or Ana or some other adult takes them to the beach, which I can't stand—I must have fried my sun-tolerance circuits as a teenager, slathered in baby oil, with an album sleeve covered in tinfoil. So I stay home and paint, sometimes a picture a day. At night we have bonfires on the beach, light Japanese lanterns, and make s'mores.

I always worked so many hours, often in the evenings when Marchesa was home, that I absolutely treasured those weeks in summer, in such a relaxing, beautiful setting, when I could just be with and enjoy close friends, and especially my daughter.

• • •

I wanted to extend the magic of those summers, to assemble a community of family and friends around me, for more than a month a year. I couldn't see myself doing that in Winchester, where I never put down roots, or in my pied-à-terre in Southie. I'd always had a fantasy of one day owning a white stucco house, somewhere like Tuscany or Provence, with french doors open to the countryside, an airy kitchen full of antique utensils and tools, and lots of bedrooms where dear friends like Kerri, Mary, and the rest of the Southie crew, Kevin Tyo, and others who know and love me just as I am, with no bullshit, no need to be sociable, no need to apologize, ever, could just hang out for whatever period of time. There would be children running around, yet plenty of private space, too, so I never felt encroached upon. In the throes of my depression, my fantasy of escape to the white stucco house became an ache.

As I fought my way back to health, the image of the stucco house stayed strong in my mind. Amazingly, I came across a replica of my vision, even with lots of my imagined details. It was not in Tuscany or Provence, but in Gloucester, on the Massachusetts North Shore, forty miles from Boston.

From the time it was founded in the 1600s, Gloucester has been a fishing port. It's lost more than ten thousand fishermen to the seas, and each new name is still recorded on a huge mural at city hall. Because it's picturesque and rocky, it's always had an arts community, with some of America's famous painters passing through, like John Sloan and Edward Hopper. But Gloucester is still an authentic, gritty working town, not some bullshit resort. There's one upscale restaurant, Short & Main, founded by alumni of Alice Waters's legendary Chez Panisse, right across the street from Virgilio's, an Italian market and bakery that upholds the culture of the Italian and Portuguese immigrants who settled the town in the 1880s. The sign above its door reads, *Bread of the Fishermen.*

Back when Annie Copps and I were roommates, a guy from Italy we knew took us to visit his relatives in Gloucester. They lived in a small dark house with a tiny electric stove, on which his aunt, who barely spoke English, made us some incredible monkfish, marinated in balsamic vinegar and crusted with cornmeal. When I got to Galleria, she hooked me up with a fishing crew who drove to the city to sell me amazing, just-caught cuttlefish, weighing it on a scale in the back of their truck. After I met Charlie, I got to know Gloucester itself because our close friends Sarah Gulati and her late husband, Patrick, had a place there, right on the ocean.

The white house of my vision is not on the ocean but just up the hill from town, on a nature preserve. It has a vernal pond, meaning that frogs breed there. There is a huge vegetable garden, a giant three-car garage with an upstairs apartment, and incredibly, a swimming pool. Brick archways and an arbor give the grounds a touch of Tuscany.

The stucco house was built by a businesswoman at the turn of the twentieth century. What a pioneer she must have been. It has a screened side porch long enough that, at one end, I could put a dining table for twenty, and at the other, set up my painting studio. Inside are archways with barnwood doors, a living room with ten-feet-tall windows looking out on greenery, and four wood-burning fireplaces. One is in the kitchen, so I can cook in it, like Mita Antolini. When I opened a kitchen drawer, it held an array of old silver serving forks, oyster knives, and some stranger implements—the antique tools of my vision!

The upstairs is rustic, which I like, with an eccentric layout of bedrooms—enough of them so that I can have both community and private space. There's enough room to host the whole family, including my (*gulp*) grandchildren. Charlie's son Adam married a wonderful woman, Amy, who works, as he does, in high tech. They have two adorable kids, Max and Olivia. One day when Marchesa reported Olivia, then about three, for peeing on the stairs, I consoled her by confessing my history as a "pissah." That was a mistake because I have yet to live it down.

Ryan just married a woman from Nepal, Anila, whom we all love, especially Marchesa. They had a quick, informal wedding; and the stucco house is the perfect place to throw them more of a bash. And I can just picture the holidays: last year at Thanksgiving and Easter, Keely and Amy pitched in to make ravioli and gnocchi. That was fun. Ryan loves to cook too and sends me pictures of his creations—for a while it was chicken wings but now it's more Indian and Nepalese food.

All my own siblings, with my grown-up nieces and nephews, would have trouble fitting under one roof.

• • •

For fifty-plus years, I lived within seven minutes of Southie, the place where I was born: where I learned to lie, steal, and fight; to take any dare and to tell anyone to fuck off; to rise above cement, piercing sharps, and newspapers damp with vinegar; to throw off the terror of hissing pipes, clammy darkness, and the stench of piss; to be staunch in friendship and values and ferocious in effort; to cook, awakening my senses, and then to create; to be open to all the possibilities of life, since, when you come from nothing, you have everything to gain.

So now my radius has expanded, beyond seven minutes, to maybe an hour, depending on traffic. I'm living proof that you don't have to go far, or ever lose sight of where you come from, to discover and embrace the whole wide world.

RECIPES

IRISH SODA BREAD WITH CARAWAY AND CURRANTS

1 cup dried currants
2 cups all-purpose flour
2 cups whole wheat flour
1 tablespoon baking soda
1½ tablespoons kosher salt
2 tablespoons caraway seeds
1½ cups buttermilk

1. Preheat the oven to 400°F. Line a sheet tray with parchment paper. In a small mixing bowl, lightly coat the currants with 1 tablespoon of the all-purpose flour. In the work bowl of a mixer, combine the whole wheat flour, the remaining 1 tablespoon all-purpose flour, the baking soda, salt, and caraway seeds. Mix on medium speed with the dough-hook attachment. Slowly add the buttermilk. Once the dough comes together, add the currants. The dough will be very wet.

2. Place the dough onto a well-floured surface and knead until you form an oblong loaf. Slice a vertical line into the top of the loaf with a serrated knife. Bake for 10 minutes, reduce the oven to 375°F, and continue to bake for an additional 35 to 45 minutes. Cool on a baking rack.

Yield: 6 to 8 servings

LAMB IN YOGURT WITH JUNIPER AND RED WINE REDUCTION, AND ROASTED CRISPY POTATOES WITH ROSEMARY

Lamb in Yogurt with Juniper

> 3 tablespoons dried juniper berries
> 1 cup Greek yogurt
> 4 garlic cloves, minced
> 1 teaspoon salt
> 1 teaspoon black pepper
> 1 (4 to 5-pound) leg of lamb, butterflied
> 2 cups dry red wine

The night before:

Lightly smash juniper berries with the back of a heavy sauté pan. Mix the juniper berries, yogurt, garlic, salt, and black pepper. Completely cover the lamb with the yogurt mixture and allow to marinate overnight in the refrigerator.

Roasted Lamb with Red Wine Reduction

1. Preheat the oven to 400°F. Remove the lamb from the yogurt marinade, reserving the yogurt marinade. Roll the lamb back into its original shape, placing the seam side

down into a heavy roasting pan. Roast for 20 minutes, then reduce the heat to 350°F. Continue to roast until the internal temperature is 130° to 135°F (for medium-rare) another 40 minutes to an hour. Allow the lamb to rest, 15 to 20 minutes.

2. While the lamb is roasting, place the wine in a medium saucepan and reduce until almost evaporated. Whisk in the reserved yogurt marinade until incorporated. Strain through a fine sieve to remove the juniper berries. Set aside until ready to serve.

Yield: 6 to 8 servings

Crispy Potatoes with Rosemary

4 large Idaho potatoes, boiled until cooked
   through
¾ cup olive oil
2 garlic cloves, chopped
4 to 5 rosemary sprigs
Kosher salt
Freshly cracked black pepper
Fleur de sel

1. Once the potatoes are cool enough to handle, peel and quarter. In a large sauté pan, heat the oil on medium-high heat, place the potatoes in the pan, and sauté for 5 to 7 minutes before turning. Add the garlic and rosemary sprigs. Continue cooking the potatoes until they are golden brown, 15 minutes at

the most. Place them in the middle of a serving platter and season to taste with salt and pepper.

2. Once the lamb is well rested, slice and place around the potatoes. Pour the yogurt sauce on top and finish with fleur de sel to taste.

Yield: 6 to 8 servings

FOCACCIA WITH OLIVE OIL, ROSEMARY, PROSCIUTTO, AND VIN SANTO–CURED CHESTNUTS

2 cups vin santo wine

2 cups whole chestnuts

2 cups lukewarm water

1 package active dry yeast

2 tablespoons olive oil, plus 2 tablespoons for
    drizzling

6 cups all-purpose flour

1 tablespoon kosher salt

2 whole cloves garlic, with ⅛ inch slice sliced off the
    top

Sea salt to taste

4 to 6 sprigs rosemary, picked and chopped well

10 to 12 slices very thin prosciutto

1. To make the vin santo–cured chestnuts: Preheat the oven to 350°F. Reduce the wine in a saucepan by half. Slice an X on the top of the chestnuts and roast until the skins pull away, about 15 minutes. Peel the chestnuts and place them in the reduced wine for 3 to 4 hours, or until the chestnuts have absorbed all the liquid.

2. To make the focaccia: Combine the water and yeast in a bowl, cover with a towel, and leave in a warm place for 10 minutes. Once you see bubbles forming, add the oil, flour, kosher salt, and mix well. Proof, allowing the dough to rise, in a generously oiled bowl covered with a towel or plastic wrap for 1 hour, or until doubled in size.

3. To cook the focaccia: Preheat the oven to 400°F. Oil a large cast-iron skillet and place in the oven. Divide the dough into 2 discs and roll each into a circle ½ inch thick. Using the tips of your fingers, make indentations in the dough. Place the rolled-out dough onto the hot iron skillet then cook for 7 minutes, until golden. Turn the dough and rub the cooked side with the garlic clove speared on the tines of the fork. Cook an additional 7 minutes then rub the second side with garlic. While still warm, season with fleur de sel. Coarsely chop the chestnuts and place on top. Layer the entire surface with the prosciutto, and drizzle with the remaining oil and rosemary.

Yield: 6 to 8 servings

ROAST PORK WITH FIG SAUCE

2 to 3-pound center-cut pork loin,
   with ½-inch fat cap on
1 tablespoon sea salt, plus more for finishing to taste
3 rosemary sprigs, leaves picked and
   chopped, stems reserved
2 cups dry red wine
1 tablespoon sugar
½ teaspoon cinnamon
1 pint fresh figs, quartered

1. Preheat the oven to 425°F. Season the roast with sea salt and the chopped rosemary. Roast for 30 minutes, then reduce the heat to 350°F. Continue to cook until the internal temperature is 145°F for medium or 155°F for well—about 25 minutes per pound. Allow the roast to rest for 20 to 25 minutes.

2. In the meantime, make the sauce. Add the wine to the roasting pan and bring to a simmer on the stove top over medium heat. Gently whisk up the browned fond (the residual bits of meat) into the wine. Add the rosemary stems, sugar, and cinnamon. Reduce the sauce by half, remove the rosemary stems, and add the figs at the very end so they are gently warmed but not falling apart. Season to taste. Serve the fig sauce on the side.

Yield: 6 to 8 servings

LIGURIAN POTATO SALAD

2 pounds russet potatoes, cut into small dice

⅓ cup cider vinegar

¼ cup minced shallots

1 to 1½ tablespoons lemon aioli or Cains mayonnaise

Zest of 2 lemons

Kosher salt

Freshly cracked black pepper

Place the potatoes in pot of cold water and bring to a boil. Simmer about 15 minutes until cooked through. Once the potatoes are cooked through, strain and place in a mixing bowl. While the potatoes are still hot, pour the cider vinegar over them, add the shallots, and fold in the lemon with aioli. Season to taste with salt and pepper. Serve warm.

Yield: 6 to 8 servings

PARMESAN SOUFFLÉ WITH PORCINI AND CHANTERELLE SAUCE

Porcini and Chanterelle Sauce

½ ounce dried porcini, rehydrated
  in 1 cup water for 3 hours
½ ounce dried chanterelles, rehydrated
  in 1 cup hot water for 3 hours
Reserved mushroom water
1 shallot, finely diced
4 to 6 tablespoons unsalted butter
1 cup dry red wine
1 tablespoon chopped fresh thyme
3 cups veal stock
Kosher salt
Freshly cracked pepper

Remove the mushrooms from the water, rinsing 2 to 3 times if they are especially gritty. Reserve the mushroom water. In a saucepot, gently sauté the shallot in 2 tablespoons of the butter until translucent. Add 2 cups mushroom water to the shallots, being careful to leave any grit in the bottom of the container. Reduce to 2 to 3 tablespoons. Add the wine and thyme, reduce by two-thirds. Add the stock and the rehydrated mushrooms. Simmer and allow the liquid to reduce again by two-thirds. Whisk in the remaining butter 1 tablespoon at a time over low heat, being careful not to break the sauce. Season with salt and pepper.

Parmesan Soufflé

4 tablespoons butter, plus more for buttering ramekins
   at room temperature
3½ ounces all-purpose flour
2 cups whole milk, brought to a simmer
   and cooled to lukewarm
½ teaspoon salt
Pinch of white pepper
Pinch of nutmeg
1 cup grated Parmesan cheese
5 eggs, separated

1. Prepare 6 ramekins (4½ ounces each) by brushing butter onto the entire surface of the ramekins. Brush butter in upward strokes from the bottom of the ramekin toward the rim. This will help the soufflés to rise. Keep the buttered ramekins in a cool place until ready to use. Preheat the oven to 375°F and prepare a water bath by filling a cake pan with enough water to go halfway up the sides of the ramekins you are using.

2. Melt the 4 tablespoons butter over low heat. Whisk in the flour and cook for 8 minutes, preventing any color from developing. Whisk in the milk slowly and allow to thicken slightly. Add the salt, pepper, nutmeg, and Parmesan, allowing the mixture to cool slightly by stirring. Incorporate the egg yolks one at a time and place in a bowl. In a separate bowl, whisk the egg whites until stiff peaks form. Incorporate one-third of your egg whites into the cheese mixture by gently folding it in with a spatula. Follow this with another

third of the egg whites, and finally the remainder of the egg whites. Fill the prepared ramekins with the soufflé batter and level off the top with a straightedge such as the back of a knife, wiping the excess batter from the ramekin lips. Place the soufflés in the water bath and cook for 20 to 25 minutes until they have risen ¼ inch above the rims and are golden on top.

Yield: 6 servings

ACKNOWLEDGMENTS

First my family, whom I love! It's amazing that we all came out of the same vessel and have survived so much. We grew up with the most amazing morals and strength ever. Life is not easy but you all made it incredible for me to grow up to be the person I am today. Love you all!

Tied for first is Charlie Petri, who I thank for the family we've built together.

Thank you to the wonderful Judith Curr, president and publisher of Atria, and the entire Atria Books team.

To Erica Spellman-Silverman, my agent at Trident Media Group, *wow*! What can I say? Your persistence in finding me and talking me into writing my story was immeasurable to say the least. Thank you for not letting me quit and for introducing me to the best writer ever and the best person to capture my voice, Elisa Petrini. I am forever grateful to you and your quenelles.

To ELISA, you, my friend, are incredible! You captured my voice like no one I could ever imagine, you knew when to back off, when to push and when to hug me, which wasn't instant for sure. I'm forever grateful to you and your amazing talent as a writer, true friend, and confidante. I truly missed you when our writing sessions were over, you made me laugh with your sense of humor, and just your all-out attitude is something I will cherish forever. Your antipasti platters will also go down in history! Love you, dear friend.

To Leslie Meredith, I knew that I had the right editor the minute I met you; your kindness and professionalism shined throughout your entire office that first day; your love of cooking and food was and still is impressive. Most of all, believing in me and believing in this powerful story in so many ways.

TO MY GANG OF GIRLS FROM SOUTHIE, I am forever grateful for all of you.

To ALL of my amazing staff, past and present. Thank you for believing in me and my vision.

To all of my colleagues who I look up to: I devour your inspiration.

To our incredible strong food community!

To all of the purveyors, farmers, stylists, artisans, and wine producers. Thank you for your passion and extraordinary products.

To all who feel my heart in my food and vision.

To all of the generations of chefs/restaurateurs who have taught me so much through the years.

To the younger generation who think it's impossible to accomplish your goals—it most certainly is possible.

And most of all, to evolution, art, and culture.

ABOUT THE AUTHOR

Barbara Lynch, a multiple James Beard Award–winner and a Relais & Châteaux Grand Chef, is one of Boston's—and America's—leading chefs and restaurateurs. Growing up in a South Boston housing project, one of seven children with a widowed mother, Lynch got her first cooking job in a local rectory at age thirteen. While waiting tables at Back Bay's prestigious St. Botolph Club, she was inspired to cook professionally by chef Mario Bonello. Largely self-trained, Lynch went on to cook under Todd English at the renowned Boston restaurants Michela's and Olives before striking out on her own as an executive chef. For her work at Galleria Italiana, she was named one of *Food & Wine* magazine's "Ten Best New Chefs in America" in 1996.

In 1998, Lynch opened her own first restaurant, No. 9 Park, in Boston's Beacon Hill. Immediately named one of America's top restaurants by such publications as *Gourmet, Food & Wine, Travel and Leisure,* and *Bon Appétit,* it won Lynch a James Beard Award as Best Chef: Northeast in 2003. That same year, she began to build a culinary empire with two South End restaurants, B&G Oysters and the Butcher Shop; an elegant greengrocer, Plum Produce; a catering company, Niche Catours (later called 9 at Home); and a demonstration kitchen, Stir.

In 2008, Lynch spearheaded the revival of Boston's Fort Point Channel neighborhood by founding Drink, an artisanal cocktail bar, and Sportello, an Italian version of a classic diner; followed in 2010 by Menton, a "modern" fine-dining restaurant. All the Fort Point restaurants received local and national "best of" designations, and Menton was certified by Relais & Châteaux, the exclusive international association of gourmet restaurants and boutique hotels, as a distinguished destination. It is Boston's only Relais & Châteaux property, and Lynch is one of just six female Relais & Châteaux Grand Chefs in the world.

In 2013, she was inducted into the James Beard Foundation's Who's Who of Food and Beverage in America, a roster of America's most accomplished culinary professionals; and in 2014, she became only the second woman to receive the Beard Foundation's highest honor, the award for Outstanding Restaurateur.

Lynch's first cookbook, *Stir: Mixing It Up in the Italian Tradition*, won the prestigious Gourmand Award for Best Chef Cookbook in 2009.

Philanthropy has always been important to Lynch. In 2012, she established the Barbara Lynch Foundation, dedicated to nutritional and culinary education for the Boston community, especially children.